CREATIVITY AND INTELLIGENCE:
A PERSONALITY APPROACH

GEORGE S. WELSH

INSTITUTE FOR RESEARCH IN SOCIAL SCIENCE
UNIVERSITY OF NORTH CAROLINA AT CHAPEL HILL
1975

Library of Congress Catalog Card Number: 75-16305

ISBN: 0-89143-060-1

Printed in the United States of America

ACKNOWLEDGMENTS

A primary debt is owed the young women and men who as students at the Governor's School of North Carolina gave so much of their time to take the battery of tests that form the research base for the present work. During the three summers of the testing program Joseph M. Johnston was superintendent and C. Douglas Carter served as principal. Philosophical orientation of the school was provided by Virgil S. Ward, consultant, and by H. Michael Lewis, coordinator of curriculum. I have since that time benefited from discussions with Professor Lewis about theoretical models. The late Eugene Burnette, former director of the Program for the Exceptionally Talented, North Carolina Department of Public Instruction, was an active participant in the research program and in some of the initial analysis of the test results. This support as well as the cooperation of the faculty and staff of the school is gratefully acknowledged.

The Governor's School supplied the testing materials and paid for commercial scoring of the Strong Vocational Interest Blank. Scoring of other tests and data analysis were made possible through grants from the University of North Carolina Faculty Research Council; the Creativity Research Institute of the Richardson Foundation, Greensboro, N.C.; and the U.S. Department of Health, Education, and Welfare, Office of Education, Bureau of Research (Project No. 7-C-009). Patricia Foil served as research assistant during much of this time period.

Permission to use copyrighted test items was granted as follows: Adjective Check List, Harrison G. Gough and Consulting Psychologists Press; Minnesota Multiphasic Personality Inventory, University of Minnesota Press (the MMPI is distributed by The Psychological Corporation); Strong Vocational Interest Blank, Stanford University Press.

During a year's leave of absence from Chapel Hill I was fortunate to have an opportunity to participate in assessment procedures at the Institute of Personality Assessment and Research at Berkeley. I wish to thank the staff and the subjects

for this experience which had a marked influence on my views of
creativity. In particular I want to acknowledge my indebtedness
to Harrison G. Gough, Wallace B. Hall, Ravenna Helson, and Donald
W. MacKinnon for their continued help and encouragement.

The initial outline and writing of the present work was
aided by a semester's Kenan leave of absence granted by the University of North Carolina. It was possible to present the personality model in its final form to many colleges and universi-
ties while lecturing in Virginia during my tenure as Visiting
Scholar, the University Center in Virginia.

I wish it were possible to thank individually all of the
students and faculty at Chapel Hill and at other institutions
for their reactions to early forms of the present work given,
in many instances, as talks before various audiences. Although
I cannot list the names of all of these persons, their comments
have helped me in many ways and have not gone unnoticed. For
continued encouragement and assistance in completing the present
work I owe a special debt to Fred L. Adair, College of William
and Mary, Williamsburg and to Amos Goor, Ben Gurion University
of the Negev, Beer-Sheva, Israel.

My colleague James C. Carpenter sketched the Jungian mandala
which was the original idea for my drawing that was professional-
ly completed by Doris Mahaffey for the cover design.

It would not have been possible to complete this project
without the assistance and support of the Staff of the Institute
for Research in Social Science. Frank J. Munger, Elizabeth M.
Fink, and Barbara B. Higgins read the manuscript in preliminary
form and urged its publication by the Institute. For expert
typing of the many revisions I wish to thank Jane Dry, Robin
Ratliff, and Bonita Samuels. I am especially grateful for
personal help as well as extensive editorial assistance to
Patricia R. Sanford.

CONTENTS

Creativity as a Human Attribute
Perspectives in Studying Creativity
The Creative Person
The Creative Product
The Creative Process
Motivation for Creativity
Time and Place for Creativity
Some Basic Features of Creativity
    Talent
    Diligence
    Intelligence
Identifying Potentially Creative Subjects

Problems of Measurement
Problems of Definition
Conceptual Definition
Definitional Relationships
Terman's Concept Mastery Test
    Follow-up Studies
    Form T
    Validational Evidence
    Score Stability
    Group Difference
Summary

Definitions of Creativity
Cognitive Approaches
    Guilford's Theory
    Getzels and Jackson
    Wallach and Kogan
    Mednick's Test
    Torrance's Tests
Need for Other Approaches to Creativity

LIST OF TABLES

Chapter VII: Personality and Interest Test Correlates
of Dimensional Scores

Chapter VIII: Cross-Validational Studies

Chapter IX: Sex, Masculinity-Femininity, and Creativity

Chapter I

INTRODUCTION

For the past two decades much psychological research has been directed to an important question: What is the relationship between creativity and intelligence? In most of these studies it has been assumed, often implicitly, that the general nature of intelligence is reasonably well understood even though it is evident that a detailed conceptual consensus has not been reached in theoretical formulation. Identification of individual subjects differing in intelligence has usually been made by means of a standard IQ test or one that has been derived from this psychometric tradition. Creativity, on the other hand, has been the unknown term in the question both conceptually and psychometrically. It has not been assumed that the nature of creativity is understood either generally or specifically and no standard creativity test has been developed that plays a role analogous to the traditional IQ measure.

In the study of intelligence the pioneering work of Alfred Binet is well-known and needs no elaboration. It must be kept in mind that he "is the departure point of every major development in theories and measures of intelligence since 1895" (Edwards, 1971:9). The importance of the Binet position is that intelligence has been conceptualized continuously as a cognitive ability and has been assessed by tests requiring knowledge based on cognitive skills for correct answers. Theory and practice have mutually reinforced each other and there is a reluctance to leave the familiar conceptual framework with its convenient IQ tests. No advance beyond this point can be made, however, if we restrict and confine our study of intelligence in this way. Shortcomings of our continued dependence on this traditional approach have been emphasized in a survey of intelligence and ability in which the author complains that "it is not only unrealistic but misleading to think of man's intellectual gifts and capabilities purely in cognitive terms" (Wiseman, 1967:7).

Nonetheless, some important research has been carried out which demonstrates the potential value of looking at intelligence from a noncognitive point of view. For example, in one extensive factor-analytic study of personality R.B. Cattell found that the second largest source of variance in peer-group description could

1

be interpreted as a bipolar factor contrasting "general intelligence" and "mental defect" (Cattell, 1946). Another example comes from the work of H.G. Gough in developing one of the scales for his California Psychological Inventory (Gough, 1964). A clearly noncognitive approach is reflected by the title of the paper in which this study was reported, "A Nonintellectual Intelligence Test" (Gough, 1953).

The corpus of work relating intelligence to noncognitive traits of personality seems to have been ignored by most authorities discussing this area of investigation. Suffice it to note that in a monumental volume, *The Nature of Human Intelligence* (Guilford, 1967), no studies like those mentioned above are cited. Indeed, the term "personality" does not even appear in the index.

Creativity, too, has been conceptualized narrowly in cognitive terms by most of the workers in this area. Tests developed for its assessment have utilized scales and tasks that require production or recognition of items very similar to the abilities tapped by conventional IQ tests. In an influential study of creativity and intelligence the authors candidly acknowledge that for them, "the term 'creativity' refers to a fairly specific type of cognitive ability reflected in performance on a series of paper-and-pencil tests" (Getzels and Jackson, 1962:16). A similar cognitive approach characterizes most of the studies made by other investigators, although these works cannot be reviewed here (see Vernon, 1970).

Two crucial questions must be asked of those espousing a cognitive concept of creativity. First, do such tests identify persons substantially different from those picked out by conventional IQ tests? Second, do persons recognized as outstandingly creative actually score higher on these tests than persons not-so-recognized when some selection in terms of general intelligence has already taken place? A negative answer to both questions has been given in this country and abroad. Studies carried out by D.W. MacKinnon and his associates at the Institute of Personality Assessment and Research (IPAR) in Berkeley, California, found little value in cognitive creativity tests (MacKinnon, 1965). In Great Britain, Liam Hudson also challenges continued reliance on the so-called divergent-thinking tests that are typical of the cognitive orientation to creativity (Hudson, 1966).

An extensive review of this problem has been made by John G. Nicholls of New Zealand in an article entitled "Creativity in the Person Who Will Never Produce Anything Original or Useful" (Nicholls, 1972). He concludes that a cognitive approach, particularly the reliance on ability tasks as exemplified by divergent-thinking tests, has hampered research. "Perhaps because of the cultural emphasis on creativity, acceptance of divergent thinking tests as creativity tests persists and leads to distortions in research design and interpretation" (Nicholls, 1972:723).

In addition to the implications for research in creativity as noted by Nicholls, there is an obvious problem for the test subject. On any test that requires specific kinds of knowledge --word meanings or items of information, for example--a person who lacks this background is at a disadvantage. He cannot answer items of this nature and will get a low score on such a cognitively-based measure whether it is called a test of creativity, divergent thinking, or even general intelligence. Thus, a subject may be classified as "uncreative" or "unintelligent" merely because he lacks some particular bits of knowledge required by such a test.

However, on personality scales that do not require the subject to give a response to cognitive items that are scored as "correct" or "incorrect," but rather to describe his own attitudes and personality traits, it is entirely possible for the subject to be recognized as having characteristics associated with intelligent behavior or creativity as manifested outside of a test situation. That is, he will not be handicapped *per se* because his background or education has deprived him of specific content required by conventional tests.

The purpose of the research described in the present report is to argue the value of a noncognitive approach to the study of creativity and intelligence. There are two basic objectives of the research, the first conceptual and the second practical. (1) It is postulated that two general dimensions of personality which we have termed "origence" and "intellectence" can account for many of the individual differences in performance on the conventional, cognitive tests currently employed. These dimensions are assumed to be independent so that their conjoint relationship leads to a fourfold typology that has conceptual implications for personality theory. (2) Special scales to assess these dimensions were developed for several widely used and easily administered personality tests so that it is feasible to employ them in the identification of potentially creative and intelligent subjects who might otherwise be missed by traditional tests requiring cognitive skills. Although the concept of intelligence has not been explicated in any ultimate sense, it has been investigated by psychologists and other specialists for many years and a number of summaries of the work done in this area are readily available. These summaries cover conceptual, psychometric, and applied problems (see, for example, Butcher, 1968; Edwards, 1971; Guilford, 1967; Hudson, 1970; Tyler, 1969; and Wiseman, 1967).

Since much less work has been done in the area of creativity, it may be helpful to give some background for the discussion of issues and methods of approaching problems in creativity research. It may be pointed out that in many instances some of the matters discussed might be applicable, *mutatis mutandi*, to intelligence as well.

CREATIVITY AS A HUMAN ATTRIBUTE

Whatever creativity may be, it seems to be considered a distinctively human attribute--no other living creature has been characterized as creative.

Many birds and animals have been called intelligent and there is no doubt that they can show remarkable ingenuity in some cases of problem-solving. One thinks of Köhler's chimpanzee uttering the anthropoid equivalent of "eureka" as he sees that a banana outside his cage can be reached by joining two sticks together (Köhler, 1957:113).

All of the higher mammals have highly developed systems for communication although they do not have the power of speech. Birds, which can learn to talk, are limited to the words that have been put in their mouths by human mentors; they are limited to repetition of specific phrases that have been taught and they cannot create a novel sentence by rearranging the words in their repertoire.

A rudimentary sense of aesthetics may be attributed to the Australian bower bird's arrangement of pebbles and bright objects before its nest, or to the Baltimore oriole's preference for colored yarn and string in its nidulation. But these birds cannot create a work of art. As Lancelot Hogben points out, "When modern man appears on the stage of prehistory, he is a picture-making animal, the only picture-making animal which has ever lived on our planet, maybe the only picture-making creature in the universe" (1949:16). To picture something and to make a picture requires an act of imagination and conceptualization that is beyond the capability of birds and animals other than man.

So it is with any other activity of these nonhuman creatures. The koala bear does not limit its diet to leaves from certain eucalyptus trees because of neurotic food faddism. The crested flycatcher does not incorporate a cast-off snake skin in its nest because of a superstitious or fetishistic hang up. The wolverine does not enter a cabin and befoul the stores of food there as an act of revenge against any specific trapper. The lion does not

decorate its den with horns of the impala it has slain. Animals
are entrapped in acting, reacting, enacting, and re-enacting a
limited and circumscribed repertoire of behavior closely tied to
their immediate physical and physiological needs.

Man alone can deliberately modify his own activities and
he alone has the power to rearrange the world to suit himself.
Man alone can picture in his imagination what the world was like
before him and what it might be like in the future. Man alone
can depict his thoughts in words and figures. The behavior of
only man can be considered creative.

PERSPECTIVES IN STUDYING CREATIVITY

Granted that creativity is a distinctively human attribute,
we are still faced with the problem of distinguishing creativity
from other characteristics of human behavior, even those that may
be shared with some other species. The fact that the term exists
and is used in an apparently meaningful way by many persons implies
that there must be some kind of agreement about what creativity is.
There is, however, a dismaying lack of consensus in definition and
rather than enumerating the various definitions that have been
proffered (Taylor [1959] has analyzed more than 100 definitions
of creativity), it may be more helpful to begin with an outline
of the various ways that psychologists have attempted to study
creativity.

In Stuart E. Golann's review (1963) he noted that "a striking
feature of the literature on creativity is the diversity of interests, motives, and approaches characteristic of the many investigators" (p. 548), and proposed that most of these could be organized under four basic *emphases*: products, process, measurement,
and personality.

More recently Marie Dellas and Eugene L. Gaier (1970) have
suggested that "most economically, the literature on creativity
can be classified into four major orientations: (a) the nature
and quality of the *product* created, (b) the actual expression of
the creative acts and the continuing *process* during the 'creation,'
(c) the *nature* of the individual, and (d) environmental factors
and *press** that tend to initiate and foster creativity" (p. 55).

---

*The term *press* was introduced by Henry A. Murray (1938) to
indicate the pressure and influence that objects or persons in the
environment have on an individual. He differentiates the actu-
ality of the situation, *alpha press*, from the subjective perception, *beta press*, by an individual.

The present writer has suggested (Welsh, 1973) a modifica-
tion and a colligation of these proposed emphases and orientations
in terms of a pentad of perspectives on creativity: person, product, process, press, and place. Translated into common grammatical
terms these nouns become the *who, what, how, why,* and *where* of creativity and may in turn be phrased as basic questions to be asked
of any research in this area of human behavior.

1. Who are the creative persons?

2. What is it that they do that can be called creative?

3. How do they do it?

4. Why do they do what they do?

5. Where do they show their creativity?

Although the question may be individually framed and the
area of study staked out separately, it must be stressed that this
is basically a matter of convenience or a research stratagem.
Every human endeavor, whether creative or not, must be understood
as a complex sequence of behavior that occurs in some context.
Delimitation and circumscription of observation and interpretation
are necessary for understanding any phenomenon. While it may be
true that the whole is greater than the sum of its parts, and that
the part has no meaning apart from its context, no one has yet
demonstrated an effective alternative to analysis and dissection
as a first step in a scientific enterprise.

To comprehend creativity in its totality we must understand
first some of the bits and pieces of human behavior that can be
observed either in contrived circumstances or in natural settings,
regardless of the fact that the observed behavior may seem at
this time to be far removed from the supernal acts of a creative
genius. This point is particularly apposite for the smallest
units of observation, test items, whether they are true-false,
multiple-choice, or "open-ended" in format and whether the test
itself is called a measure of "creativity," "creative thinking,"
"originality," or whatever. Golann has clearly pointed out the
discrepancy between psychometric observations and other kinds of
behavior. "The point that needs to be stressed is that these data
are in a sense arbitrary: intelligence is not performance on a
test; creativity is more than test performance or being judged as
creative" (1963:560). Yet test data themselves may be an appropriate starting point for the kind of conceptual reorganization
that he feels is necessary before creativity can be understood in
any comprehensive way. They should not be rejected in advance on
a priori grounds.

One of the basic assumptions of the present work is the legitimacy and the utility of psychological tests for the study of creativity--a measurement approach, or emphasis in Golann's terms.

THE CREATIVE PERSON

There are some individuals whose accomplishments were so outstanding during their lifetimes and so enduring that there is little disagreement in recognizing them as creative individuals. The names of Aristotle, Galileo, Leonardo, Mozart, Shakespeare, Newton, Darwin, and Einstein, for example, quickly come to mind. It may be noted that they are also recognized as having been highly intelligent.

Were these men different in kind from their contemporaries? Were they distinguishable at an early age? What were their identifying personality characteristics? We have to rely on the reports of biographers, or autogiographical statements when available, and the judgments of historians for answers since these men were never subjects in psychological studies during their lives. In many cases these persons did show some of the characteristics associated with creative genius such as intellectual precocity, intense curiosity, and early exhibition of outstanding talents. But in other cases these qualities were conspicuously absent. Liam Hudson (1966) cites four examples of this point: Turner, Rilke, Kepler, and Darwin. In the latter's case Hudson comments that "nothing of Darwin's previous development could possibly alert us. It simply is not the case that psychologists, even with the benefit of hindsight, can detect the signs of his dormant gifts" (p. 121).

It is, however, possible that had these men been examined early by means of standard psychological tests, their creative and intellectual potential might have been recognizable. Cox (1926) estimated the probable childhood intelligence quotient of 300 geniuses by evaluating biographical data. Judging from her report, it is evident that had IQ tests been available and actually administered, these individuals would have scored high enough to be identifiable as unusually intelligent children.

When it comes to personality traits, which are not related to overt behavior in the straightforward way that cognitive characteristics seem to be, tests may be invaluable. It is entirely possible that the systematic and quantifiable observations available by means of objective personality tests would detect some of the subtle characteristics which elude casual and undirected observation in naturalistic settings.

Certainly many studies of adults utilizing psychometric evaluation, for example, those of Roe (1952) and MacKinnon (1965), are consistent with this possibility. Indeed, after a review of more than two dozen studies in this area, Dellas and Gaier conclude that "this evidence points up a common pattern of personality traits among creative persons and also that these personality factors may have some bearing on creativity in the abstract, regardless of field" (1970:65). They reach similar conclusions after summarizing a series of studies with subjects of a younger age. "Generally, the data indicate that the personality characteristics of young creatives bear similarity to those of creative adults, and, therefore, the conclusion seems tenable that these traits develop fairly early. Their manifestation at this level suggests that these characteristics may be determinants of creative performance rather than traits developed in response to recognition of creative behavior" (p. 66).

According to the summary of these authors, the creative person is characterized by the following personality traits: (1) independence in attitude and social behavior, (2) dominance, (3) introversion, (4) openness to stimuli, (5) wide interests, (6) self-acceptance, (7) intuitiveness, (8) flexibility, (9) social presence and poise, (10) an asocial attitude, and (11) unconcern for social norms. Two additional traits seem to be more closely related to aesthetic than to scientific creativity: (12) radicalism, and (13) rejection of external constraints.

The creative person, then, appears to have certain personality characteristics that can be delineated, and these characteristics may be recognizable in younger individuals before adult accomplishment has been demonstrated.

THE CREATIVE PRODUCT

The study of creativity by means of products seems in many ways so obvious and natural that it is often assumed or implicit even when it is not singled out for special study. Indeed, there is very little that we can know about a person, whether creative or not, unless he does something or says something. To be sure, we sometimes make judgments about someone because of his appearance or his reputation, but it is largely on the basis of what a person has done--what he has produced--that we decide his worth or value as an individual. This seems to be particularly true for the creative person.

In some cases the role of the product is explicitly recognized. "Creativity may be defined, quite simply, as the ability

to bring something new into existence" (Barron, 1965:3). Morris I.
Stein suggests that creativity "results in a novel work that is
accepted as tenable or useful by a group at some point in time"
(1963:218). More comprehensive in scope and comprising both the
novelty and the social judgment positions of the previous definitions, is that offered by Donald W. MacKinnon. True creativity

> involves a response or an idea that is novel or
> at the very least statistically infrequent...
> [that]...must to some extent be adaptive to, or of,
> reality. It must serve to solve a problem, fit a
> situation, or accomplish some recognizable goal.
> And...[it]...involves a sustaining of the original
> insight, an evaluation and elaboration of it, a
> developing of it to the full. (1962:485)

Thus, an extremely complex judgment is required to determine whether any product is truly creative. It may be noted that
MacKinnon's research group at Berkeley used products more as symptoms or signs of creativity rather than as objects for special
study. Products do have the advantage that they can be studied at
leisure--independently of the creative person himself. Although
creative products have intrinsic value and interest it is doubtful
that a product can tell us anything about the personality of the
individual who produced it. Studies of artists (Wittkower and
Wittkower, 1963) and of philosophers (Hook, 1960) fail to find
any direct and systematic relationship between the person and his
production.

Harold G. McCurdy, however, arrives at different conclusions
in his studies of the literary products created by one authentic
creative genius, William Shakespeare (1953, 1968), and by other
outstanding writers, D.H. Lawrence, and Charlotte and Emily Bronte
(1961). The rationale for his research methodology seems psychologically sound.

> If the little stories made up in response to
> TAT pictures have some value in personality as-
> sessment, why should this not be true of the great
> stories which constitute imaginative literature
> --novels, dramas, poems? It is a natural conclu-
> sion from general Freudian theory that such
> material should reveal the personality of the
> author, in much the same way as dreams are sup-
> posed to. (McCurdy, 1961:413)

Although he demonstrates some consistencies between their
literature and their lives for Lawrence and the Brontes, the case

for Shakespeare cannot be considered compelling. He acknowledges
that "in taking up the plays of Shakespeare, I was assuming, rather than trying to test the hypotheses, that an author's fictional
productions reflect his personality and the circumstances of his
life" (1961:419). Since practically nothing is known of Shakespeare's actual personality, there is no way of determining the
degree to which McCurdy's assumption was justified.

The late Gordon W. Allport believed that inferring personality from formal literary productions was not always warranted, although he did feel that informal writings such as letters and
diaries might be useful in some instances. He pointed out that
"so far as personal documents are concerned, it must be borne in
mind that the more exacting the prescription in terms of task,
the less value the document has in terms of expression or projec-
tion" (1942:112). The rigid requirements of the sonnet form, for
instance, leave much less possibility for stylistic expression
than free verse. At any rate, it is unlikely that a poem, even
though based on a dream like Coleridge's *Kubla Khan*, tells as
much about the personality of the author as the direct and unem-
bellished recounting of a dream by a naive subject. Finally, Allport's observation still seems valid that "as yet no one has established an invariant relation between any one stylistic feature
and a corresponding attribute of personality" (p.113).

It may well be that spontaneous expression and unselfcon-
scious utterance do reveal something about an individual's personality; but whether consciously produced literature that is often
edited and rewritten many times can be relied upon as data of di-
vulgence remains to be convincingly demonstrated. In the case of
some contemporary poets, at least, there is evidence that better
artists reveal less personal material about themselves in their
work than the less gifted (King, 1969). If this relationship were
generally true for other fields and for artists of earlier time
periods, it would surely cast doubt on the unqualified use of creative products to infer the personality of the producer.

THE CREATIVE PROCESS

Products, whatever their limitations in studying creativity,
at least have the advantage of being tangible and available for
public scrutiny. We can examine the drawings made by Paleolithic
man 15,000 years ago in the caves of Lascaux as well as the most
recent paintings of a contemporary artist. Even the transitory
acts of a stage performance can be recorded for later review.
Processes that are not overt, however, cannot be studied directly
but must be inferred from other observations and thus have an inherent intangibility that makes them elusive and indeterminate.

Nonetheless, there is an impressive literature on the creative process, much of it organized around the areas of thinking and problem-solving. Some have argued that the creative process actually consists of four identifiable stages: preparation, incubation, illumination, and verification (Wallas, 1926). Others find six discernible steps: realizing the need, gathering information, thinking through, imagining solutions, verification, and putting the ideas to work (Harris, 1959). More useful, according to some, is a functional analysis of the interrelationships of the various steps rather than studying distinct stages (Crutchfield, 1961).

More interesting, and perhaps more helpful despite its anecdotal rather than laboratory flavor, is the report made by the creative person himself based on his own introspections. A classic example is that of the famous French mathematician, Henri Poincaré, who stressed the role of the unconscious in the sudden illumination of solutions to baffling problems (Hadamard, 1954: 12-15). Brewster Ghiselin, himself a poet, has edited the reports of 38 gifted men and women in a volume with an appropriate title, *The Creative Process* (1955). These accounts are obviously more literary than scientific, although they do furnish some leads to experimental work. It is difficult, however, to translate their insights about the creative process into practical research techniques that can be applied in systematic studies of different groups of subjects.

MOTIVATION FOR CREATIVITY

The "why" of creativity is obviously an integral part of personality and there has been a tendency to distinguish dynamic, motivational aspects of behavior from structural characteristics of personality. The former focuses more on concepts of need and drive while the latter stresses the concept of trait. It must be admitted, at the same time, that psychologists have been neither clear nor consistent in either their terminology or their conceptual framework. At any rate, two quite different viewpoints regarding motivation have been expressed. One is negative in orientation and finds the source of creativity in hidden and unacceptable impulses; the other is positive and sees creativity as the natural outcome of the realization and expression of man's fullest potentials.

Most of the proponents of the first viewpoint have worked within a psychoanalytic framework and have stressed such features as aggression, hostility, destructive urges, anxiety, guilt, need for restitution, sublimation, and other classic Freudian concepts.

Practically all the work in this reductionistic camp has concerned
artistic rather than scientific creativity and has followed the
case history tradition rather than an experimental or research
model. Thus it is difficult to translate such insights as have
been gained into workable methods of identifying creative persons
or judging the nature of their motives. Even when this is possible, however, support is often found for the opposed positive
viewpoint rather than the proposed psychoanalytic formulation
(Münsterberg and Mussen, 1953; Myden, 1959). The second point of
view is typified by Carl Rogers (1959) who utilizes the concept
of "self-actualization" and sees the creative individual as motivated by a need to complete himself by realizing and maximizing
his potential capabilities. Although self-actualization and similar global concepts of this kind are also difficult to apply in
specific research projects, results compatible with this view have
been found in a number of carefully conducted studies.

Golann, for example, proposed "the creativity motive" (1962)
and obtained empirical support for the self-actualizing position.
Subjects selected by means of high scores on an art scale "preferred the ambiguous, evocative figures, indicated preference on
a questionnaire for activities and situations which allowed more
self-expression and utilization of creative capacity" in contrast
to subjects low on the scale "who preferred more routine, structured, and assigned activities" (1963:556).

Other researchers using specific concepts stemming from the
self-actualization viewpoint have also demonstrated findings consistent with this approach. Representative are the following:
greater striving and need for excellence (Torrance and Dauw, 1965);
need for quality and novelty (Maddi, 1965); need to achieve and
test limits (McClelland, 1963); willingness to take risks (Pankove,
1967); need to impose a personally derived kind of order, commit-
ment to deep philosophical and aesthetic meanings in one's work
(Barron, 1968).

Many other motivational factors have been proposed but most
of them have received very little empirical support. This may be
in part a function of inadequate measuring devices (Taylor and
Holland, 1964), or, as suggested by Salvatore R. Maddi (1965), because of the "child-oriented" view of creativity held by many
researchers. This view stresses relaxation, playful meandering,
aimlessness, whimsicality, and lack of purpose. "The major difficulty is that it does not include any active push, intention,
motivation that leads a person inexorably, at whatever cost toward creative functioning" (Maddi, 1965:335), and this view fails
to recognize "the long period of purposeful, relentless, organized
thought that must have preceded the creative insight" (p. 336).

The creative person, then, is held to be characterized by motivation that is serious, meaningful, and directed, rather than casual, incidental, and accidental. Research organized around the latter elements will not succeed in identifying him on the one hand, or in understanding the nature of his behavior on the other. Whether the creative person is driven by one motive or many, whether he differs from noncreative persons in the intensity or the direction of his motivation, research questions cannot be answered without practical means for locating creative or potentially creative subjects for special study.

TIME AND PLACE FOR CREATIVITY

The "where" of creativity will be touched on briefly for the sake of completeness, and simply to indicate that this approach has been viewed temporally and spatially in both historical and geographical frameworks.

Typical of the humanistic orientation in this approach is Jacob Bronowski who finds two great peaks of creativity, Greece between 600 and 300 B.C. and the renaissance. "The sciences and the arts have flourished together and they have been fixed together as sharply in place as in time" (1958:60). In addition Bronowski believes that artists and scientists are similar in their motivation: "A man becomes creative...when he finds a new unity in the variety of nature...a likeness between things which were not thought alike before, and this gives him a sense both of richness, and of understanding" (p. 63). This latter view could easily be cast in objective terms for empirical studies. Indeed, there is no reason why historical data could not be utilized for research in creativity.

Some workers believe that time and place may not be crucial at all. Maddi (1965) writes, "I suspect that the overwhelming majority of people we remember as significantly creative would have been so regardless of the kind of environment in which they found themselves" (p. 331).

It is difficult to know how to resolve these contradictory views. If a person has been truly creative, it is possible to evaluate in some way what the effect of the environment and the historical period may have had on him and his work. But of a noncreative person, can we say with any assurance that he would have been creative if he had lived in different times and different circumstances?

Contemporary experimental efforts to stimulate creative thinking have been attempted by group activities such as

"Brainstorming" (Osborn, 1953) and "Synectics" (Gordon, 1961); other research has compared the productivity of the individual with that of the group (Taylor, 1961). While some interesting findings have been reported, it must be acknowledged that results have not been consistently convincing.

SOME BASIC FEATURES OF CREATIVITY

Despite the diverse viewpoints of research workers in the area of creativity and differences in the kind of data they favor, it still may be possible to find some agreement among them about basic features of creativity. That is, there may be some broad general principles upon which anyone who has studied the litera-ture on creativity can agree.

Talent

One of the most obvious features of creativity is talent, that is, an above average aptitude and ability in some specific area. The talent may be manifested in any sense modality or form of expression, but it must be outstanding. It may be verbal in the case of a novelist who sets down his ideas in words or for the poet who is especially sensitive to nuances and implications of symbolic language. To draw or paint the artist needs both visual talent and a skilled hand. Ability to deal with three-di-mensional relationships is needed by the sculptor and the architect. Musicians must be talented in auditory areas, dancers and athletes in kinesthesis, and chefs in gustation and olfaction. It seems likely that there are specific cognitive talents required for such fields as theoretical physics, the higher mathematics, and other intellectual endeavors, but there seems to be no person of out-standing creativity who is not unusually talented in at least one kind of function and some, like Leonardo da Vinci, may be excep-tionally gifted in a number of different areas.

Is it possible to be creative without talent? An eminent art historian, Max Friedlander, refers to the famous Dutch im-pressionist painter, Vincent Van Gogh, as "genius without talent." But what he seems to mean by this phrase is that Van Gogh's "great-ness of soul" and "strength of spirit" overshadow his "visual gifts" (1960:141). The Dutch painter certainly had a high degree of talent, even though he may not have possessed the exquisite hand of Rembrandt. In the latter's case Friedlander says, "Indeed, to apply the concept of 'talent' almost sounds like blasphemy" (p. 140). Talent may not always be fully realized for many reasons; in Van Gogh's case periodic mental illness may have prevented him from achieving his full potential.

Three kinds of relationships are possible: highest talent
and highest creativity, lesser talent and highest creativity, and
greater talent without creativity. What does not seem possible is
for great creativity to be expressed without some degree of talent
as a necessary but not sufficient condition.

Diligence

A second feature, related to the first, is that talent must
be developed and brought to skillful use for some purpose--it is
not enough to have a naturally keen eye, a deft hand, or any other
outstanding ability. To go beyond the level of dilletantism requires inordinate practice and exercise of a special talent and
this, in turn, implies motivational characteristics of perse ver-
ance and diligence. No person who has attained more than superficial success has done so without a lot of hard work. That this
is true for creativity as well as for intelligence has long been
recognized by psychologists. "High but not the highest intelligence, combined with the greatest degree of persistence, will
achieve greater eminence than the highest degree of intelligence
with somewhat less persistence" (Cox, 1926:187).

It must be stressed that the creative person does not work
for work's sake nor does he display a talent for mere exhibition
of skill. There is a direction and a goal orientation to be seen
in his efforts that transcends the persistence and perseverance of
ordinary endeavor and the neurotic perseveration of the pathologi-
cally compulsive person.

Intelligence

A third feature of creativity is a normal degree of intellectual ability, that is, intelligence as commonly understood.
The general question of the relationship between creativity and
intelligence has been alluded to earlier but the specific point
to be argued here is that the creative person must be intelligent.

Mentally retarded individuals show very little in the way of
intelligent behavior and there is no evidence that their behavior
can be described meaningfully as creative. In fact, it may be
pointed out that Donald W. MacKinnon states very clearly that his
creative subjects were all above average in general intelligence
(1962:488).

The well-known study of Jacob W. Getzels and Philip W. Jackson (1962) seems to have been interpreted widely as though

intelligence counts for much less than creativity. Indeed, these
authors themselves tend to disparage intelligence by relating it
to characteristics that they cast in negative terms. But the
fact is that all of their subjects, including those labeled creative, were far above average intelligence.

The possession of intelligence by itself, however, does not
guarantee creativity. Lewis M. Terman and his co-workers studied
more than a thousand subjects identified when they were children
because of unusually high IQ scores on the Stanford Binet. As
adults, these highly intelligent subjects showed superior intellectual performance and achieved a higher degree of success academically and vocationally than the average person. Nonetheless,
in a review of these studies on the gifted and talented it is
pointed out that "most strikingly, the group [Terman's subjects]
did not produce any great creative artists" (Fliegler and Bish,
1959:410).

Outstanding talent in the absence of adequate and organized
intelligence leads to nothing but the exercise of the talent itself. There are many cases of the so-called *idiot savant*--mental-
ly retarded individuals with exceptional ability of a specific
nature. Some of these individuals can tell immediately on what
day of the week any given date in the past or the future falls.
Others have perfect musical pitch and some can reproduce exactly
any musical phrase or melody after hearing it once (Scheerer,
Rothman, and Goldstein, 1946). Many mathematical prodigies have
been found who are only average in general intelligence and some
actually retarded (Bryan, 1970). These talents are always expressed in a reproductive or a repetitive way and never do those
persons possessing them manifest any originality or creativity.

IDENTIFYING POTENTIALLY CREATIVE SUBJECTS

The problem then, is how to identify potentially creative
subjects. There is no way of knowing exactly what the true incidence of creativity may be. Certainly it is usually considered
to be rare or infrequent in occurrence, and the number of noncreative persons in the world must surely outnumber those considered
to be creative no matter what criterion is used.

If, as discussed above, three prerequisites for creativity
are talent, intelligence, and motivation, we ought to be able to
increase the likelihood of locating a creative person by looking
in a group that has been selected for these characteristics. In
this present study such an opportunity was available in the Governor's School of North Carolina. This is a residential summer

program for high school students who are especially selected because of outstanding ability and achievement in academic subjects
and in arts areas. Students are not nominated for the school
merely because they are "gifted" in a narrow, psychometric, high
IQ sense, but rather because they have intellectual and artistic
aptitudes that have been demonstrated in actual performance both
in the classroom and in extracurricular activities. A more detailed description of the Governor's School and the students will
be given later in Chapter V.

It is assumed that in the Governor's School the incidence
of potential creativity is likely to be greater than in a randomly
selected group of high school students. There is, admittedly, no
way of knowing exactly what the difference in likelihood of adult
creativity may be. In fact, there can be no complete assurance
that there will be any creative persons at all in the Governor's
School group. We can only hope that there will be and assume
that the chances are better than zero.

There is a second important reason for using high school age
subjects in this research project. If we start with creative subjects who have been identified as adults, there is no way of knowing what they were like as youngsters except by retrospective
analysis. The loss of accurate information because of the erosion
of time and distortion of memory is self-evident. Very few schools
or administrative agencies keep systematic records and, in any
event, they are not likely to record exactly the same kinds of information in exactly the same kind of way. Different units will
maintain different kinds of records for different purposes making
accurate comparison of individual subjects or groups difficult if
not impossible.

Furthermore, attitudes, interests, and personality characteristics are much less likely to be available than academic grades
and easily measured intellectual abilities. As a number of writers
have pointed out, it is the former traits that may be of more value in understanding creativity.*

A longitudinal study seems called for, then, which includes
data that are not restricted to standard cognitive and intellectual measures, a study in which theoretical personality factors

---

*Even a staunch proponent of a cognitive approach to cre-
ativity, J.P. Guilford, has finally conceded the importance of
noncognitive factors and asks research workers to determine "which
needs, interests, and attitudes help the individual to be produc-
tively creative" (1967b:12).

hypothesized to be related to creativity are measured.* The argument for a longitudinal approach has been stated succinctly by Robert S. Albert: "While much has been discovered about creative behavior, giftedness, and genius *qua* eminence by working backward, a fully scientific understanding of them will be achieved only by working forward and predicting their occurrences" (1969:752).**

In addition to testing the validity of the actuarial argument that the Governor's School students as a group are likely to produce relatively more creative adults than a randomly selected high school sample, a second claim is set forth. A prediction is made that within the Governor's School a subgroup of subjects can be identified that will show a higher incidence of creative behavior as adults than the remainder of the group. This prediction is based on personality and temperamental characteristics rather than cognitive factors. Intelligence and cognitive functions are, of course, important as will be discussed in the next chapter, but the approach taken here considers personality dimensions to be basic parameters of creativity in their own right.

-----

*Dellas and Gaier have pointed out, "there is a necessity to develop creativity measures based on personality study rather than on task performance" (1970:70).

**Dellas and Gaier also express a similar viewpoint: "The necessity of longitudinal studies is obvious for determining qualities that contribute to creative performance, personality changes within the developing creator, and the interaction of personality, cognitive and environmental variables in the creative versus the noncreative" (1970:70).

Chapter II

MEASUREMENT OF INTELLIGENCE

There is a widespread belief held by most laymen that intelligence is fairly well understood by "science" and that there are many tests available to measure intelligence precisely. Psychologists differ primarily in degree from this view--although one would think that their training and experience would have led them to a somewhat more sophisticated attitude. However, reports of research procedures to the effect that "groups were equated for intelligence" or that "subjects were matched on IQ" without any further specification of how the equating or matching was achieved belie the assumption that psychologists are very much more advanced in their basic understanding of intelligence or in the use of related terms than an educated layman.

In a refreshingly straightforward paper dealing with this problem Alexander G. Wesman commented:

> It is my conviction that much of the confusion which plagued us in the past, and continues to plague us today, is attributable to our ignoring two propositions which should be obvious:
>
> 1. Intelligence is an attribute, not an entity.
> 2. Intelligence is the summation of the learning experiences of the individual.
> (1968:267)

While not all psychologists would agree with the second proposition as being obvious, most would accept the first since they recognize the inferential nature of intelligence as a concept. It might help reduce confusion and ambiguity, even though it would be awkward, to require everyone to employ the phrase "intelligent behavior" instead of saying "intelligence" or, even worse in terms of accuracy, "IQ."

"Intelligence Quotient" had at first a reasonably rigorous definition in terms of the measuring procedures on which it was based. But, as time passed, popular usage by laymen and sloppiness on the part of psychologists (even the abbreviation, I.Q., was reduced to IQ) have eroded the term to a vague synonym for intelligence itself.

It may be just as well to restate what was initially obvious. First, that an IQ is basically a *score* on a test, that is, a number given to a subject on the basis of how many items he gets correct. Formerly, the number of correct items (Mental Age, in the form of a score) was divided by the number of items a child of the same age ought to answer correctly (Chronological Age, again, merely a score). In this context "ought" means a statistical average. These two numbers, actually based on the number of items arbitrarily included in the test but converted to units based in terms of time (months and years), were divided and the quotient then multiplied by 100 to get rid of the decimal point. The formula shows this clearly:

$$\frac{\text{Obtained Score (MA)}}{\text{Expected Score (CA)}} \times 100 = IQ$$

If the ratio were 1, it would become an IQ of 100. If it were .75, it would become an IQ of 75, and would indicate that the subject did not get as many items right as the average child at the same age. To say that a child with an IQ of 75 is below average in intelligence and that one with an IQ of 125 is above average is an inference, justified perhaps by experience with the test and by acknowledging the psychometric assumptions, but an inference nonetheless that is a long way from observations of the child's actual nontest behavior in ordinary surroundings.

It must be pointed out that the use of the term IQ is inaccurate psychometrically at the present time because most users of standard intelligence tests have abandoned the use of ratio scores (which had serious drawbacks, both numerical and conceptual, from the beginning). In common use now are standard scores derived by completely different statistical procedures even though these scores are usually expressed in the same kind of numerical values (see Anastasi, 1968:45-49, 57-58).

PROBLEMS OF MEASUREMENT

Another widespread belief is the assumption that there can be no measurement unless there is something to be measured. It is perfectly legitimate, of course, to ask a psychologist to measure the intelligence of a child by means of the Stanford-Binet test. But what is it that is measured? Can we say that *intelligence* is being measured?

Anne Anastasi is willing to answer that question. Strictly speaking, she says, "No psychological test can do more than measure behavior" (1968:23). What is measured, then, by the test is not some entity--intelligence (or aptitude, achievement, ability, or whatever)--but the behavior of a subject who is asked to perform certain tasks in a specified way. Anastasi continues, "Whether such behavior can serve as an effective index of other behavior can be determined only by empirical tryout" (p. 23). In other words, we are comparing two sets of behavior, test behavior and nontest behavior. Nontest behavior includes such activities as school grades, ratings by teachers, extracurricular experiences, and so on. Such nontest behavior is often conventionally, if misleadingly, called "the criterion." For consistency and clarity it might be better to keep the phrase "criterion *behavior*" in mind when the term is used.

Admittedly, it is difficult not to reify the terms of a statement such as "intelligence and academic achievement are related." It seems insufficient to say that, strictly speaking, we mean only that one set of numbers derived fairly systematically from a test, say the Scholastic Aptitude Test, is correlated with another set of numbers, Grade Point Average, which is derived from a much less systematic procedure.

Now it may well be that many psychologists do hold an objective view about the conceptual terms that they use and keep in the back of their minds, at least, the measurable behavior that must form the basis for conceptual elaboration. Yet Gordon W. Allport, whose classic book on personality (1937) probably has had more influence on the thinking of psychologists working in this area than any other writer outside of Freud himself, was able to state in the ultimate revision of his book, "Most philosophers and psychologists (except for the modern positivists)...prefer to define personality as an objective entity, as something that is 'really there'" (1961:25). There is no doubt in reading Allport's last words on the subject that he still maintained that when he used the term "trait," for instance, he meant something that had an independent existence apart from the conceptualization of the psychologist and that it had an objective reality of its own. A trait he asserted is "a neuropsychic structure" (p. 347). In a monograph on objective tests as instruments of psychological theory, Jane Loevinger clearly expresses a similar conviction: "Traits exist in people; constructs...exist in the minds and magazines of psychologists" (1967:83).

PROBLEMS OF DEFINITION

Psychologists, if we accept the argument thus far, can no more define intelligence in any ultimate sense than biologists can define "life" or physicists "light." But it does not follow that such terms are meaningless or that it is futile to attempt definitions. We should be sympathetic to the psychologists at a symposium held many years ago who gave up in despair and concluded that intelligence is whatever is measured by intelligence tests. This is not as bad as it sounds since it offers at least a starting point for systematic investigations of intelligence that may help us to understand the concept, even if we do agree that no ultimate definition is possible.

To hold that intelligence is what such tests measure is essentially an "operational" or working definition. The psychologist may say that for his purposes intelligence will be defined by scores on the Stanford-Binet or on the Wechsler Scale, for example. Persons who have studied the behavioral nontest correlates of the scores (and even those who have not) will have some understanding in a general way of what it means to say that Group A had an average IQ of 120 on the test while Group B averaged 105. The fact that these values are expressed in quantitative form and seem to imply some amount or capacity should not mislead us.

There are, of course, many other kinds of definition in addition to that of the operational type, but it is not crucial for our purposes to explore them all and only two other types will be considered.

One type comprises a class of definitions that is pragmatic or practical and closely tied to the common sense observations of daily life. We note that some persons "catch on" more quickly to new problems, that they have more knowledge about the world, that they can define unusual words, that they can solve mathematical puzzles, and so on. It is on this pragmatic level that certain distinctions are often noted between persons in terms of their success in ordinary pursuits of life. We may say that two persons are equally intelligent as judged by observations of their general behavior but that one succeeds and the other fails because of differences in "ambition" or "business sense" or, even, just plain "luck." Differences in the performance of students are sometimes ascribed to levels of "motivation." Often a teacher is surprised to find on the record of pupil A, who has attained outstanding course grades, an Otis IQ, say, of 110 but a score of 125 opposite the name of pupil B whose academic work has been indifferent.

Many factors will influence test behavior and hence the test score, just as many different kinds of influence will affect the nontest behavior of ordinary life. Scores have no more claim to be "true" or accurate than the judgments of peers or parents or psychologists.

Although it is implicit in the argument advanced above that there is a core of common sense agreement in a general way about the connotations of the term intelligence, it must be noted that this holds at the school age level only. In a systematic statistical analysis of a group of subjects tested and retested with intelligence tests from the age of 2 months to 18 years, three distinct factors of intelligence were found that referred to quite different kinds of nontest behavior. "The term 'an intelligent' child seems to refer to a lively (alert) infant at first and to a rather stubborn child at an age of three before it acquires the connotations [manipulation of symbols] which predominate all through the school-age" (Hofstaetter, 1954:163).

It may be that a fourth and different factor will emerge for the adult years. If so, this would cast doubt on the implicit assumption that we can freely generalize from one situation to another on the same basis. In particular, it may be misleading to expect at different ages and at different levels the same kind of relationship between intelligence defined operationally in terms of some psychometric instrument, and the behavior observable in practical everyday behavior. An adult with a test score of 110 on the Wechsler Scale may be just as intelligent from a pragmatic point of view as someone with a score of 125, and may actually accomplish more in the world of affairs.

Figure II-1 depicts the relationship between pragmatic and psychometric intelligence in diagrammatic form. The broken line represents the assumed direct linear relationship that seems to be implied by laymen and by psychologists; that is, the higher the IQ score, the brighter the person. The solid line in the figure offers an alternate hypothesis, namely, that although there may be a consistent relationship between test score and nontest behavior at the lower levels, this begins to change at the average level of test score. At higher levels of test score there may be very little systematic relationship between the two kinds of intelligence and we should not be surprised to find discrepancies between test and nontest behavior. It seems likely that attitudes, interests, motivation, and other personality characteristics may be related both to practical success and to test scores. Some persons have the ability to obtain high scores but are indifferent to standardized psychometric situations, others do well in the safely structured testing room but not in the uncertain demands of the outside world.

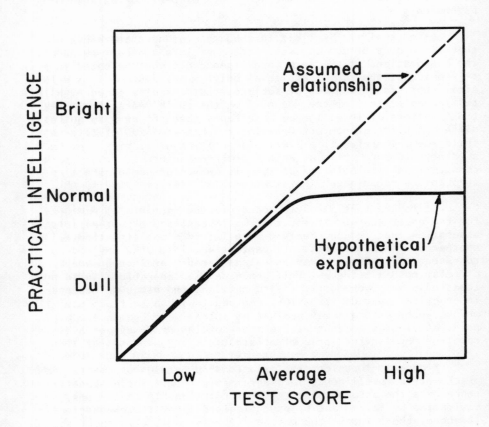

Figure II - 1

A person with verbal interests may do well on a vocabulary test but perform poorly on a nonverbal intelligence test (Welsh, 1967; 1971). Emotional states and conditions such as anxiety have been shown to affect scores on intellectual tests (Baughman and Welsh, 1962: Chap. 13).

In a study demonstrating good memory and certain kinds of problem-solving ability among mentally deficient school children, it was noted that they "do not resemble each other for merely having scored the same I.Q. rating on a given test. Pupils with an I.Q. of 70...are quite different in temperament, in personality, and in quality of intelligence" (Gaudrea, 1968:302). It was found that "at least 20% of normal subjects turn out to be less success-ful than their deficient age-compeers in the solving of easy tasks in learning" (p. 305).

The relationship between social intelligence and the kind of intelligence measured by a standard IQ test was studied by Ralph Hoepner and Maureen O'Sullivan (1968). Scores on the Henmon-Nelson Test of Mental Ability for a group of juniors in a middle-class high school were correlated with six tests of social intel-ligence derived from Guilford's Structure-of-Intellect theory (see pp. 41-45). The correlations ranged from .17 to .42, and when corrected for statistical attenuation yielded an average value of .40. this finding seems to imply that social intelligence and IQ intelligence are rather clearly related and are not indepen-dent.

The authors reported, however, that when the actual scatter-plots of the correlations were examined, triangular rather than eliptical distributions were apparent. Thus, while high IQ sub-jects tended to have equally high social intelligence scores, low IQ subjects showed high social intelligence scores almost as often as showing low scores. They argue that many persons may have supe-rior social intelligence yet not be identified by standard intel-ligence tests.

There is evidence, then, that there is not necessarily a di-rect and linear relationship between intelligence as defined opera-tionally by IQ scores on a conventional intelligence test and the kind of behavior subsumed by intelligence defined in pragmatic and practical social terms.

CONCEPTUAL DEFINITIONS

The last general class of definitions that will concern us is the theoretical or conceptual. Many writers shy away from this kind of definition. J.P. Guilford, for example, in *The Nature of Human Intelligence* (1967), does not offer a definition of his own at this level but quite clearly ties his theory of Structure-of-Intellect to operationally-defined tests of his own design.

On the other hand, Cyril Burt, after reviewing evidence from various sources, social and physiological as well as psychological, concludes that intelligence is "a general mental factor which enters, with varying degrees, into all types. of cognitive processes" (1967:280). He concludes further that this hypothetical mental factor is "largely dependent on the individual's genetic constitution" (p. 280). T.R. Miles believes that it is justifiable to say that intelligence is a "factor of the mind" only in the sense that there can be discovered "factors of the body" to which the former can be related (1967:176).

Many other psychologists, to be sure, have offered conceptual definitions of intelligence as well as psychometric methods of describing intelligence by test performance, but it is not necessary for our purposes to review them. It is of interest, though, to look at the views of the great pioneer in the testing of intelligence, Alfred Binet. Translations from extracts of his writings are available in Anastasi (1965).

> It seems to us that in intelligence there is
> a fundamental faculty, the alteration or lack of
> which is of the utmost importance for practical
> life. This faculty is judgment, otherwise called
> good sense, practical sense, initiative, the
> faculty of adapting one's self to circumstances.
> To judge well, to comprehend well, to reason well,
> these are the essential activities of intelligence.
> (p. 38)

The important point is that Binet saw very clearly the need to relate conceptual definitions of intelligence, the psychometric methods of measuring intellectual functions, and the practical demands of real life. It is to these interrelationships that we now turn.

DEFINITIONAL RELATIONSHIPS

We may conclude, then, that in the context of the present study there is no need to assume that intelligence is an entity. The basic argument is this: Intelligence can be understood as a hypothetical concept in a theoretical framework which is inferred from certain observations that are in turn dependent on certain measurements.

The relationship between the three types of definitions offered above are summarized in Figure II-2. These definitions may
be organized on two different levels, observations and inferences.
Pragmatic and practical definitions are related to the more or less
casual and unsystematic observations of everyday life, while operational and psychometric definitions refer to the controlled and
systematic observations made possible by a test or by some experimental procedure. Conceptual and theoretical definitions are not
directly observable but must be inferred from the observations
that can be made directly either in a common sense situation or in
a scientific setting. The double-headed arrows connecting the
three definitions are intended to show the mutual influence and
the interrelationship of all three.

Binet's well-known test of intelligence was developed in
response to a practical problem, namely that some children in
French schools did not seem to be able to learn very much. The
success of his psychometric instrument then influenced general
theories of intelligence (see also Goodenough, 1949: Chaps. 4, 5).
Guilford, on the other hand, starting from a conceptual model of
Structure-of-Intellect (1967), has developed a large number of
tests that may prove to be related to some of the practical problems of intellectual performance.

It is shibbolethic dogma to assert that one must start with
a concept and develop a test from that point. Movement can just
as legitimately be made in the other direction. We can start from
observations of ordinary behavior and develop both a conceptual
frame of reference to help comprehend these observations and also
devise measuring instruments for accurate assessment of the behavior.

The influence must be mutual for all three points of view.
When there are discrepancies between test scores and ordinary behavior, we should examine not merely the psychometric device but
also the conceptual framework of our testing procedures. In the
long run, of course, someone--if not the individual investigators
who choose a particular position--must organize a comprehensive
way of resolving all three points of view and must develop a complete system of explanation.

TERMAN'S CONCEPT MASTERY TEST

As indicated earlier, the point of view taken in the present
study is an operational one and is based on a psychometric approach
to research that relies on standard tests to differentiate among
subjects and to explore systematically relationships and interrelationships of different aspects of their behavior. The test used

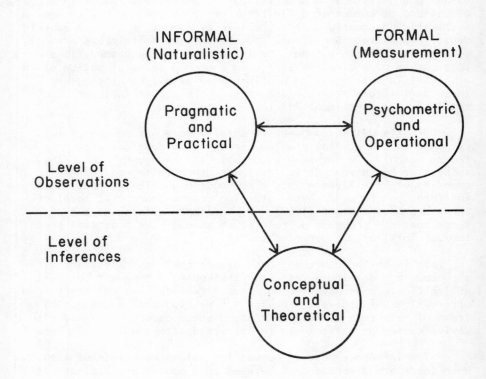

INFORMAL
(Naturalistic)

FORMAL
(Measurement)

Pragmatic
and
Practical

Psychometric
and
Operational

Level of
Observations

Level of
Inferences

Conceptual
and
Theoretical

Figure II - 2

here as a measure of intellectual ability or intelligence is the
Concept Mastery Test (CMT) developed by Lewis M. Terman in the
course of his well-known study of gifted children.

Terman became interested in the study of intelligence as a
result of required work in one of his college classes.

> My first introduction to the scientific prob-
> lems posed by intellectual differences occurred
> ...when I was a senior in psychology at Indiana
> University and was asked to prepare two reports
> for a seminar, one on mental deficiency and one
> on genius. Up to that time, despite the fact
> that I had graduated from a normal college as a
> Bachelor of Pedagogy and had taught school for
> five years, I had never so much as heard of a
> mental test. The reading for those two reports
> opened up a new world to me, the world of Galton,
> Binet, and their contemporaries. (1954:222)

The interest that was aroused by this required report carried over to his graduate study, and to his doctoral dissertation
at Clark University in 1903 which was an experimental study of
the "intellectual processes of fourteen boys, seven of them picked
as the brightest and seven as the dullest in a large city school"
(p. 222). These subjects were given an extensive battery of tests
(many of them derived from Binet's work) that required 40 to 50
hours of Terman's time for each subject. Although he modestly dis-
claims that his experiment contributed anything to science, it did
contribute to his future thinking and "sold" him "completely on
the value of mental tests as a research method" (p. 222).

At Stanford he pursued this interest in intellectual behavior
and after several tentative translations and adaptations of Binet
and Simon's tests, in 1916 he published the famous Stanford Revision of their work which became "the standard for all testing in
the United States" (Goodenough, 1949:62). Reliance on Stanford-
Binet scores as a universal metric is still a common practice
(see p. 46 below).

In the extensive standardization of the Stanford-Binet, Terman noted at each age level the contrast in behavior between the
highest and the lowest scoring children; these observations reinforced and intensified the interest that had been aroused by his
college report and his dissertation. He resolved to study the
gifted end of the intellectual continuum and in 1921 received a
grant from the Commonwealth Fund of New York for research on subjects of superior intelligence. By means of individual and group

intelligence tests given in school classes from kindergarten level
to the 8th grade, about 1500 subjects were identified in California
schools who averaged about 150 in IQ scores on the Stanford-Binet.
His aims in this research were typically straightforward: "First
of all to find what traits characterize children of high IQ, and
secondly, to follow them for as many years as possible to see
what kind of adults they might become" (Terman, 1954:222). This
long-term study of the intellectually gifted aroused the interest
of the general public as well as that of psychologists and educa-
tors.

Follow-up Studies

Terman and his associates made a series of follow-up studies
of his gifted children and have reported details of their physical,
social, and psychological characteristics which show a general
superiority of the subjects throughout life (see especially Terman and Oden, 1947; 1959).

It was necessary to devise a new measure of intelligence for
the longitudinal study since it was not feasible to use an individually administered test like the Stanford-Binet even though it
had been revised in 1937. (The current revision, 1960, abandoned
the use of ratio IQ scores as discussed above.) Not only was the
test prohibitive in terms of time that would be required for administration, but it was also unsuitable because the content was
developed essentially for children and there were not enough difficult items to differentiate at the extreme upper end of adult
intelligence. After a survey of various kinds of tests and the
results that they yielded, two different types of items were
chosen: pairs of words (synonyms or antonyms) and analogies.
The test was entitled the Concept Mastery Test because it seemed
to involve abstract ideas. In the test manual Terman states that
"abstractions are the shorthand of the higher thought processes,
and a subject's ability to function at the upper intellectual
levels is determined largely by the number and variety of concepts at his command and by his ability to see relationships between them" (1956:10).

The original form of the CMT was devised in 1939 and is now
referred to as Form A; details of its derivation have been described by Terman and Oden (1947). A revised form (previously
known as Form B, but now called Form T) was prepared in 1950 by
eliminating some of the excess top items that not even the grown-
up gifted subjects could answer, and extending the level downward
so that spouses of the subjects might be included in the range
of scores (Terman and Oden, 1959).

Form T

Form T is described in the manual and directions for administering and scoring the test are outlined. The CMT now comprises 190 items, 115 word pairs in Part I and 75 analogies in Part II. Since the CMT is untimed it may be considered a "power" test rather than a "speed" test. The manual suggests that "those for whom the test is intended will ordinarily complete it within forty minutes" (p. 3) but in practice it takes a class hour of fifty minutes for college students when the time for giving instructions, handing out and collecting the booklets and answer sheets are taken into account. Scoring is completely objective and may be carried out by machine or by hand.

To take account of the possibility of getting answers correct on a sheer guessing basis, wrong answers are penalized and the subject is told on the face sheet of the test booklet to "omit those items that you could answer only by pure guess." A right-minus-wrong formula is used for Part I, and for Part II the score is the number right minus half of the wrong answers (the half point occurring for an odd number of wrongs is dropped before subtraction).

This so-called "correction for guessing" should result in a zero score for a subject who answers every item and answers on a strict guessing or random basis. In actual fact, however, negative scores do occur, particularly for subjects who do not answer many items and who either have bad luck or who have incorrect knowledge of the few items answered. Terman and Oden (1947) found that 4 of 690 spouses of the gifted subjects obtained negative scores. There were relatively more cases in the much younger gifted students from the Governor's School; 16 out of 1163 had negative scores.

Validational Evidence

What evidence is there that the CMT really works? To say that an intelligence test "works" actually means, in this context, that there should be some systematic relationship between the psychometric test behavior and the pragmatic nontest behavior. Groups considered to be more intelligent as commonly understood should get higher scores on the CMT than groups less highly regarded. Further, there should be some differentiation within groups; that is, individuals who show higher levels of intellectual accomplishment should get higher scores than those with lower accomplishment.

In Terman's follow-up studies two different forms of the CMT were given to the original gifted subjects; about 950 were tested in 1939-40 and more than a thousand in 1951-52. "On both tests they scored on the average about as far above the generality of adults as they had scored above the generality of children when we selected them" (Terman and Oden, 1947:223). Thus the CMT shows them to be as superior a group psychometrically as had been shown earlier on the Stanford-Binet.

Within this group of gifted subjects there is a clear-cut relationship between adult CMT scores and childhood IQ scores. Subjects whose IQ's were above 170 earned an average of 156 on the CMT, those from 160-169 scored 146, and so on, down to subjects with less than 140 in IQ points who averaged only 114 on the CMT (Terman, 1956: Table 3). Thus, as adults, the gifted subjects ranked in approximately the same relative position in intellectual ability as they had when tested in childhood.

There is also a positive relationship between CMT scores and educational achievement. Subjects obtaining a Ph.D. degree averaged 159; the LL.B., 149; M.A. (or equivalent) and M.D., 144; and so on, down to those with a high school education whose CMT average was 118 (Terman, 1956: Table 4). The same table in the manual also shows that spouses of the gifted subjects, although averaging somewhat lower in CMT scores than their mates, still show the same ordering of educational attainment and CMT scores.

A group of Air Force Captains scoring much lower on the CMT in absolute level, compared to the groups discussed above, also demonstrate the hierarchical relationship with education. Those with a college degree averaged 74; those with some college, 61; high school, 57; and less than high school, 35 (Terman, 1956: Table 5).

Finally, CMT scores and undergraduate grade point average show a significant relationship. The coefficient of correlation for these measures for two different groups of students is .37 and .49 (Terman, 1956: Table 6). Even within a single course, the CMT seems to differentiate level of academic achievement; in the present writer's "Tests and Measurements" course final grades correlated .41 with the CMT for one section of 47 students and .58 for another group of similar size.

The evidence indicates, then, that Terman's Concept Mastery Test may reasonably be regarded as a measure of intelligence or intellectual ability as ordinarily understood in the sense that there are meaningful and systematic relationships between nontest intellectual status and score level on the CMT.

Score Stability

A question that has both practical and theoretical importance is the stability of scores on a test; that is, do the scores
tend to change over time? If there are changes in scores, are
these consistent or inconsistent?

A great deal of effort was spent on the problem of the "con-
stancy of the IQ" during the 1920s and 1930s that is now seen as
partly a psychometric pseudo-problem reflecting misconceptions
about both the nature of intelligence and the implications of measurements related to this concept. Many persons conceived of intelligence as a relatively innate ability that should show a relatively constant increase during childhood like height or weight;
during adolescence the amount of increase with age should dimin-
ish and then level out.

By using a ratio of scores as outlined previously it was
hoped that a metric could be established to achieve score stability such that a child with an IQ of 100 at the age of 6 would have
the same IQ when he was 8 or 12 years of age. Elaborate statistical corrections were employed in the 1937 revision of the Stanford-
Binet in an effort to accomplish this type of score stability.
They were unsuccessful and were abandoned in favor of a more tenable psychometric treatment of raw scores using standard scores
for conversion (see Anastasi, 1968:195-198).

There is no reason to assume, however, that a person's intelligence test scores *should* remain constant over time. Just as
fluctuations in our weight "scores" change from time to time and
may have implications for our physical health and psychological
well-being, so changes in intelligence test scores may have similar implications. A depressing environment and poor instruction
in school may well lower scores on measures of intellectual performance that can be reversed by favorable environment and good
instruction. It is known that anxiety and emotional problems may
affect intellectual functioning and alter test scores (see Baughman and Welsh, 1962: Chap. 13).

Further, there is no reason to assume that intelligence stops
increasing during the teen-age years and remains constant until
senility unless accident or disease causes a premature decline.
Test scores should reflect changes in educational opportunities
and improved instruction. "When cultural conditions have improved
over the interval, a significant rise in the mean intelligence
test performance of the population has generally been found"
(Anastasi, 1968:575-576).

It should be noted, however, that if every subject tested at one time gained the same amount in score, the relative position of the subjects would remain the same. The person with the lowest score the first time would have the lowest score the second time, and so on. The coefficient of correlation for the test-retest scores would be 1.00 and imply a psychometric stability over time but would not necesarily reveal the fact that there had been a constant increase for all subjects. If the amount of increase is not the same or proportional for each subject, then the correlation will be less than 1.00.

To refer specifically to the CMT, the test manual lists test-retest correlations based on the earlier and more difficult Form A and the current Form T ranging from .86 to .94 for different groups of subjects (p. 8). But the gifted subjects, as Terman pointed out, gained in ability: "In the twelve year interval between the two tests, 90 percent increased their intellectual stature as measured by this test" (1954:223).

Were these subjects more intelligent on the second testing, or should we say merely that they had learned more information and knew more words so that they obtained higher scores on that basis? If we accept Wesman's argument they are in fact more intelligent.

Some evidence bearing on the stability of CMT scores during adolescence comes from the Governor's School. A group of 32 students who attended the first summer session was chosen from all of the areas of study at the school to fairly represent the diverse interests of the school. These students came back the following summer as "returnees" and repeated the battery of tests with the current student group. Thus it was possible to determine whether or not there were any significant shifts in scores on this test.

The test-retest correlation was .89 and reflects the fact that the relative standing of the students was very similar in intellectual ability as measured by the CMT one year later. The mean score for the two years, however, showed that there was a marked shift upward from 60.75 (*SD* 30.52) the first summer to 74.81 (*SD* 34.30) the second. Examination of individual scores revealed that all but four subjects increased their scores and one made a remarkable gain of 47 raw score points; the average increase, including the four losers, was 14 points.

By chance, some former Governor's School students have been in sections of the present writer's "Tests and Measurements" course where the CMT is given to illustrate intellectual assessment. One

of the students showed an increase of only 13 points in a four
year interval and another had gained 17 points in five years.
But in the latter time period five other students showed much
larger increases in scores: 34, 39, 42, 44, and 54 points.

In sum, it may be said that the CMT exhibits the conventional psychometric stability of scores held necessary for any
measuring instrument, but that meaningful shifts in scores may
occur for this test.

Group Differences

A summary of statistical characteristics for the groups
discussed above and for a number of other groups obtained from
various sources is given in Table II-1. For each group the total
number of subjects (N), the arithmetic mean (M), and the standard
deviation (SD) are reported. The table comprises 24 different
groups that are listed in descending order of the magnitude of
mean scores.

The highest scoring group in the table is not the original
California gifted subjects, although they rank second, but a small
group of creative writers studied at Berkeley's Institute of Personality Assessment and Research (IPAR), with an average score of
156. The lowest mean in the table, 22, was obtained by a large
group of freshmen in a community college. The discrepancy between
the highest and lowest means is 134 points, representing more than
70% of the total number of possible points on the CMT.

In general, most of the groups listed in the table fall at
expected positions along the hierarchy of means. One notable
exception is Group 22, which was obtained from W.S. Miller in the
manual (1960) for his own difficult intelligence test, the Miller
Analogies Test. It is reported there as "graduate students in
various departments in a southern university" (p. 17), without
any further identification. It may be noted parenthetically that
the CMT and the Miller Analogies Test were highly related for
this group with a correlation coefficient (r) of .73; a similar
value of r was reported for these two tests for the subjects of
Group 11 who were "graduate students in psychology in a western
university" (p. 17).

Although the community college freshmen earned the lowest
average score of all of the groups in Table II-1, it must be
pointed out that within this particular group there was a very
wide range of individual scores, from a low of -26 to a high of
124. In other words, there was at least one freshman who scored

TABLE II-1.   SUMMARY STATISTICS ON CONCEPT MASTERY
               TEST FOR VARIOUS GROUPS*

GROUP	M	SD	N
(1) Creative writers[b]	156	22	20
(2) Original gifted subjects[a]	137	29	1004
(3) Female mathematicians[b]	132	34	41
(4) Graduate students, California[a]	119	33	125
(5) Research scientists and engineers[b]	118	29	45
(6) Graduate and medical students, California[b]	118	33	161
(7) Ford Foundation fellowship applicants[b]	118	35	83
(8) Irish management leaders[g]	114	35	37
(9) Creative architects[b]	113	38	40
(10) College graduates, California[a]	112	32	75
(11) Psychology graduate students[e]	108	26	77
(12) Undergraduates, California[a]	102	33	201
(13) Public Health Education applicants[a]	97	29	54
(14) Spouses of original gifted subjects[a]	95	43	690
(15) Electronics engineers and scientists[a]	95	37	95
(16) Students, Tests and Measurements course[c]	82	24	85
(17) Engineering college seniors[b]	80	28	40
(18) Undergraduates, Stanford[a]	78	26	91
(19) Candidates for M.Ed. degree[d]	69	27	85
(20) Military officers[b]	60	32	344
(21) Governor's School students[c]	57	29	1163
(22) Graduate students, southern university[e]	53	32	207
(23) Independent inventors[b]	51	35	14
(24) Community college freshmen[f]	22	24	236

Sources: a, Terman (1956); b, MacKinnon (1961); c, Welsh (1969a); d, Adair (1969); e, Miller (1960); f, Saunders (1968); g, Barron and Egan (1968).

*N = sample number; M = mean; SD = standard deviation.

higher than the average of all but the three top groups. Likewise, candidates for the Master of Education degree (Group 19), although averaging only 69, had a score range from 12 to 132. Creative architects ranged from 39 to 179 (MacKinnon, 1962:487) and research scientists from 54 to 183 (H.G. Gough, personal communication).

The Governor's School adolescents, subjects of the present research, ranged all the way from -32 to 161. A few of these young students actually scored higher than the average adult creative writer.

Exact score ranges for the other groups cannot be determined directly but can be inferred from the size of the group and the magnitude of the standard deviation.* The group with the largest *SD*, 43 points, is the spouses of the original gifted subjects (Group 14) which, as previously noted, had several scores below zero. The smallest *SD*, 22, appears for the top group of creative writers; although the range is not reported directly, Barron noted that only two members of this group made scores below the mean of the original gifted subjects (1965:69).

The important point to be stressed is that the CMT gives an unusually wide range of scores within any particular group, whether the average score for the group is relatively high or low as contrasted with other groups of subjects. To the extent that the test is "a measure of ability to deal with abstract ideas at a high level" (Terman, 1956:3), we should be able to identify within the Governor's School students those who differ markedly in this ability despite the fact that they are all highly selected in terms of general intelligence. By systematic study of subgroups that obtained extremely high and extremely low CMT scores, we should be able to determine some of their traits and personality characteristics and to see how they are related to intellectual functions.

A good example of this approach may be found in Harrison Gough's paper (1953), "A Nonintellectual Intelligence Test." For the study he assembled a series of items, some selected from standard personality tests and some especially written, that on *a priori* and on theoretical grounds might be expected to covary with intellect. The item pool was administered to several groups of students from which subgroups were identified that fell at the upper and the lower 25% in scores on conventional intelligence tests. Response tendencies to the pool for these

---

*Statistical methods for estimating range of scores may be found in Snedecor (1946:98).

two subgroups were analyzed and those items that significantly differentiated them were assembled as a personality scale. Gough describes the personological correlates of subjects falling high on this scale as reflecting factors which stress "dependability, intellectual clarity, persistence, and planfulness. The decision was made to call the scale a measure of 'intellectual efficiency' in order to reflect these properties" (p. 246).

Thus, a theoretical concept and a scale for measuring it were both developed from analysis of a series of opinion, attitude, and self-description items. The scale has proven to be very useful in personality assessment (Gough, 1964) although it did not by itself differentiate more and less creative architects (MacKinnon, 1962:490). Nor did the CMT, it must be pointed out, show any correlation with rated creativity in these architects (p. 487). This was also true for research scientists (Gough, 1961:111-8).

One implication of these findings is that intelligence as measured by a standard intellectual test and by a personality scale related to it may not by itself be adequate for predicting degree of creativity or for identifying creative persons.

For this reason, a decision was made not to study the Governor's School students solely on the basis of CMT scores but to utilize in addition another measure that has shown some relationship to creativity. This measure, an objective personality test scale, will be discussed in detail in Chapter IV.

SUMMARY

We have, then, discussed in this chapter the problems involved in defining intelligence and have put forth three major points of view in the field: 1) operational or working definition (intelligence is what intelligence tests measure); 2) pragmatic or practical (intelligence is what can be defined by observations of general behavior, *e.g.* levels of performance); and 3) the theoretical or conceptual (considers intelligence as a fundamental faculty of the mind). Ultimately, because of the interrelationship of these three points of view we had to decide on a method to pursue that would encompass all three. Thus, the approach used in the present study is an operational one based on a psychometric approach to the research relying on standard tests to differeniate among subjects and to explore systematically relationships and interrelationships of different aspects of the subjects' behavior. The test used here as a measure of intellectual ability, or intelligence, is the CMT developed by Lewis M. Terman.

    One implication of the above studies in the field is that
intelligence as measured by a standard intellectual test and by
personality scales related to it may not by itself be adequate
for predicting degree of creativity or for identifying creative
persons.   Therefore, the decision was made to combine the CMT
scores with an *objective* personality scale (to be discussed in
Chapter IV).

Chapter III

WHAT IS CREATIVITY?

Very few persons, laymen and psychologists alike, assume
that creativity is well understood and susceptible to accurate
measurement. This is quite to the contrary of the assumption
that introduced intelligence in Chapter II. In some ways this
may be an advantage since there may be fewer prejudices or biases
to overcome. There are problems, on the other hand, since there
has been less exploration of the area by scientific investigations
and there are fewer psychometric instruments available for measurement of what may be even tentatively called creativity.

The most recent edition of the *Mental Measurements Yearbook*
(Buros, 1972), a standard source of information about tests of
all kinds, devotes a section of 236 pages to "Intelligence" but
the Table of Contents does not even list a section for creativity.
The third edition of Anastasi's *Psychological Testing* (1968),
which is a standard and widely used textbook in courses on tests
and measurements, does contain a section on creativity in Chapter
14, "Special Aptitude Tests," but the section itself is less than
nine pages in length.

DEFINITIONS OF CREATIVITY

In the last chapter, intelligence was considered from the
point of view of three different major types of definitions: operational or working definitions, pragmatic or practical definitions, and theoretical or conceptual definitions. It was shown
that these three are interrelated and that although an investigator may want to start, for convenience or because of his particular interest, with one definition or approach rather than another,
in the long run he must be able to show systematic and comprehensible consistencies between and among the three points of view.

Suppose we start with paraphrases of the prototypical definitions offered for intelligence: (1) creativity is what is measured by "creativity" tests, (2) creativity is what leads to "creative" solutions of problems in life, and (3) creativity is a
general mental factor which enters, with varying degrees, into
all types of (?) processes. The quotation marks around *creativity*
in the operational definition and *creative* in the pragmatic

definition, followed by a question mark before *processes* in the conceptual definition have been employed to indicate doubt and skepticism at this stage. The typographic stylism serves, then, to reinforce the statements of tentativeness in the opening section of the present chapter.

There is much less agreement here about tests than in the intellectual area, and construction of what may eventually come to be called creativity tests is in a rudimentary stage compared to intelligence testing. There is much less agreement here about the meaning of creative solutions to the problems of life and some doubt that there is any obvious way at all to clearly distinguish creative and noncreative behavior at the problem-solving level. Finally, there is much less agreement (some feel that there is practically none at this time) about the concept of creativity itself. Is creativity to be conceptualized as a cognitive factor like intelligence or as a noncognitive factor? If it is cognitive how does it differ from intelligence? If it is noncognitive should it be conceptualized as a dimension of attitude, interest, temperament, or some other aspect of personality?

COGNITIVE APPROACHES

Frank Barron has written extensively on this topic and he seems to view creativity largely from an intellectual or cognitive point of view. He commented in discussing early research efforts: "The end of the first half of the twentieth century saw the profession of psychology well furnished with tests of 'intelligence' but as yet poorly furnished with tests of that aspect of intelligence we call creativity" (1965:7).

If creativity is an aspect of intelligence, how does it differ from other aspects of intelligence?

Guilford's Theory

One answer to the question above has been supplied by J.P. Guilford, whose views have influenced a large wing of research in creativity and have led to the development of a number of practical tests.

Guilford conceptualizes intelligence in a three-dimensional model that he terms the "Structure-of-Intellect" (1959b). There are three basic parameters in his model: operation, product, and content. Each of the parameters is divided into categories; there are five kinds of operations, six kinds of products, and

four classes of content. He has represented this model in graphic form as a cubical space subdivided into 120 different areas
(5x6x4), each of which would be represented by a specific test.

Of special interest to us are the five operations that he
employs in his model: evaluation, convergent production, divergent production, memory, and cognition.

He uses the term cognition here in a more limited way than
ordinarily understood, and has commented:

> Tests of many factors simply determine how
> much the examinee knows or can readily discover
> on the basis of what he knows. Such factors of
> knowing or discovering were recognized as cogni-
> tive abilities. In adopting this label for the
> category, a very apt and descriptive one for
> the purpose, it was realized that reference has
> traditionally been made to *cognitive abilities,*
> a term that is meant to include all intellectual
> abilities. The use of the term cognition in the
> more limited way seems more appropriate. After
> all, we do have the term intellectual to use for
> covering the whole range of abilities; there is
> no point in having two labels for the larger
> class of abilities. (1967:62)

Although many persons may feel that Guilford's point is
well taken, the fact is that most psychologists still tend to use
the term cognition in the general sense that it has traditionally
been used. Very few, if any, outside of Guilford's camp have
actually adopted the restricted meaning of the term that he has
recommended: "The primary cognitive abilities have to do with
the possession of information--its discovery and its rediscovery
or recognition" (1959a:365).

In Guilford's schema, two of the five operations are of
specific interest in our discussion; these are convergent and
divergent thinking or *production* as he now prefers to call these
operations "to avoid the ambiguity of the term *thinking*"(1967:62).

In an earlier presentation Guilford wrote, "The convergent-
thinking class of abilities takes its name from the kinds of tests
involved. In general they call for one right answer (at least
one *keyed* answer), which can be determined closely, if not exactly, from the information given" (1959a:376). Thus, convergent
thinking or production "leads to a recognized best or conventional
answer" (1959b:470). More recently he has stated that "in

accordance with the information given in the item, the examinee must converge upon the one right answer" (1967:62).

It can easily be recognized that what Guilford has termed convergent production will seem to many persons to correspond very closely to the kind of intellectual or cognitive ability tapped by most conventional tests of intelligence. That is, information is supplied and only one answer, which has been determined in advance by the psychometrist, is counted as correct (*e.g.*, "*Kepi* is to *sabot* what *head* is to __?__" "In what way are a *wimple* and a *snood* alike?" "What is a *caftan*?" and so on). Guilford himself, however, does not seem to equate the two and states that "the convergent-production category of abilities and functions has been relatively neglected in exploration by factor analysis and rather slighted in traditional intelligence tests" (1967: 183).

In contrast to the one-best answer approach to assessment of intellectual functions, "divergent thinking is defined as the kind that goes off in different directions. It makes possible change of direction in problem solving and also leads to a diversity of answers, where more than one answer may be acceptable" (1959a:381).

Many persons in addition to Guilford have been interested in tests that give the subject a chance to demonstrate some imagination, originality, or cleverness in responses to test items, but most standard intelligence tests, as noted above, require a predetermined answer that is more or less conventional. On the Similarities Test of the Wechsler Adult Intelligence Scale, for instance, the manual (Wechsler, 1955:39) gives examples very clearly indicating that a clever or unusual answer is penalized. To the item "In what way are *wood* and *alcohol* alike?" answers of "organic substances," "have carbon," or "hydrocarbons" earn two points. One point is given for "burns," "used in manufacturing," or "used as fuel." But no credit at all is given for "tree products," "alcohol comes from wood," "both useful," or "both can knock you out." To answer that a *fly* and a *tree* are alike because "they both have limbs" is listed as a zero response.

A subject, then, must either curb his inclination to give clever and unusual answers or be prepared to earn lower scores than he should on conventionally scored intelligence tests. School examinations may also reflect this bias, as pointed out by Alexander Calandra (1968).

The refusal to give credit for imaginative replies in tests of intelligence may have its roots in historical circumstances:

Since divergent-production tests require ex-
aminees to produce their own answers, not to
choose them from alternatives given to them, it
is not surprising that any such tests would be
conspicuous by their absence in modern tests of
intelligence, particularly after machine scoring came into the picture. Their absence from
individual tests is also well known, a fact that
can probably be traced to Terman's early experience (1906) with his seven "bright" and seven
"stupid" children that were not discriminated
by a test of creative imagination in line with
other tests. In recent years it has become
known that children of high IQ can be either high
or low on divergent-production tests. With only
seven cases in his "bright" group, Terman could
have had an adverse selection on divergent production, which precluded any superiority of
this group over his low one, particularly if
the judges who selected the bright children did
not include imagination among their signs of
brightness. For whatever reasons, the divergent-
production abilities have historically been outside the domain of intelligence tests and conceptions of intelligence. (Guilford, 1967:138-39)

It may well be, as Guilford argues, that the vagaries of small-
sample research groups or biases of judges in nominating subjects
have deprived intelligence testing of items requiring imaginative
responses. Certainly, the Stanford-Binet, as has been pointed
out above, had a profound influence on the development of group
as well as individual tests of intelligence and on psychometric
theories of intelligence.

Many research workers have utilized Guilford's terminology,
if not his Structure-of-Intellect theory, in differentiating between standard intelligence tests and tests requiring ingenuity,
cleverness, originality, and imagination by referring to the former as convergent tests and the latter as divergent tests. Others
have made a contrast between intelligence tests and "creativity"
tests. This latter terminological distinction has been made popular by the well-known studies of Jacob W. Getzels and Phillip W.
Jackson which will be discussed in some detail. Liam Hudson at
the University of Edinburgh prefers the term "open-ended" to refer
to the divergent-production type of tests and feels that it is a
mistake to use the term *creative* in this manner for such tests.

The crucial question for Hudson is this: "Do people who are creative in the normal sense of the word (great scientists, writers, painters, and so forth) score unusually well on these tests, or not?" (1966:37). If they do not--and Hudson finds no evidence that truly creative subjects do so--then it is indeed misleading to call them creativity tests.

Getzels and Jackson

A study that has proven in many ways to be a landmark in the study of creativity was conducted by Jacob W. Getzels and Phillip W. Jackson in the late 1950s. Major findings from their researches were published in 1962 in a book entitled *Creativity and Intelligence: Explorations With Gifted Students.*

Their basic position is set forth quite directly: "Giftedness in children has most frequently been defined as a score on an intelligence test, and typically the study of the so-called gifted child has been equated with the study of the single [sic] IQ variable" (Getzels and Jackson, 1962:6). Although rejecting the value of intelligence tests *per se* in studying giftedness, their approach to creativity is clearly a cognitive one: "...such other intellectual functions as creativity,... Are there not other intellectual qualities--qualities not presently sampled by the intelligence test--that are also representative of giftedness?" (p. 3).

The contrast between two aspects of intelligence that they proposed to investigate was clearly made:

> It is possible to begin by identifying two basic
> cognitive or intellectual modes. The one mode
> tends toward retaining the known, learning the
> predetermined, and conserving what is. The sec-
> ond mode tends toward revising the known, explor-
> ing the undetermined, and constructing what might
> be. A person for whom the first mode or process
> is primary tends toward the *usual and expected*.
> A person for whom the second mode is primary
> tends toward the *novel and speculative*. The
> one favors certainty; the other risk. (Getzels
> and Jackson, 1962:13-14)

Subjects for their studies came from a private school in the Chicago area that enrolls children from mostly middle and upper-middle class families. Students at this school are very intelligent in terms of standard intellectual tests since their average IQ score is reported to fall two standard deviations above the mean. From a group of almost 500 students in the sixth grade up to the last high school year, two specific subgroups were selected; one subgroup scored high on conventional intelligence tests but not so high on special creativity tests, the other subgroup had high creativity scores but were not so high on standard intelligence.

Intelligence scores were "either a Binet or a Henmon-Nelson [a group test] IQ...although perhaps a dozen were WISC [Wechsler Intelligence Scale for Children, an individual test]. All scores were converted by regression equation to comparable Binet IQ's" (Getzels and Jackson, 1962:16). Thus the Stanford-Binet, as the prototypical test of intelligence, and its method of expressing IQ scores as a standard metric were followed.

Scores for creativity were determined not by one standard test but by a series or battery of tests related to, but also differing from, classic IQ measures. "As it is used in this study, the term 'creativity' refers to a fairly specific type of cognitive ability reflected in performance on a series of paper-and-pencil tests" (p. 16).

The five tests in the creativity battery were:

1. *Word Association*. Give as many definitions as possible to stimulus words such as "bolt" or "bark." It may be pointed out that this differs from the assessment of vocabulary as typically employed in standard intelligence tests by virtue of using relatively common and easily defined words as items, and also by awarding points for the total number of different definitions supplied by the subject rather than for one "correct" answer.

2. *Uses for Things*. This requires the subject to give as many different uses as he can think of for some common object such as "brick." This test, derived from Guilford's work, has been frequently used as a creativity measure in the sense of divergent production and is sometimes called the "Unusual Uses" or "Alternative Uses" test.

3. *Hidden Shapes*. This is basically a perceptual test in which the subject has to locate a simple geometric figure that is "hidden" in one of four complex figures which follow each stimulus item. The test is derived from the work of R.B. Cattell (1965).

4. *Fables*. The subject has to make up different endings for the omitted last line of four different fables.

5. *Make-up Problems*. This is a mathematical task which requires the subject to derive as many different kinds of problems as he can from a paragraph containing a series of numerical statements.

Scores on the five tests were summed to give a creativity score. The summing was justified by showing that all of the tests were positively correlated with each other. For 292 boys the correlations ranged from .159 to .420; for 241 girls the range of correlations was from .197 to .525. Critics of the study were quick to point out that the five creativity tests showed correlations almost as great with the standard IQ measure (see, for example, Thorndike, 1963). For boys, these values went from .131 to .378, for girls, from .115 to .393. In other words, the correlational evidence could be interpreted as reflecting one general intellectual dimension rather than two different cognitive measures as Getzels and Jackson claimed.

Nonetheless, subjects were selected who were in the upper 20% on intelligence scores but not so high on creativity scores for one subgroup which was contrasted with a second subgroup showing the opposite pattern of scores, top 20% on creativity but not on intelligence. There were 15 boys and 11 girls in the High Creative subgroup and 17 boys and 11 girls in the High Intelligence subgroup.

Getzels and Jackson were able to demonstrate that the two subgroups differed on a number of important variables related to school achievement, perception by teachers, parental characteristics, and several personality traits. The content of their findings will not be reviewed here since they are tangential to the purpose of the present study. It is important to note, however, that these authors themselves recognize the inadequacies of a narrowly defined kind of cognition.

> Description of the two groups on the basis of test scores alone neglects certain significant qualitative differences.... It must be emphasized that the qualitative differences are as important as the quantitative, and indeed the concept of *style* of cognitive functioning is much more central to the objectives of this study than any linear notion of "more or less" intellective ability or even the concept of "level" of cognitive functioning. (Getzels and Jackson, 1962:21)

That is, they consider the manner in which a subject attempts to
solve a problem to be as important as whether or not a correct
answer is achieved.

Many persons felt that the kind of design that Getzels and
Jackson employed was incomplete. That is, they did not study
subjects high on creativity *and* intelligence, nor subjects low
on both tests.

Wallach and Kogan

Among the critics of the Getzels and Jackson study were
another pair of workers, Michael A. Wallach and Nathan Kogan,
whose own report, *Modes of Thinking in Young Children: A Study
of the Creativity-Intelligence Distinction*, appeared in 1965.
The research design that they employed rectified the incomplete
method of Getzels and Jackson since they examined all four groups
of subjects selected conjointly on two variables: high/high,
high/low, low/high, and low/low.

The Wallach and Kogan study differed in a second important
way, the concept of creativity from which their techniques for
assessing this dimension stemmed was explicitly formulated from
a previously enunciated theoretical position. They employed an
associative concept of creativity related to the views of Sarnoff
A. Mednick. Mednick had defined the creative thinking process
as "the forming of associative elements into new combinations
which either meet specified requirements or are in some ways useful. The more mutually remote the elements of the new combination, the more creative the process of solution" (1962:221).

Although Wallach and Kogan subscribe to Mednick's associative theory of creativity they pointed out that their "operation-
alization follows a different approach from his" (1965:14). That
is, they did not employ the specific test developed by Mednick
to explicate his theoretical position since its scoring procedures
require giving points for the single correct answer to each item.
They used instead a series of tasks that were presented to their
subjects, a group of 151 5th-grade pupils, which were more in the
nature of games to be enjoyed rather than tests to be endured.
They felt that "an attitude of playfulness rather than evaluation"
would be more likely to maximize the "generation of associative
material" (p. 19).

The method used for assessing creativity was a battery of
five tests, each containing from four to ten items:

1. *Instances.* Name all the (<u>round</u>) things you can think of.

2. *Alternate Uses.* Tell all the different ways you could use a (<u>newspaper</u>).

3. *Similarities.* Give the ways in which a (<u>potato and a carrot</u>) are alike.

4. *Pattern Meanings.* Tell the different things the drawings could be.

5. *Line Meanings.* Tell the different things the line makes you think of.

Two scores were derived from each test, the total *number* of responses to each item in the test and the number of responses for each item that were statistically *unique*. Creativity was thus derived as a measure from ten different scores.

Intelligence was measured by three subtests of the Wechsler Intelligence Scale for Children (WISC)--Vocabulary, Picture Arrangement, and Block Design; two scores from the School and College Ability Tests (SCAT)--verbal and quantitative; and five tests from the Sequential Tests of Educational Progress (STEP)--mathematics, science, social studies, reading, and writing. There were thus ten scores that would serve as indices of intelligence.

Matrices of intercorrelations were generated first for the sexes separately and then combined, which showed that the creativity scores tended to be fairly highly intercorrelated with each other but showed low correlations with intelligence scores and *vice versa*. The average intercorrelation among creativity scores was .41, among intelligence scores .51, and between intelligence and creativity only .09. "Clearly," they concluded, "a dimension of individual differences has been isolated that possesses generality and yet is quite distinct from intelligence as classically defined" (p. 56).

Although the empirical findings on these particular subjects seem fairly convincing, the theoretical hypothesis has been challenged by A.J. Cropley (1968). In a study of Australian university students he found that the Wallach-Kogan creativity tests, even when administered in group form (rather than individually as games), did indeed show high intercorrelations among these tests while remaining practically uncorrelated with standard measures of intelligence. However, a factor analysis of the entire intercorrelational matrix showed a large general factor on which both the creativity tests and the intelligence tests were

substantially loaded. That is, both types of tests could be arrayed on a single dimension rather than requiring two independent
dimensions. Although a second, weaker factor did appear with the
two groups of tests loaded on opposite poles (and hence quite
different statistically), Cropley concludes that "it is by no
means clear that they elicited a new and separate intellective
mode" (p. 200).

Whether or not the Wallach-Kogan results support their conceptual hypotheses or their operational test procedures is not
crucial for the present study. What is important to note is
that although they did employ a more complete design than Getzels
and Jackson, they used a similar kind of approach, namely a cognitive concept of creativity.

Mednick's Test

In addition to the concept of creativity, Sarnoff A. Mednick has contributed to the study of this phenomenon by a practical test that was developed from the theoretical position mentioned above. His test is called the Remote Associates Test or
RAT (Mednick and Mednick, 1967). The thirty items on the test

> are intended to require the testee to perform
> creatively. That is, he is asked to form as-
> sociative elements into new combinations by pro-
> viding connective links. Since the test situ-
> ation is contrived, the combination must meet
> specified criteria that are experimenter im-
> posed. (Mednick, 1962:228).

Each item comprises three words such as *rat, blue,* and *cot-
tage*; the subject has to supply a fourth word "which could serve
as a specific kind of associative connective link between these
disparate words" (p. 229). The required answer is *cheese*. The
RAT is thus quite similar to conventional measures of intelligence
in the sense of convergent thinking since it requires the subject
to give a response which has been contrived in advance by the
tester and can be achieved by cognitive functions on the basis of
information supplied.

In practice, the RAT has indeed proven to be fairly highly
correlated with conventional tests of intelligence for many different groups of subjects. For 106 high school students Lorge-
Thorndike scores correlated .43 with the RAT; for 269 subjects
in grades 7 through 12, IQ scores on the WISC and the RAT gave a
correlation of .55; both Scholastic Aptitude Test scores for 234

college freshmen were significantly correlated--.34 for SAT verbal and .19 for SAT mathematical (Mednick and Andrews, 1967:429).
In a study using 75 nurses, the highest intertest correlation of
seven different variables appeared for the RAT and a conventional
intelligence test, the Shipley-Hartford Scale, with a correlation
of .47 (Day and Langevin, 1969).

McNemar's Hypothesis. It has been suggested (McNemar, 1964)
that the disparity in reported relationships (some quite low, others fairly high) between creativity tests and conventional intelligence tests may be in part a statistical artifact. That is,
although there may be a significant, but low, positive correlation over the entire range of intellectual ability, at the upper
end of the intellectual continuum there may be much more variation in creativity scores than at the lower end. The distribution of scores would fan out and the regression line would be
shaped like the lower one shown in Figure II-1 (p. 51). Such a
hypothesis implies that the correlation of RAT and intelligence
scores would be greater on lower levels of intelligence than at
the upper end.

Martha T. Mednick and Frank M. Andrews (1967) tested this
hypothesis with the RAT and SAT scores for 1211 university freshmen. Not only were overall correlations fairly high, .43 verbal
and .20 math, but when five subgroups differing in absolute level
of SAT scores were studied separately, there was no tendency for
the magnitude of the correlations to drop with high levels of intellectual ability. In fact, there was a slight trend in the opposite direction. In addition to rejecting the nonlinear hypothesis, they commented on the continued evidence that the RAT is
correlated with intelligence tests.

> It seems clear that any measure designed as a
> predictor of creative performance must be shown
> to be a predictor which is superior to any
> existing measure of ability, including intel-
> ligence tests. That is, the creativity measures
> must prove to be more useful than the conven-
> tional, well-standardized, well-validated mea-
> sures which are already available. (p. 431)

The "fan-shaped" hypothesis was also rejected by Gerald P.
Ginsburg and Robert G. Whittemore (1968) who found a linear relationship between levels of intellectual ability measured by the
ACT (English) and the RAT for 292 freshmen at a western university; a similar relationship was obtained with 107 Australian
schoolboys. "Therefore, despite the persistent finding of a
moderate, positive, and reasonably homoscedastic relationship

between RAT and verbal intelligence measures, the two appear
to be measuring different (albeit overlapping) abilities" (Ginsburg and Whittemore, 1968:136).

RAT scores do not seem to be related to factors affecting
the manifestation of creative ability by scientists. Frank M.
Andrews administered the RAT to 355 scientists from a larger
group of over one thousand. Data were available from the scientists themselves, from peers, and from supervisors relating to
scientific or technical contributions and overall usefulness to
the research organizations.

> Results were clear. Creative ability, as
> measured by the RAT showed no strong rela-
> tionship to any of the measures of scientif-
> ic performance.... Adjusting the performance
> measures to hold constant various background
> effects--differences in education, length
> of work experience, type of research setting,
> and time between BS and PhD or age at BS--
> had little effect on the relationships.
> (1965:145)

Jacobson's Criticisms. Mednick's views have been challenged both psychometrically and conceptually by Leonard L. Jacobson and
his co-workers (Jacobson, Elenewski, Lordahl, and Liroff, 1968).
These authors raise three problems that have emerged in studies
based on the Mednick model. The first is the adequacy of the
theory itself, which they hold to be overly simplistic in its
view of the associative process and not strongly supported by
empirical data. The second is based on Mednick's failure to account theoretically for the quantitative aspect of associations--
that the RAT shows higher correlations with quantity of associ-
ations than with originality of response. The third problem con-
cerns the conceptual differentiation of intelligence and creativity which they consider to be generally approached by Mednick with
superficial empiricism. "Tests of creativity and intelligence are
correlated and low correlation between the two are taken as indicative of a kind of construct validity. The underlying assumption
appears to be that if the test is not measuring intelligence it
must be measuring creativity" (p. 431).

Such an approach, these authors feel, ignores an important
conceptual difficulty. Since some of the behavioral characteristics associated with high scores on the RAT (and ostensibly with
creativity) are ones generally assumed to be related to intelligence, the demonstration of statistical independence between two
such tests is not adequate. Such demonstration

> does not by itself necessarily provide informa-
> tion concerning the characteristics which each
> test predicts, nor does it guarantee that each
> measure will predict different constellations
> of behaviors. It is necessary to identify the
> relationships among the tests and processes con-
> cerned and behavioral characteristics in vary-
> ing situations. (Jacobson *et al.*, p. 432)

Here we may refer back to the conceptual model outlined in
Chapter II (Figure II-2, p. 28). What Jacobson and his colleagues
have called for is a statement of the interrelationship of the
three elements in the diagram--behavioral, psychometric, and theoretical.

Although two tests show some degree of correlation, they
may be in fact quite different conceptually, just as the physical
characteristics of height and weight are highly correlated but
are obviously different physical concepts arrived at by quite
different measurement methods, both practically and theoretically.
But, as M.T. Mednick and Andrews have pointed out, if two tests
are highly correlated statistically and if both tests are related to the same kind of observable nontest behavior, then, in
the absence of any compelling conceptual differences between
them, it must be said that the theoretical justification for considering them to be different is weak.

In Jacobson's report the correlation of RAT scores and WAIS
Vocabulary, used as an operational index of intelligence, was .34
for their group of 115 subjects.

> The present data raise fundamental questions con-
> cerning the RAT as well as the general conceptu-
> alization of intelligence and creativity. With
> regard to the latter, it is unclear whether in-
> telligence and creativity refer to cognitive di-
> mensions (inferred hypothetical organismic states),
> behavioral dimensions (personality variables), or
> both simultaneously. (p. 435)

Further, these authors feel that although creativity is assumed to have personality correlates by Mednick, almost all studies employing the RAT have concentrated on cognition. "The personality correlates, which for many investigators would be fundamental to any theory of creativity, have not been adequately explored or even clearly specified" (p. 435).

Finally, Jacobson and his colleagues assert that there are no grounds for assuming that the cognitive dimensions themselves and the kinds of processes measured by the RAT are any more related to some unique aspects of cognition called creativity than many of the Wechsler intelligence subtests such as Similarities or Block Design. "Theoretically, it is not clear why the effective use of remote associates has some unique quality which sets it apart from the variety of abilities measured by intelligence tests" (p. 436).

Torrance's Tests

Another cognitive approach to the study of creativity may be found in the work of Paul Torrance and his followers. They have assembled a series of different kinds of tasks, "The Minnesota Tests of Creative Thinking" (MTCT), that comprises both verbal and nonverbal stimulus items (Torrance, 1962). Many of these tests have been widely used in studies of creativity.

Wallach and Kogan, whose approach has been summarized above have pointed out that most studies employing the MTCT battery of tests have found little or no positive correlation between the verbal and the nonverbal parts of the battery. In contrast to intelligence tests where verbal and nonverbal (performance) indices are highly correlated, "We find a distinction being made between two kinds of 'creativity'--verbal and visual--which are found to be largely independent of each other" (1965:7). These authors also point out the lack of independence of the MTCT from traditional measures of intellectual ability.

One of Torrance's collaborators, Kaoru Yamamoto, studied the Lorge-Thorndike Intelligence Test and the Minnesota Tests of Creative Thinking in large groups of 5th-grade children. When appropriate statistical corrections for restriction of range and for other sources of variance were made, the "true" correlation was seen to be as high as .88. The tests of intelligence and of creativity were not at all independent. He concludes that "we should regard creativity tests as complementary components in new and more inclusive measures of human intellectual behavior, and not as a measure wholly independent and exclusive of the general factor of intelligence" (1965:305).

George F. Madaus also studied the MTCT to determine whether they were independent of intelligence. Subjects were middle-class high school students and included entire freshman and sophomore classes with the exception of those in special classes for the educable mentally retarded. He used the same scoring procedures

as Yamamoto for the Minnesota tests. Intelligence was measured
by the School and College Ability Test (SCAT) including the verbal and quantitative part scores. A rotated factor analytic solution of the intercorrelational matrix of the measures produced
three distinct factors: verbal divergent thinking, nonverbal divergent thinking, and intelligence. Thus, the tests of creative
thinking could not be arrayed on the same dimension. At the same
time, Madaus concluded, "However, whether or not these Minnesota
tests form a separate underlying dimension distinct from intelligence is not entirely clear from these data" (1967:233).

The Minnesota Tests of Creative Thinking, then, like the
RAT, have not been found to be entirely satisfactory.

NEED FOR OTHER APPROACHES TO CREATIVITY

Tests that are alleged to measure creativity in the operational sense that has been discussed above should show positive
intercorrelations among each other and should show some kind of
independence from measures of intelligence. It is, of course,
not necessary that the creativity measures yield intercorrelations
of 1.00 and cross-correlations of .00 with intelligence scores.
It has been noted that height and weight ordinarily show correlations in the neighborhood of .50 for most groups, yet it is obvious that both are needed to describe physical stature. Nonetheless, when the measures employed in the well-known and influential
study of Getzels and Jackson showed that the creativity tests they
employed were about as highly correlated with the intelligence
tests as they were with each other, some doubt must be cast on
the methodology of the study as well as their substantive conclusions. Many other studies in addition to those already reviewed
have also failed to demonstrate the necessary intercorrelations
for creativity measures and have reported insignificant or very
low coefficients (Barron, 1955; Getzels and Csikszentmihalyi,
1966; Eisenman and Robinson, 1967; Piers, 1968). A notable exception is the well-conducted study of Wallach and Kogan discussed
above.

It must be concluded that the search for an easily administered test of creativity that is independent of traditional
tests of intelligence has not been successfully demonstrated by
those working within a cognitive framework. Conceptual clarifica-
tion of creativity has not been achieved, nor has a practical
metric for the assessment of creative behavior been developed.
Whether or not such an instrument is available for this task remains to be seen.

We turn now to a somewhat different and more comprehensive approach, the personality assessment method, that has as a starting point the pragmatics of everyday life and is thus more closely related to that type of definition and also to the product perspective as discussed above.

PERSONALITY ASSESSMENT

Donald W. MacKinnon organized the Institute for Personality Assessment and Research (IPAR) at the University of California, Berkeley, in 1949 and with his colleagues and co-workers has been studying creativity for more than two decades. There can be no doubt that this group has influenced investigators in this country and abroad and has made important contributions to the field.

The starting point for IPAR studies is not some particular psychometric test nor a well-structured theoretical position, but rather with the identification of men and women who are considered by their peers and by other knowledgeable persons to be creative to some degree in their particular field of endeavor. This corresponds to the practical or pragmatic type of definition that has been outlined above.

The method of procedure at IPAR is a research technique known as "living-in assessment" in which nominated subjects come to the Institute and live there for two or three days with the psychologist "assessors." In small groups and individually, these subjects participate in an extensive series of experiences including interviews, batteries of tests, experimental procedures, and observations both in contrived situations and ordinary experiences such as eating lunch and dinner.

At the end of the assessment period the psychologists record their impressions of the subjects systematically by means of a series of ratings and evaluations using check lists, scales, and other psychometric devices, many of which have been especially developed for this purpose by the IPAR staff. A more detailed account of the assessment method and the procedures may be found in writings of Frank Barron (see 1965:9-13; 1968: Chaps. 3,4,5).

The Creative Person

The IPAR group held a conference on "the creative person" at the University of California Alumni Center, Lake Tahoe, California, and individual staff members reported specific findings whch appeared then in the proceedings of the conference (MacKinnon,

1961). Although the IPAR group was not formed to test some well-specified theory of creativity as noted above, it does not imply that they started in complete ignorance of the field or that they had no general concept of creativity from which to inaugurate their assessment procedures. Their general position was summarized in the introductory remarks of MacKinnon:

> The first task which must be faced by any group who would study creativity is to decide what they will consider creativity to be, since creativity has been so variously described and defined. It has seemed to us that true creativity fulfills at least three conditions. It involves a response that is novel or at least statistically infrequent. But novelty or originality of behavior, while a necessary aspect of creativity, is not sufficient. If a response is to lay claim to being a part of the creative process, it must to some extent be adaptive to, or of, reality. It must serve to solve a problem, fit a solution, or accomplish some recognizable goal. And thirdly, true creativity involves a sustaining of the original insight, an evaluation and elaboration of it, a developing of it to the full.

> This view sees creativity as a process which has a time dimension. It may be brief, as in a musical improvisation, or it may involve a considerable span of years, as was required for Einstein's creation of the theory of relativity.

> * * * *

> The process of creativity is not easily come by, nor are all of its phases easy to endure. We should then perhaps be prepared to discover that those who have high potential as well as those who have demonstrated true creativity will show a disposition to undertake problems where the degree of difficulty and frustration is great and will have a drive toward completion and accomplishment that is persistently strong. What I am suggesting is that the creative person is likely to possess, in addition to superior intelligence and cognitive skills, a distinctive motivational structure and personality. (pp. I-1, I-2)

It *is to the last point, the nature of distinctive personality characteristics in creative individuals, that the present
research is directed. The analyses to be reported later are an
attempt to approach systematically a new conceptualization of
two dimensions of personality.*

GOVERNOR'S SCHOOL STUDY

A number of standard tests given in the IPAR assessment
procedures were included in the test battery given to the Governor's School adolescents. This makes possible a comparison between these two groups--adults on the one hand who have been recognized for actual creative behavior and adolescents on the other
hand who are specially selected high school students and are, perhaps, potentially creative.

Among the measures used at IPAR and with the Governor's
School subjects is an art scale from a figure preference test
that has proven to discriminate effectively between more and less
creative groups of subjects, and within groups, has shown systematic relationships to ratings or rankings of creativity. This
scale will be described in some detail in the next chapter and
justification for its use in the present study will be given at
that time.

As noted earlier in Chapter I, the students who attend the
Governor's School are highly selected in terms of intelligence
and intellectual ability, as well as for special talents, aptitudes, and skills. No doubt they are different from the ordinary
high school student in motivation, although the implication of
that term in MacKinnon's usage relates to long-term goals and the
ability to sustain a drive toward that goal over a longer period
of time than an eight-week summer program. The goals that the
Governor's School students will actually attain must wait for a
follow-up study that must be carried out some years hence.

But the personality characteristics of the students while
they are attending the school can be determined. Their personali-
ties can be described by means of standard psychometric instruments. Immediate comparisons can be made with IPAR test results
and similarities and differences in personality characteristics
can be noted.

There is no way of determining exactly what the IPAR subjects were like as adolescents. Not merely the elapse of time
but, more importantly, the inevitable lapses and unavoidable distortions of recall make the retrospective reconstruction of their
adolescent time period by creative adults subject to serious error.

If, however, some of the Governor's School students become recognized as creative adults, it will be possible to say what they were like as adolescents. What we can do now, though, while "waiting for the criterion to mature" is to compare our adolescents with IPAR adults and try to interpret the results of the comparison.

Chapter IV

AN OBJECTIVE TEST RELATED TO CREATIVITY

While it has been shown in Chapter III that there does not seem to be any standard cognitive test of creativity that is independent of conventional tests of intelligence, there remains the possibility that a noncognitive measure related to temperamental or personality characteristics may be found for research in this area. The operational approach taken in the present study requires that some test or scale be utilized for the selection of subgroups on this basis. As mentioned briefly in discussing the assessment procedures at IPAR, there is available an objective measuring instrument that has shown some promise in distinguishing between creative and noncreative groups of subjects and in differentiating more and less creative subjects within groups. It must be emphasized at this point that the instrument is not to be considered in any way a specific measure of creativity, but must be regarded as an operationally definable starting point for research into some of the temperamental or personality characteristics associated with creativity. In this chapter a brief description of the test scale will be given and some justification for using it will be presented.

A FIGURE PREFERENCE TEST

The Welsh Figure Preference Test (WFPT) is an outgrowth of a study begun in the late 1940s which attempted to distinguish types of psychiatric psychopathology using non-language stimulus material as items (Welsh, 1949). The task set for a subject was to express his preference for each item by a dichotomous response, either "Like" (L) or "Don't Like" (DL). In the original study, 200 stimulus items were prepared by drawing in India ink on 3x5 cards figures that ranged from simple geometric forms to complex and diverse shapes and patterns. Some of the figures were drawn with freehand line and some with ruled line and they appeared in many variations, that is, thin line, thick line, reversed figure and ground, and so on. The original pool of items was expanded to 400 and these have been assembled in a booklet with a special answer sheet on which a subject can record his preferences (Welsh, 1959).

Factor Analysis

In the original study a factor analysis was undertaken to determine the dimensionality of the test. A set of 16 different scales was utilized that had been determined *a priori* fashion by inspection of the items; that is, ruled line, freehand line, angular figures, *etc.*, were grouped together in scales. For 61 neuropsychiatric patients most of the common variance could be accounted for by two major dimensions, the first of which was the total number of items placed in DL. The second factor was bipolar and had highest positive loadings on simple, symmetrical, and ruled line scales, with highest negative loadings on complex, third-dimensional, and freehand line scales. "For convenience this second dimension was referred to as 'simplicity-complexity' although it is obviously more complicated than that" (Welsh, 1959:22). Further studies with additional scales and different types of subjects have shown that a two-factor solution is inadequate. Indeed, some work with the much larger group of Governor's School subjects indicates that as many as eleven meaningful factors may emerge from a factor analysis of WFPT scales (Welsh, 1969a:26).

Informal Analysis

A less statistically rigid and far less formal analysis of the subjects in the original study was carried out by contrasting those subjects in the experimental group with those in the normal control group who had extremely high positive or negative factor scores on the second dimension.

> They seemed to be quite different sorts of persons. Among other things, it was noted that the high positives (who preferred simple and symmetrical figures) tended to be quite conservative and conventional, while the high negatives included a number of the artists as well as some rather deviant personalities (among the control group) whose behavior tended toward the anti-social and psychopathic, though not without creative aspects to the rebellion.

> A group of psychologists who were acquainted with some of these high positive and high negative scorers in the control group were asked to suggest ways in which the two groups differed from one another. The consensus was that the positive scorers were enthusiastic,

optimistic, conservative, organized, and
conventional, while the negative scorers
were cynical, pessimistic, depreciative,
overtly hostile, and in general rather
socially dissident. It remained for one
of the negative scorers to suggest that an
additional characteristic of his group was
that it had good taste. The fact that the
few artists in the original sample all
clustered together at the negative end of
this factor lent some weight to the view.
(Barron and Welsh, 1952:200)

DEVELOPING AN ART SCALE

Whether the differences between the positive and negative
groups were a function of aesthetic taste and discrimination or
of personality characteristics associated with artistic temperament, or both, was not immediately apparent from the original
data and its analysis. It must be emphasized that the original
items were deliberately drawn to avoid obvious aesthetic or
artistic standards of visual perception. The intent had been,
rather, to generate a wide variety of different types of items.
Accordingly, an eminently straightforward empirical procedure
was followed.

Responses to the 400 items in the enlarged pool for two
groups of subjects were compared, one a sample of 150 people-
in-general including many older persons without college education, and a second, smaller group of 37 artists and art students.
An item analysis revealed statistically significant differences
between the groups for 65 items—40 liked more by people-in-
general and 25 liked more by artists. For the most part the
items were consistent with the original findings; that is, artists tended to prefer complex and asymmetrical figures and to
reject simple, symmetrical items.

Using the 65 items as a scale scored in the direction of
the artists' preferences successfully discriminated between the
two groups with a mean score for artists of about 40 and that for
the non-artists of only 17. A cross-validation on two new
groups of 30 artists and 30 non-artists gave means of 39 and 18,
again highly significant statistically (Barron and Welsh, 1952).
In a much larger group of unselected males*(N = 343) a mean of

*Not selected for artistic interests *or* lack of it.

13.9 with a standard deviation of 11.2 was obtained (Barron, 1962:22).

Subsequently, three of the scale items (one L and two DL) were eliminated and the 62 items are now generally referred to as the Barron-Welsh Art Scale (BW). When used for research purposes the BW scale has an undesirable feature in the sense that the imbalance of items (38 DL and 24L) tends to produce a positive correlation between BW and the total number of items checked as "Don't Like." In fact, a subject who puts all of the WFPT items in the DL category will get a BW score of 38, close to the average of artists.

To eliminate the forced correlation with total DL scores, a revision of the original BW scale was carried out by an item analysis on a larger group of subjects for which an equal number of L and DL items were selected (Welsh, 1959:9). This Revised Art Scale (RA) has 60 items, 30 L and 30 DL. The two scales are highly correlated with each other; for a group of 100 neuropsychiatric patients who tend to fall at the lower end of the art scale and to have a somewhat limited range of scores, a correlation of .85 was obtained.

The Governor's School students in the present research yielded for both boys and girls correlations of .96 between the BW and RA scales. Thus, for practical purposes the two scales may be considered equivalent and the term "art scale" will be used to refer to either or both of the scales, although BW or RA will be used for reference to the specific scale when necessary. The items on these two scales have been made available in a separate booklet apart from the complete WFPT by the test publisher.* The longer 400-item test booklet has the advantage that a number of other interesting scales such as Conformance, Femininity-Masculinity, and Movement can be scored (see Welsh, 1969a). Some of the correlates of these scales will be discussed later.

Construct Validity

Determination of the "meaning" of the art scale is related to the concept of *construct validity* (Cronbach and Meehl, 1955) since there is no objective criterion or single set of behaviors independent of the test scores that can serve as such a measure. "Construct validity must be investigated whenever no criterion or universe of content is accepted as entirely adequate to

---

*Consulting Psychologists Press, 577 College Ave., Palo Alto, California.

determine the quality to be measured. Determining what psychological constructs account for test performance is desirable for
almost any test" (Cronbach and Meehl, 1955:282).

Anastasi, whose book has been cited previously, puts the
matter in these terms:

> The construct validity of a test is the ex-
> tent to which the test may be said to mea-
> sure a theoretical construct or trait. Ex-
> amples of such constructs are intelligence,
> mechanical comprehension, verbal fluency,
> speed of walking, neuroticism and anxiety....
> It requires the gradual accumulation of in-
> formation from a variety of sources. Any
> data throwing light on the nature of the
> trait under consideration and the conditions
> affecting its development and manifestations
> are grist for this validity mill. (1968:114-
> 115)

One of the kinds of evidence that is important for any construct
validity of the art scale and which is crucial for its use as
an operationally-defined measurement in the present study is its
relationship to creativity. A number of studies have been conducted in which the art scale was administered to subjects nominated as creative. Some of these have involved persons widely
recognized in their fields, such as those reported by the Institute of Personality Assessment (IPAR). Other studies have dealt
with creative students at the grade school, high school, and college level. Material related to the construct validity of the
art scale is found in still other studies dealing with concepts
often associated with creativity, such as originality, aesthetic
interests, independence, and personal complexity.

A summary of some representative studies is given below to
substantiate the validity of using the art scale in studying creativity. For those interested in examining the actual statistical findings on which the summary is based, Appendix A includes
a detailed review of the original research reports.

Summary of Research Results

Four groups of creative subjects studied at IPAR scored
higher on the art scale than people-in-general, a finding which
is consistent with scores originally obtained by artist groups
in the derivation and cross-validation of the scale. It is

important to note that the IPAR subjects included not only persons in primarily visual professions such as architecture, but also in fields such as mathematics, scientific research, etc. Even within these highly selected groups of creative subjects the art scale differentiated subgroups manifesting the greatest degree of creativity from those who were less highly rated.

Similar findings have been reported for various student groups including subjects in art, writing, and science. The validity of the art scale seems to hold across different cultures as shown by studies in India where creative musicians as well as creative artists were discriminated from control groups by the art scale.

By way of contrast it has been found that groups not especially selected for creativity or artistic ability tend to score relatively low on the art scale. Some of the groups studied in this regard include: graduate students, medical students, medical inpatients, psychiatric patients, student engineers, business leaders, managers, and military personnel.

Consistent with the findings on creative subjects are the results obtained in a number of researches in which related concepts were studied. For example, in an extensive investigation of originality in military officers, the art scale clearly differentiated the more original subjects from those manifesting less original behavior in a series of experimental tasks. Independence of judgment was found to be related to the art scale in a student study where subjects low on the art scale yielded to a contrived and incorrect report, while those high on the scale resisted the pressure of a false consensus.

In many other studies concepts that on logical or psychological grounds would seem to be related to creativity have shown consistent findings on the art scale. Students scoring high on the scale tended to show better aesthetic judgment and to prefer modern and experimental styles of painting, while those low on the scale preferred conventional and traditional works. Even in such matters as conformity in dress for college women, the high art scale scorers were less conforming. Self-description by experimental subjects shows a similar kind of distinction; that is, low-scoring persons tend to describe themselves as conforming and more accepting of themselves and others. High scoring subjects, on the other hand, see themselves as independent, autonomous, and self-oriented.

STABILITY OF SCORES

The general concept of stability of scores has been discussed above in connection with measurement of intelligence and
exemplified with data from the Terman CMT (pp. 27-38). It is
important for the art scale, as well, to know whether or not
subjects will be consistent in their responses and tend to fall
in the same relative position when tested again. However, if
the temperamental and personality traits associated with the art
scale change during a period of time, then the scores should reflect this fact. On the other hand, no measuring instrument is
perfectly accurate, so that some of the shift may be attributed
to error variance that is basically psychometric and not psychological.

In general, scores on the art scale are quite stable over
time as shown by test-retest correlations. A group of 26 patients in psychotherapy retested at the end of a six-month period
showed a correlation of .91 on BW (Barron, 1965:21). Lawrence S.
Wrightsman and his colleagues (Wrightsman, Wrightsman, and Cook,
1964) retested a subgroup of 75 of the college students in their
study of attitudes during a period of several months. The average time interval for retesting was 166 days and the test-retest
correlation coefficient was .80.

A comparison was made of the art scale in two different
formats: the original 400-item card form of the WFPT and an abbreviated 144-item booklet. Two groups of undergraduate students were tested one week apart with reversed order of presentation. For one group of 29 students a test-retest correlation
of .94 on the RA was obtained and for a second group of 35 the
correlation was .90 (Welsh, 1959:21).

For the 32 returnees from the Governor's School mentioned
in connection with the CMT, the test-retest correlation after
one year was .70. Unlike the CMT, which showed an increase in
scores that is probably meaningful, the individual scores on the
art scale are about as likely to change in one direction as the
other. Scores increased for 13 subjects and decreased for 18,
while one score was exactly the same. The average change in
score was slightly under 2 points and the means for the two years
reflect this shift, dropping from 30.50 (*SD* 14.01) to 28.53 (*SD*
12.45).

Another comparison of the art scale in two different formats was made with 30 subjects using a paired-comparison/forced-
choice form on one occasion versus the box form of the test several weeks later. A test-retest correlation coefficient of .75

was obtained (Welsh, 1959:24). For a larger group of subjects, $N = 41$, a correlation of .75 also resulted from the two methods of presenting the test items.

Thus, it seems fair to say that scores on the art scale are about as stable from a psychometric point of view as those usually obtained in intelligence testing.

ART SCALE SUMMARY

The correlates of the art scale, as shown by the studies cited above and reported in detail in Appendix A, are indeed complex. While it is no simple matter to pull them all together, some trends can be discerned and there may be some common threads that bind the findings. To help in that colligation, Table IV-1 has been prepared by way of a summary listing major differences between groups as reported in various researches.

In some cases a term has been supplied for one side or the other when the study did not employ a contrasting term, but merely implied a difference in degree or in kind. Hence, the opposition implied by some of the pairings is not to be taken too literally and must be seen as a suggestive, rather than a definitely established, correlate of the art scale.

One general feature that seems to cut across many of the descriptive categories is the subjects' predilection at the lower end for obvious and explicit structure. This takes the form of preference for simple and symmetrical figures in visual perception and for the regularity of formal rules which are externally imposed in social interaction. At the upper end, the predilection is for subtle and implicit structure; figure preferences are for complex and asymmetrical figures that are less easily grasped at a single glance. In social exchange the emphasis is on personal and informal decisions that may transcend or be free from ordinary rules and regulations.

Further implications for the personality dimension assessed by the art scale will appear in the analyses of the Governor's School data to be presented later, and a more general formulation will be attempted at that time.

TERMINOLOGY

From the viewpoint of construct validity it is difficult to find a single concept or a general rubric that will encompass all

TABLE IV-1.   SUMMARY OF DIFFERENCES BETWEEN GROUPS
               SCORING RELATIVELY HIGH OR LOW ON THE
               ART SCALE

Lower Art Scale Scores	*Upper Art Scale Scores*
Uncreative, noncreative, less creative	Creative, more creative
Unoriginal, less original	Original, more original
Non-artistic, less aesthetic interest, poorer discrimination, bad taste	Artistic, more aesthetic interest, better discrimination, good taste
Men, boys, masculine	Women, girls, feminine
Adult, older, mature, non-student, civilized	Children, younger, immature, student, primitive
Mentally retarded, neuropsychiatric patient	Mentally normal, non-patient
Conforming, conventional, yielding	Non-conforming, unconventional independent
Controlled, orderly, planful, productive, responsible	Impulsive, disorderly, playful, less productive, irresponsible
Conservative, traditional cautious, incurious	Radical, modern, daring, curious
Repressive, rigid, prejudiced	Expressive, flexible, unbiased
Socially oriented	Self directed

of the findings from the various researches and reports that
have been summarized above. It is tempting to utilize the term
creativity itself and to refer to the art scale as a creativity
test. But the writer agrees with Hudson (p. 48 above) that none
of the cognitive tests such as the Unusual Uses or the RAT can
fairly be designated in that way; this argument seems to hold for
the art scale as well despite evidence that persons identified
as creative and original do tend to get relatively high scores

on the scale. It will be recalled that divergent-thinking tests do not discriminate effectively according to Hudson. Although there is hazard in proposing new terms and resistance to them, it may be better in the long run to do so than to use older terms that carry too many connotations with them.

The proposed term is "origence" which was coined by combining the element *orig-* as found in origin, original, originality, and other forms, with the noun suffix, *-ence*, which signifies action, state, quality, or degree. *Origence*, then, refers to the personality or temperamental dimension tapped by the art scale and related measures. A subject scoring high on the scale may be called an "origent" person, and, if necessary, he can be described as behaving "origently."

To free the present approach from the excess implications of the word intelligence, a new term, "intellectence," is suggested for the personality dimension related to performance on intellectual measures such as the Terman CMT. These two dimensions will be approached operationally in the present context with origence defined by scores on the art scale and CMT scores defining intellectence.

Subjects from the Governor's School were selected on these two dimensions conjointly by a method to be described in Chapter V. These tests serve as independent variables; dependent variables in the initial research analysis are three standard tests of interest and personality: Gough's Adjective Check List, the Minnesota Multiphasic Personality Inventory, and the Strong Vocational Interest Blank.*

---

*For a detailed description of these three tests, see Appendix B, pp. 228ff.

Chapter V

RESEARCH DESIGN

THE GOVERNOR'S SCHOOL OF NORTH CAROLINA

The Governor's School of North Carolina* is a special summer program for talented and gifted high school students selected
from all parts of the state. It was inaugurated in 1963 to offer
distinctive and unusual educational experience for exceptional
secondary school boys and girls. It is different in character and
in intensity from ordinary programs in the regular high school.
At the same time it serves as an experimental laboratory for innovative instructional practices on the part of the teachers who,
when freed from conventional curricular constraints, can test out
new methods and techniques for working with students of unusual
ability.

Students attend the school without paying any fees or tui-
tion; supplies and materials as well as room and board are provided free of charge. There are no financial requirements and
the rich and poor alike are all eligible to attend the school if
selected. It is important also to note that no grades or unit
credits are given at the Governor's School so that a student's
motivation for attendance must come from his own desire to participate in a challenging and an enriching educational experience.
Self-aspiration is the goal here, not the accumulation of academic
points.

Any student who is a rising junior or rising senior in a
public high school or private preparatory school in North Carolina
is eligible to attend the Governor's School. Since there are almost 200,000 students at this level and only 400 can be accommodated at each summer session, the selection rate is 1 in 500 and
the school comprises .2 of 1% of the population of boys and girls
nominally eligible.

---

*A general account of the Governor's School describing its
background and history may be found in the Carnegie Corporation
Quarterly (1964, January:1-4). This report also covers the philosophy of education that was followed in organizing the school
and describes briefly the selection procedures followed. Further
descriptive material appears in a report by Welsh (1969a); see
also Lewis (1969) for an extensive discussion of the theory of
the school.

There is, however, one constraint in the selection procedures: To ensure wide geographic distribution over the 100 coun-
ties of North Carolina and to afford small schools an opportunity
to send students, each of the more than 150 school districts in
the state has a quota of nominations based in part on its total
student population.

The Governor's School differs from many traditional programs
for the gifted since it recognizes the importance of artistic as
well as academic excellence and there are two sectors of the
school, each with somewhat different selection procedures. The
Academic Division comprises the specific areas of English, French,
Mathematics, Natural Science, and Social Science. Selection for
these areas follows the more or less conventional methods of selection and is based on an outstanding academic record including advanced course work in one of these areas, evidence of superior
achievement and intellectual ability, and recommendation by school
officials. Final selections are based on a careful evaluation of
the scholastic record of each nominated student.

The Arts Division comprises the areas of Painting, Drama,
Dance, Vocal Music, and Instrumental Music. In this division,
the nominated applicant must appear in person before an audition
board of professionals who are highly qualified in one of the
areas. The boards for the different areas judge the performance
(or product in the case of Painting) of each student and rank him
according to his demonstrated ability. Final selection is then
made from the rankings within each area.

It might be expected that the somewhat different methods of
selection would lead to some differences in the characteristics
of the students in the two divisions. Indeed, slight differences
do occur in the expected direction. Since the students in the Academic Division are more highly selected on the usual intellectual
criteria, it follows that their average score on intelligence
tests is higher than the Arts Division. The latter division, however, averages higher on measures of creativity and on masculinity-
femininity scales.*

While these differences in averages are of interest statistically and have important theoretical implications as well, it
must be stressed that from a practical point there is more similarity than difference between the divisions. That is to say,
there is a great deal of variability within each area and for all

---

*The extent of these differences may be seen in a report of
the psychometric characteristics of the groups at the Governor's
School (Welsh, 1969a).

of the test scores there is substantial overlapping in range.
Many individual students in Painting, for example, scored far
above the average for the English area on the intelligence tests,
while some students in English scored higher on creativity measures than the average student in Painting. It may be noted that
the differences that do appear between groups are not necessarily
a function of the selection procedures *per se*, although that is a
likely explanation, but may be the outcome of differences in interest and aptitude on the part of students in the various areas.
It has been found, for example, that students with high verbal
interests score relatively higher on a verbal test of intelligence
than on a nonverbal intelligence test (Welsh, 1967; 1971) when
matched for total intelligence scores.

Testing Program at the School

During the first three summers (1963, 1964, and 1965) of the
operation of the Governor's School an extensive battery of tests
was administered, teacher's ratings were obtained, and descriptive
biographical information collected from the students. The test
battery was intended to cover intellectual aptitude and ability,
creativity, personality, adjustment, interests, values, attitudes,
and motivation. Some especially designed devices were used but
most of the tests were standard ones that are suitable for group
administration and objective scoring. Many of these tests have
been used in the IPAR assessment program, so that it is possible
to compare the Governor's School adolescents of 16 and 17 years
who are, perhaps, potentially creative with groups of adults who
have actually demonstrated their creativity in various fields.

A summary of results for six of the tests in the battery has
been published (Welsh, 1969a) and may be consulted to see the actual extent of the divisional and area differences in distributions
and average scores noted above. Certain differences in test scores
between males and females are apparent also in these test results
and have some interesting theoretical implications. The tests
covered in this report are:

1. D-48 Non-verbal Intelligence Test (D-48)[*]

2. Terman's Concept Mastery Test (CMT)

3. Welsh Figure Preference Test (WFPT)

4. Gough's Adjective Check List (ACL)

---

[*]For a description of the D-48 Non-verbal Intelligence Test,
see Appendix B.

5. Minnesota Multiphasic Personality Inventory (MMPI)

6. Strong Vocational Interest Blank (SVIB)

"INTELLIGENCE" AND "CREATIVITY"

The general, theoretical question, "Are intelligence and creativity independent or are they related?" has been discussed previously. If we now ask the specific, technical question, "Are scores on the CMT and RA related or not?" then a straight-forward answer is possible. A correlation of -.06 was obtained between the sets of scores for 1155 Governor's School students who had completed both tests. This value is essentially zero although it does reach the nominal .05 level of significance be-cause of the large number of cases. For the boys (N = 527) the correlation is -.10, for the girls (N = 628) it is -.02. Again, because of the size of the N the boys' correlation does fall at the .05 level although the girls' correlation is not statistical-ly significant.

Another intelligence test was included in the test battery during the second and third summers, the nonverbal D-48 test (Black, 1963). Like the CMT scores, the RA and the D-48 were essentially unrelated although the correlation of -.12 for 349 Governor's School boys did reach the .05 level of significance. The corresponding correlation coefficient for 419 girls, how-ever, was only -.02.

For the test results during the second summer, correlations were calculated for the two divisions separately--on the CMT and the D-48, with each other, and with the RA (Welsh, 1966). The two intelligence tests were highly correlated with each other but neither showed any correlation with the RA. The results are sum-marized in Table V-1.

It is important to note that the relative statistical in-dependence of the CMT and D-48 scores from the RA for the Gover-nor's School students is consistent with studies comparing other intellectual measures to the art scale. Day (1968a) has reported a correlation of .02 for 394 seventh, eighth, and ninth grade stu-dents on the BW and the Dominion Group Test of Learning Capacity --Intermediate Form. Littlejohn (1966) found a correlation of -.03 between the RA and the California Mental Maturity IQ score for 554 ninth grade students. A similarly low correlation, -.07, was obtained by Harris (1961) for the RA and Otis Quick-Scoring Mental Ability Test with 390 ninth and tenth graders. For 80

Creativity and Intelligence

TABLE V-1. CORRELATIONS OF INTELLIGENCE TESTS AND
            ART SCALE SCORES FOR GOVERNOR'S SCHOOL
            SUBJECTS

TESTS	ACADEMIC DIVISION ($N=$ 207)	ARTS DIVISION ($N=$161)	TOTAL ($N=$368)
CMT & D-48	.27	.51	.49
RA & CMT	.07	.00	-.03
RA & D-48	-.01	-.02	-.07

adolescents in an "Upward Bound" program, nonsignificant correlations of the RA with intellectual measures were obtained; the
values are -.10 for Form I of the Otis and .03 for Form II, with
-.13 for the D-48 (Adair, 1969).

In a study of college students by Wrightsman and Cook (1965),
all of the scales included from the Guilford-Zimmerman Aptitude
Survey were independent of the art scale. The correlations are:
verbal comprehension, .14; general reasoning, -.01; perceptual
speed, -.04; and numerical operations, -.15.

Among psychiatric patients, two studies indicate that the
art scale is unrelated to intelligence test scores. Lim and Ullman (1961) found RA and verbal scores on the Shipley-Hartford to
be independent for 125 cases using a chi-square analysis. At a
Veterans Administration hospital, a nonsignificant correlation between Otis and RA scores was obtained for 30 subjects. (Richard
Cave and Charles Boutwell, personal communication, 1963).

The relative independence of the art scale and intellectual
measures seems to hold at the lower end as well. A nonsignificant
correlation of .12 between RA and intelligence test scores has
been determined for 78 mental retardates in a California state
hospital (Arthur L. Mattocks, personal communication, 1960). He
found, however, that none of the patients having IQ's below 50 on
a standard test of intelligence was able to respond in a meaningful way to the figure preference items. At the higher levels
there was no difficulty in administering the Welsh Figure Preference Test and for some patients a modified group procedure was
succesfully employed. In a study of educable mentally handicapped
children, Mitchell (1968) reported a correlation of -.24 (significant at the .05 level) for 112 boys on RA and IQ scores; the

correlation of -.08 for 71 girls was nonsignificant. The intelligence tests given were mostly the Stanford-Binet although some were Wechsler or Slossom (Marlys Mitchell, personal communication, 1969).

Although it is supportive of the general argument to find the relative independence of different kinds of intelligence tests from the art scale, it is essential for the development of the data analyses to be discussed below that we have further reassurance that the specific intellectual measure employed here, the CMT, shows this trend. In the IPAR study of creative adults, MacKinnon (1961) found a nonsignificant correlation of .23 for 40 creative architects and Gough (1961) reported an r of only .03 for 45 scientists for the BW scale and CMT scores.

Among undergraduate college students who are, perhaps, in many ways more similar to the Governor's School subjects than the IPAR adults, the present writer has found a correlation of -.09 between the RA and CMT for 40 students in an introductory psychology class. A correlation of -.08 was obtained for 30 members of a course in "Tests and Measurements." In another section of this course, a modified version of the art scale was employed in which the items are arranged in a paired-comparison format. This modified art scale correlated .16 (nonsignificant) with the CMT for 49 students.

In a group of 87 adults who were candidates for a Master's Degree in Education, a correlation of .03 was found for the RA and D-48 with an equally nonsignificant r for the RA and CMT of -.07 (Adair, 1969). Finally, Saunders (1968) in a study of 236 freshmen in a community college reported an inconsequential correlation for RA and CMT scores of .04.

At the same time it may be of interest to point out that the Remote Association Test, discussed above in connection with creativity, seems to be uncorrelated with the art scale although it was noted that RAT scores are highly correlated with measures of intelligence. Colman (1966) found an inconsistent relationship between the RA and RAT scores for two small groups of college students with r's essentially zero. Martha T. Mednick has reported that the art scale and the RAT showed no significant correlation for collegiate samples (personal communication, 1964).

These results clearly support the contention that art scale scores and intelligence test scores are statistically independent. If one wants to equate the art scale with "creativity" and the Terman Concept Mastery Test with "intelligence," then it would have to be claimed that these two dimensions are themselves independent.

But for reasons advanced earlier, such a direct equation of tests
with concepts will not be followed. Instead, some personality
characteristics of Governor's School students falling high or low
on RA and high or low on the CMT conjointly will be systematically studied to learn what differences in personality there may be
among the four subgroups formed by these configurations.

SELECTION OF GROUPS

The general design used is similar to that employed by Wallach and Kogan (1965) whose work has been discussed earlier (pp. 48-50).
That is, they employed four groups of subjects identified as falling above or below the median of their intelligence tests and also
above or below the median of their creativity tests. These four
groups--high on both measures, low on both measures, high on intelligence but low on creativity, and low on intelligence but high
on creativity--were contiguous. Because they had only 151 subjects, 70 boys and 81 girls, they employed median splits on each
dimension for the analyses carried out, and did not eliminate any
subjects in forming the four groups. Even so, the largest group
size was 22 for the girls and 19 for the boys.

Since the Governor's School afforded a large number of subjects, noncontiguous groups were formed by selecting subjects
scoring at the extremes of the distributions of the RA and CMT
for reasons discussed below. A scatterplot of the two scores on
orthogonal axes was made for all of the subjects and inspection
of the scatterplot confirmed the independence of the measures as
revealed by the correlation coefficients discussed above. Cases
were distributed nicely over the entire surface of the scatterplot with no "bunching" in any segment of the bivariate plot.
From this graphic display, cases were selected that fell in the
extreme "corners" with each group representing approximately 5%
of the total number of subjects. Each group contained 60 cases,
30 boys and 30 girls, and each of the three summer sessions was
equally represented. Thus, any differences between sessions or
between the sexes would be equated over the groups.

It will perhaps be easier to follow the method of selecting
the four groups by referring to Figure V-1. The values in the
figure are given in raw score terms with the approximate means
for the groups indicated by light line while the means on the two
measures for the entire Governor's School are shown in heavy line;
the dotted line encloses the ranges of raw scores for the four
groups. Thus, for Group I (high RA/low CMT), the mean for the RA
was 47 with a range from 40 to 57; on the CMT the mean was 21 with
a range from 0 to 43, including a few negative scores (see p. 31).

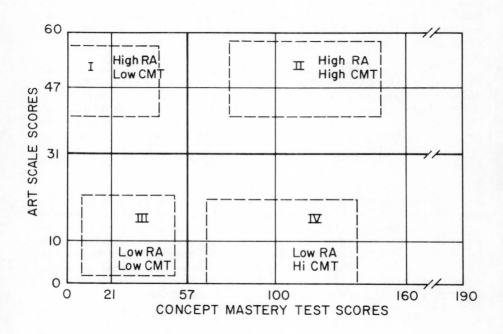

Figure V - 1

The use of extreme, non-overlapping groups minimizes the chances of misclassification. When distributions are cut at the median and two cases fall only one raw score point apart, they can hardly be very different in terms of the characteristic being measured. Indeed, on a repeated testing they might very well reverse their standings so that by chance the former high scorer would become the low scorer. When cases are selected that fall some distance apart on the distribution of scores--as has been done here with the Governor's School subjects--the likelihood of real differences in the characteristics being measured is increased and the possibility of misclassification because of measurement error correspondingly decreased.

The general effect of misclassification is to obscure actual differences between groups (see Dahlstrom and Welsh, 1960:335-36) rather than to falsely indicate their existence. Thus, by using clearly demarked groups, any differences that do appear in analyses of the contrasting groups are very likely to be actual differences rather than chance occurrences of a statistical nature.

ITEM ANALYSIS

To discover differences in personality and temperamental characteristics for these four groups of Governor's School students, a systematic item analysis was carried out on three of the tests from the battery. These tests were chosen for analysis because they each comprise a large pool of items that are potentially relevant for personality study. The three tests are: Gough's Adjective Check List (ACL), the Minnesota Multiphasic Personality Inventory (MMPI), and the Strong Vocational Interest Blank (SVIB).[*] (For a detailed description of these three tests, see Appendix B, pp. 228ff.)

The ACL (Gough and Heilbrun, 1965) is a brief, easily administered personality test consisting of a list of 300 adjectives arranged alphabetically from "Absent-minded" to "Zany." The subject is asked to put a check mark before each term that he considers to be "self-descriptive." A series of scales have been developed and are described in the ACL test manual. Some of these scales have been discussed in an analysis of Governor's School subjects by Cashdan and Welsh (1966). As previously noted, the

---

[*]The Strong Vocational Interest Blank is construed as a personality test in this context and will be so designated (see Holland, 1966). "Attempts to differentiate interest tests sharply from other types of personality tests are probably not worthwhile" (Horst, 1968:22).

ACL has been used extensively in the IPAR assessment procedures and MacKinnon has commented "It is remarkable that so simple a device as a list of three hundred adjectives can reveal so much about a person" (1963:263).

To carry out the item analysis, a frequency count was made for each of the four groups on every item in the tests. Then items that were either infrequently or preponderantly answered in a given direction by all of the subjects were eliminated. That is, if 90% or more of all students in each group gave the same response to a particular item, it would not be an effective item for discriminating between groups. Items showing marked differences in response frequencies for the sexes were also eliminated as far as possible.

The remaining items were then searched to find those items that showed the maximum differentiation of one group from the remaining three groups—with a minimum difference between these three groups. For example, suppose that on Item 4 of the ACL, *Adventurous,* the frequencies of responses (checks) for the four groups were as follows: Group I, 55; Group II, 42; Group III, 39; and Group IV, 40. Three of the groups are quite similar in response to this item but it is clear that Group I, high RA/low CMT, responds to Item 4 on the ACL differently from these groups and would thus be a useful item in discriminating Group I from them. Or, in the logic of the theory of objective personality tests (Meehl, 1945), a subject who describes himself as "adventurous" is more likely to be correctly classified as falling into Group I than into any of the other groups. The greater the number of items that a subject answers in the same direction as a given group, the greater the likelihood of correct identification in terms of group membership.

Many of the items on the three tests met the criteria for selection—response frequency, no sex difference, and group discrimination. The numbers of items from each test for the four groups are summarized in Table V-2 where it can be seen that the proportions of discriminating items ranged from 17 (6% of the total test) in the case of Group III on the ACL to 56 (14%) for Group II on the SVIB. The content of the items that emerged from the item analysis will be discussed in Chapter VI.

To simplify reference to these items considered as scales, the following nomenclature has been adopted: ACL—A-I, A-II, A-III, and A-IV; MMPI—M-I, M-II, M-III, and M-IV; SVIB—S-I, S-II, S-III, and S-IV. It will be understood, then, that A-I refers to the items on the ACL discriminating the students falling high on origence and low on intellectence from the other three

TABLE V-2.   NUMBERS OF DISCRIMINATING ITEMS BY GROUPS
FROM ANALYSIS OF THREE PERSONALITY TESTS

SVIB: 400 TOTAL ITEMS

High Origence/ Low Intellectence S-I: 32	High Origence/ High Intellectence S-II: 56
Low Origence/ Low Intellectence S-III: 35	Low Origence/ High Intellectence S-IV: 33

MMPI: 550 TOTAL ITEMS

High Origence/ Low Intellectence M-I: 54	High Origence/ High Intellectence M-II: 53
Low Origence/ Low Intellectence M-III: 50	Low Origence/ High Intellectence M-IV: 42

ACL: 300 TOTAL ITEMS

High Origence/ Low Intellectence A-I: 21	High Origence/ High Intellectence A-II: 25
Low Origence/ Low Intellectence A-III: 17	Low Origence/ High Intellectence A-IV: 24

groups; M-II refers to the MMPI items for the high origence/high
intellectence group; S-III refers to the low/low items from the
SVIB; and so on. This nomenclature for the scales has been in-
corporated in Table V-2 to show their relationship to the original groups.

Thus, the assumption is that these scales will show consistent correlations in the directions implied by the groups used
in their derivation. All of the Group I scales should be positively correlated with each other since they were all obtained
from the homogeneous grouping of subjects; the same reasoning
applies to II, III, and IV. The scales for Groups I and II, however, should be uncorrelated since their similarity on RA scores
is counteracted by the dissimilarity on CMT scores. For analogous reasons, the other adjacent scales--the I's and III's, the
III's and IV's, and the II's and IV's should also be uncorrelated. The scales in the opposite corners, on the other hand,
the I's and IV's, and the II's and III's should be negatively
correlated, since when one group is high on either the RA or CMT
the other group is low.

The above statement of expected relationships follows the
paradigm suggested by Campbell and Fiske (1959) in their paper,
"Convergent and Discriminant Validation by the Multitrait-Multi-
method Matrix." In this article they state:

> In order to examine discriminant validity,
> and in order to estimate the relative contri-
> butions of trait and method variance, *more than
> one trait* as well as *more than one method* must
> be employed in the validation process. In many
> instances it will be convenient to achieve this
> through a multitrait-multimethod matrix. Such
> a matrix presents all of the intercorrelations
> resulting when each of several traits is mea-
> sured by each of several methods. (p. 81)

In the instance of the Governor's School analysis there are
two personality traits being assessed, a temperamental trait measured by RA scores and an intellectual trait by the CMT. Each
of the three personality tests used in our analysis (the ACL,
MMPI, and SVIB) constitutes a different method of assessing the
traits. Further, since the traits are being measured conjointly
and are statistically independent, there are 4 different configurations for each of the 3 methods comprising 12 scales in all.
Finally, the correlation coefficients were computed separately
for each sex so that a replication of the matrix is possible.

An additional condition may also be stipulated. It is assumed that the 12 scales will show the expected relationship to the tests initially used in selecting the four groups from which the scales were derived. The Group I scales should show negative correlations with the CMT but positive with RA; the Group II scales, positive with both tests; the Group III scales, negative with both; and the Group IV scales should be positively correlated with the CMT, but negatively with the RA.

The entire matrix--or replicated matrices--of correlations is given in Table V-3 and the success of the argument may be judged by the magnitude and direction of the r's obtained. In order to ensure a more exacting test of the hypotheses, a somewhat stringent statistical requirement of a .01 level of significance was adopted. It is to be noted that the ACL intratest correlations are actually partial correlations. All of the four ACL scales were highly positively correlated with the total number of adjectives checked, thus acting as an artifact to obscure their basic relationship to one another. The correlations with total number checked were partialled out by conventional statistical procedures and the resulting partial correlations appear in the table. The intertest correlations of the ACL scales with the scales from the MMPI and the SVIB, however, are the actual correlations as originally computed.

Inspection of Table V-3 reveals overwhelming support for the hypotheses in terms of both the magnitude and the direction of the correlations. There was not a single instance where the opposite scales, Group I's with IV's and II's with III's, failed to show a highly significant negative correlation. These values range from a low of -.16 for the girl's Group S-II with A-III, and A-I with M-IV, to a high of -.84 for the boy's A-II with A-III. A frequency distribution of these 36 negative diagonal values is given below:

Correlation	Frequency
-.89 - -.80	1
-.79 - -.70	2
-.69 - -.60	1
-.59 - -.50	4
-.49 - -.40	6
-.39 - -.30	10
-.29 - -.20	9
-.19 - -.10	3

TABLE V-3. MATRIX OF INTERCORRELATIONS FOR INTELLECTENCE/ORIGENCE SCALES ON GOVERNOR'S SCHOOL SUBJECTS

	COMPOSITE SCORE		INITIAL TESTS		SVIB				ACL				MMPI			
	INT	ORIG	CMT	RA	S–I	S–II	S–III	S–IV	A–I	A–II	A–III	A–IV	M–I	M–II	M–III	M–IV
INT	_INT_	(.07)	.74	(-.04)	-.62	.54	-.58	.50	-.40	.30	-.41	.24	-.52	.63	-.59	.46
ORIG	(.08)	_ORIG_	(.02)	.39	.38	.50	-.49	-.49	.24	.50	-.35	-.29	.55	.51	-.53	-.56
CMT	.72	(.09)	_CMT_	(-.02)	.42	.42	-.37	.43	-.28	.27	-.25	.25	-.40	.43	.42	.32
RA	(.05)	.33	(-.02)	_RA_	.23	.23	-.19	-.27	(.09)	(.08)	(-.11)	-.19	.20	.19	-.15	-.20
S–I	-.59	.38	.44	.23	_S–I_	(-.08)	.12	-.60	.30	(.01)	.15	-.21	.40	-.23	.14	-.36
S–II	.52	.50	.44	.23	(-.08)	_S–II_	-.45	(-.02)	(-.07)	.39	-.23	(.07)	(-.04)	.46	-.37	(-.04)
S–III	-.54	-.55	-.39	-.19	.12	-.44	_S–III_	(.05)	.13	-.28	.34	.34	(.10)	-.42	.53	(-.11)
S–IV	.43	-.50	.31	-.27	-.59	-.16	(.10)	_S–IV_	-.28	(-.07)	(-.03)	.28	-.35	(.10)	(-.08)	.32
A–I	-.38	.33	-.25	(-.03)	.27	(.00)	(.09)	-.23	_A–I_	(-.07)	(.07)	-.45	.32	-.16	(.09)	-.28
A–II	.35	.52	.33	(.08)	(-.06)	.44	-.32	(-.06)	(-.03)	_A–II_	-.84	-.17	.17	.35	-.37	-.21
A–III	-.45	-.34	-.25	(-.11)	.20	-.16	.34	(-.04)	(.08)	-.56	_A–III_	-.17	(.05)	-.38	.34	(-.02)
A–IV	.26	-.30	.25	-.19	-.21	(.10)	(.07)	.28	-.45	-.22	(.08)	_A–IV_	-.17	(.03)	(.03)	.14
M–I	-.45	.53	-.29	.15	.22	-.11	(-.03)	-.22	.34	.15	(.05)	-.38	_M–I_	(-.01)	(-.03)	-.79
M–II	.58	.55	.47	.19	-.23	.40	-.45	(.04)	(-.02)	.39	-.30	-.16	(.09)	_M–II_	-.53	(-.06)
M–III	-.55	-.54	-.39	-.27	.18	-.31	.48	(-.01)	(.05)	-.35	.40	(-.08)	(-.07)	-.53	_M–III_	(-.01)
M–IV	.47	-.50	.27	-.13	-.21	(.10)	(-.05)	.23	-.16	(.06)	(.08)	.11	-.77	(-.09)	(-.01)	_M–IV_

NOTE: Boys above diagonal, N = 522 to 529; Girls below diagonal, N = 616 to 632. (r) signifies correlations not significantly different from zero at .01 level. ACL intratest correlations are partial r's.

Similarly, every one of the positive diagonal values--intertest I's, II's, III's, and IV's--showed a significant correlation. The lowest r of .11 was obtained for the girl's A-IV with M-IV. For the boy's S-III with M-III a correlation of .53 was the highest value. A summary of the 24 correlational values is given below:

Correlation	Frequency
.50 - .59	1
.40 - .49	6
.30 - .39	10
.20 - .29	5
.10 - .19	2

Scales lying adjacent on the two dimensions were predicted to be uncorrelated for the reasons outlined above. However, not all of the coefficients in Table V-3 for these scale correlations met the statistical requirements and some were significantly different from zero. Nine of the boys' correlations and seven of the girls' exceeded the .01 significance level stipulated. Of these, only three were intratest correlations, Group A-II with A-IV for both sexes and S-I with S-III for the boys. All of the MMPI intratest correlations fell into the predicted pattern.

For the intertest correlations the failures were about equally distributed over the tests: SVIB, five cases; ACL, six; and MMPI, five. For the four scale types, however, more failures occurred on the high RA scales than on the low. The frequencies are: I's, six; II's, five; III's, three; and IV's, two cases.

The values for these adjacent correlations ranged from .00 for girls' S-II with A-I to -.23 for both sexes on S-I with M-II. A frequency distribution of these correlations is given below:

Correlation	Frequency	Correlation	Frequency
-.24 - -.20	4	.20 - .24	1
-.19 - -.15	3	.15 - .19	4
-.14 - -.10	2	.10 - .14	8
-.09 - -.05	14	.05 - .09	17
-.04 - -.01	14	.00 - .04	5

The correlations are approximately evenly distributed in positive and negative deviations from 0 with 37 negative instances, one absolute 0, and 34 positive correlations.

By way of summary it may be noted that of the 132 correlations in this portion of Table V-3, 116 met the statistical requirements in magnitude and direction of the correlation coefficient. This is an accuracy rate of 88%--convincing evidence of the predicted systematic relationship among the scales of items.

Finally, we may note the correlations of the 12 scales with the RA and CMT. All of the correlations in Table V-3 are in the expected direction, although four of the RA values for boys and three for girls failed to achieve the .01 level of significance. All but one of these correlations occur for the ACL and it is possible that the length of these scales, shorter by far in terms of items (see Table V-2) than for the MMPI and the SVIB, leads to these lower correlations.

On the basis of the results obtained, one subsequent step was carried out to complete Table V-2, namely, to compute a composite score on the two personality dimensions for each of the Governor's School students. The raw scores for each of the 12 scales of items were converted to standard scores so that inter-test summations could be made. Then all the Group I scores were summed, likewise for the II's, the III's, and the IV's. To obtain a composite score for the personality dimension measured by the CMT, a difference score was obtained by subtracting the summed Group I scale scores and the summed III's (low CMT) from the summed II's and summed IV's (high CMT). The RA difference score was similarly obtained by subtracting the Group III and IV sums from the Group I and II sums.

It will be recalled that in Chapter IV a suggestion was made to refer to the personality dimension associated with the art scale as *origence* and the dimension related to the CMT as *intellectence*. Since the difference scores obtained from the personality scales are assumed to be measures of these dimensions, for consistency in nomenclature, these scores will be referred to in abbreviated form as ORIG and INT.

To make the computational method for these composite scores clear, the formulas are summarized below:

$$A-I \quad + M-I \quad + S-I \quad = \Sigma \ I$$

$$A-II \quad + M-II \quad + S-II \quad = \Sigma \ II$$

$$A-III + M-III + S-III = \Sigma \ III$$

$$A-IV \quad + M-IV \quad + S-IV \quad = \Sigma \ IV$$

$$INT = (\Sigma \ II + \Sigma \ IV) - (\Sigma \ I + \Sigma \ III)$$

$$ORIG = (\Sigma \ I \quad + \Sigma \ II) - (\Sigma \ III + \Sigma \ IV)$$

These differences scores were then distributed and their means and standard deviations calculated so that they could be converted to standard scores (T scores) for subsequent analyses.

The first two rows and columns of Table V-3 show the correlations of the composite dimensional scores with the original test scores and with the 12 special scales. All of these values are in the predicted direction and all of them are highly significant statistically. A "bootstraps" effect may be noted in the sense that the correlations for the composite scores with the special scales are higher than for their correlations with the initial tests. Only one correlation fails to show this increment but it is a trivial point; for boys' A-IV the correlation with the CMT is .25 while it is only .24 for INT.

It should be noted that the composite scores are independent in a statistical sense since for the boys and the girls the correlations of INT and ORIG are essentially zero. At the same time, the correlations with the initial tests from which the four sets of scales were derived are highly significant for both sexes. The values of the r's for the Governor's School boys and girls on INT with the CMT are .74 and .72 respectively. These coefficients are as high as those usually found when two conventional intelligence tests are correlated with each other; for the CMT reported r's range from .70 to .52 (Terman, 1956). Indeed, even in the Governor's School itself, the correlation of the nonverbal D-48 and the CMT reached only .44 for the 770 students enrolled during the second and third summer sessions.

Although the magnitude of the correlations of ORIG with RA scores, .39 and .33, is not as great as that reported above for the intellectual dimension, the values are highly significant from a statistical point of view. Practically speaking, most of the commonly used tests of creativity show very little intercorrelation as summarized above (Chap. III), and in some instances are actually negatively correlated.

In sum, these scoring procedures have been developed from standard personality tests to measure two theoretical dimensions, "intellectence" and "origence." The two corresponding scores, INT and ORIG, have been found to be uncorrelated with each other but to be highly correlated in expected directions with special personality scales and with the objective tests used in their derivation.

Chapter VI

INTERPRETATION OF SCALE ITEMS: A TYPOLOGY

In this chapter we turn to the content of items in the four scales developed in Chapter V. We will investigate the nature of the two dimensions, origence and intellectence, and the fourfold typology that results from their conjoint relationship (I, high origence/low intellectence; II, high origence/high intellectence; III, low origence/low intellectence; and IV, low origence/high intellectence).

The plan of analysis followed in this chapter will be to discuss each test separately beginning with the Strong Vocational Interest Blank, then the Adjective Check List, and finally the Minnesota Multiphasic Personality Inventory. For each test in turn, the four scales will be examined in detail to identify clusters of items within each scale that seem similar in meaning and in psychological implication. The aim is to arrive at a coherent picture of the psychological characteristics of each scale. As these features are discerned for each of the three tests, a summary of these characteristics for the four scales will be given.

When the summaries for all three tests have been completed, a general overview will be made by looking at the basic features common to all of the tests for each scale. That is, a typology will be presented that reflects the general psychological characteristics of four types of subjects as inferred from their responses to the items on the four sets of scales.

STRONG VOCATIONAL INTEREST BLANK

The SVIB has been widely used for several decades but it is important to note here that the earlier 400-item form of this test (Strong, 1959) was administered since the current 399-item revision* (Campbell, 1966) was not generally available during the testing period of the Governor's School. The basic comparability of the two forms has been established, although certain cautions have been noted (Williams, Kirk, and Frank, 1968) in assuming that scale patterns necessarily have the same interpretive significance.

---

*Form 399 T is scored on 291 unchanged items carried over from the previous form.

The girls, as well as the boys, at the Governor's School took the Men's Form (Machine Scored Edition, Form M) and evidence has been presented (Welsh, 1969a) to illustrate the feasibility and utility of this psychometric tactic. That is, the Men's Form proved suitable for the Governor's School girls in terms of their interests as shown by meaningful and consistent patterns of scores on the occupational scales (see also, Helson, 1966; Naor, 1970).

The task of searching for clusters of items on the SVIB is made somewhat easier by the logical grouping of items in the test booklet.* Both the previous and the current form of the test use a format of items arranged in eight parts. The test heading for each part and the number of items in each part are as follows:

I.	Occupations	100
II.	School Subjects	36
III.	Amusements	49
IV.	Activities	48
V.	Types of People	47
VI.	Order of Preference of Activities	40
VII.	Preference between Two Items	40
VIII.	Your Abilities and Personality**	40

Each subject responded to the items in each part by placing a check mark by the appropriate response on a special answer sheet: "Like," "Indifferent," or "Dislike"; "Like Best," "Like Least"; "Yes," "?", or "No." The process of selecting the "group identifying" items as described in Chapter V was then carried out, and the results are summarized in Tables VI-1,2,3, and 4. The actual item numbers as they appear in the SVIB test booklet are given in Appendix C.

---

*Reprinted from *Strong Vocational Blank for Men* (revised) Form M, by Edward K. Strong, Jr., with the permission of the publishers, Stanford University Press. Copyright 1938 and 1945 by the Board of Trustees of the Leland Stanford Junior University.
**The current version has only 39 items in the last part.

TABLE VI-1.   SUMMARY OF GROUP-IDENTIFYING ITEM CLUSTERS FOR
              HIGH ORIGENCE/LOW INTELLECTENCE ON SVIB SCALES

TEST HEADING	LIKE	INDIFFERENT	DISLIKE
I. Occupations	Music teacher, office manager	Editor, office clerk	Author of technical book; civil engineer; statistician
II. School subjects	Dramatics		Calculus, chemistry, math, physics
III. Amusements	Amusement parks, "rough house" initiations, full-dress affairs		Bridge, chess, solving mechanical puzzles, making a radio set
IV. Activities	Organizing a play, being called by a nickname, acting as a yell-leader		Teaching adults
V. Types of People			People who get rattled easily

	PREFERRED MOST	PREFERRED LEAST	
VI. Order of Preference of Activities	Enrico Caruso, singer; chairman, entertainment committee		

	ITEM PREFERRED	(TO)	OTHER ITEM
VII. Preference between Two Items	Selling article, quoted 10% above competitor	(to)	Selling article, quoted 10% below competitor
	Physical activity	(to)	Mental activity
	Many acquaintances	(to)	Few intimate friends
	Jealous people	(to)	Conceited people

	DESCRIBE BEST		
VIII. Your abilities and personality	Put drive into the organization; win confidence and loyalty		

TABLE VI-2. SUMMARY OF GROUP-IDENTIFYING ITEM CLUSTERS FOR
            HIGH ORIGENCE/HIGH INTELLECTENCE ON SVIB SCALES

TEST HEADING	LIKE	INDIFFERENT	DISLIKE
I. Occupations	Artist, astronomer, author of novel, cartoonist, college professor, consul, editor, explorer, foreign correspondent, magazine writer, poet, reporter (general), sculptor	Building contractor, ship officer	Athletic director, bank teller, cashier in bank, factory manager, office clerk, office manager, typist
II. School Subjects	English composition, literature, philosophy		
III. Amusements	Chess, art galleries, poetry, "Atlantic Monthly"	Bridge, "New Republic"	
IV. Activities	Arguments, continually changing activities, climbing along edge of precipice		Operating machinery, methodical work
V. Types of People		Irreligious people, people who have done you favors, people w/ gold teeth, blind people, fashionably dressed people, carelessly dressed people	People who always agree with you

	PREFERRED MOST	PREFERRED LEAST	
VI. Order of Preference of Activities	Freedom in working out one's own methods of doing things, Booth Tarkington; author; chairman, program committee	Steadiness and performance of work	

	ITEM PREFERRED	(TO)	OTHER ITEM
VII. Preference between Two Items	Gardening	(to)	House to house canvassing
	Activity which is enjoyed for its own sake	(to)	Activity which produces tangible returns
	Taking a chance	(to)	Playing it safe
	Reading a book	(to)	Going to the movies
	Belong to few societies	(to)	Belonging to many societies
	Few intimate friends	(to)	Many acquaintances

	DESCRIBE BEST		
VIII. Your abilities and Personality	Describes me: Have more than my share of novel ideas. Does not describe me: Am quite sure of myself, plan my work in detail		

TABLE VI-3.   SUMMARY OF GROUP-IDENTIFYING ITEM CLUSTER FOR
LOW ORIGENCE/LOW INTELLECTENCE ON SVIB SCALES

TEST HEADING	LIKE	INDIFFERENT	DISLIKE
I. Occupations	Athletic director, bookkeeper, certified public accountant, laboratory technician, pharmacist, playground director, worker in YMCA, K.of C. etc.	Machinist, orchestra conductor	Poet, ship officer
II. School subjects	Arithmetic, bookkeeping, physical training		
III. Amusements	"Popular Mechanics," pet canaries		Poker
IV. Activities	Giving "first aid" assistance, regular hours for work, saving money, contributing to charity		Arguments
V. Types of People	People who are natural leaders, very old people, blind people, deaf people, deaf mutes, fashionably dressed people		

	NEITHER BEST NOR LEAST		PREFERRED LEAST
VI. Order of Preference of Activities	Create a new artistic effect		Freedom in working out one's method of doing the work

	ITEM PREFERRED	(TO)	OTHER ITEM
VII. Preference between Two Items	Chauffeur	(to)	Chef
	Head waiter	(to)	Lighthouse tender
	Activity which produces tangible returns	(to)	Activity which is enjoyed for its own sake
	Playing safe	(to)	Taking a chance

	DESCRIBE BEST
VIII. Your abilities and Personality	Describes me: Stimulate the ambition of my associates. Does not describe me: Have more than my share of novel ideas.

TABLE VI-4. SUMMARY OF GROUP-IDENTIFYING ITEM CLUSTERS FOR LOW ORIGENCE/HIGH INTELLECTENCE ON SVIB SCALES

TEST HEADING	LIKE	INDIFFERENT	DISLIKE
I. Occupations	Politician, scientific research worker, statistician	Artist, corporation lawyer	Auto racer, building contractor, employment manager, playground director
II. School Subjects	Algebra, calculus, geometry, mathematics, physics		
III. Amusements	Bridge, solving mechanical puzzles		
IV. Activities	Methodical work	Meeting and directing people, continually changing activities	Interviewing men for a job
V. Types of People	Optimists	People who assume leadership	

	PREFERRED MOST	PREFERRED LEAST	
VI. Order of Preference of Activities	Treasurer of a society or club	Chairman, entertainment committee; Enrico Caruso, singer; Charles Dana Gibson, artist; opportunity to understand just how one's superior expects work to be done	

	ITEM PREFERRED	(TO)	OTHER ITEM
VII. Preference between Two Items	Inside work	(to)	Outside work

	DESCRIBE BEST		
VIII. Your abilities and Personality	Best-liked friends are equal to me in ability. Become annoyed at times when handling complaints. Never make wagers. *Not sure:* Stimulate the ambition of my associates, win confidence and loyalty.		

Descriptive Summary of SVIB Scales

S-I (high origence/low intellectence). This scale reflects
an orientation toward people both in terms of seeking them out and
in working directly with them. There is a need to stimulate and
to be stimulated by others, to be amused by and to entertain them.
Personal contacts are sought for these reasons and also at times
to persuade others, to sell them something, even against their
will, as if it were a personal challenge to influence others.
There is an egocentric and self-seeking quality and many of their
activities seem to be self-oriented rather than motivated by a
genuine love of or respect for other persons. Social interaction
thus may be more lighthearted or superficial rather than based on
deep-seated emotional involvement with another person. Overt physical action is favored over mental or intellectual activity. Problems, whether in the form of puzzles or the demands of school subjects, are rejected. Responsibility is shunned although attention-
getting devices are favored--the center of the stage, both literally and figuratively, is sought.

S-II (high origence/high intellectence). The emphasis in
this scale is on intellectual matters, particularly literary or
artistic, in impersonal or apersonal settings. Rather than working directly with people or meeting them socially, there is a
preference for activities "about" people--reading about them,
writing about them, and thinking about them. Although a few
friendships may be sought, superficial social acquaintances are
shunned; a somewhat introversive trend may be detected. There is
a marked self-orientation, not so much egocentric as that of a
strong ego with prominent features of self-reliance, self-motiva-
tion, and self-direction. Adventure, excitement, risk--even dan-
ger--are sought. Chances are taken, whether in intellectual matters or in games, and personal challenges which pit one against
another are accepted. Independence and originality, particularly
in the realm of ideas as they may be expressed through the humanities in an academic setting, are strong features of the scale.
Personal and intellectual freedom is an essential aspect of all
activities.

S-III (low origence/low intellectence). A genuine liking
for people of all kinds is evidenced by this scale that may even
take the form of indiscriminate tolerance although it may also
lead to the assumption of civic duties. Independence and freedom
are rejected in favor of letting other persons take responsibility,
assume control, and give direction. Working for others and car-
rying out routine and petty details in business and in the community are welcomed. "Be a faithful follower" seems to be the
watchword. Be cautious, play it safe, look for practical results.
Regularity and a tangible system that works are sought.

S-IV (low origence/high intellectence). This scale seems to reflect some social distance from other persons. That is, leadership is sought to influence people by means of ideas or intellectual activities rather than by direct and personal contact. It may be that people are seen as an intellectual challenge to be solved just as puzzles or scientific problems can be solved by the application of rules and general principles abstracted from the sciences and mathematics. The world may be seen as a research arena and conceptualized by the same principles. Regularity exists; it remains only to discover this by hard work and study. Risk and uncertainty can be avoided by application of what has been learned. Art and literature can be tolerated but they do not lead to "real" knowledge.

GOUGH'S ADJECTIVE CHECK LIST

Items for the four ACL scales are shown in Table VI-5, and the item numbers for the ACL test booklet are given in Appendix C. A rather consistent picture of four different personality types emerges from the adjectives on these scales since the items reflect many basic characteristics such as social and personal attitudes toward other persons, level of emotionality and responsiveness, personality style and manner, and orientation and approach to the world.

Descriptive Summary of ACL Scales

A-I (high origence/low intellectence). The person depicted by this scale seems to like people and to have them around. But there is a hint that this is not so much genuine social interest in others as it is a self-centered desire to exhibit personal charm and attractiveness for others to admire. In manner he is easygoing and seems best at lighthearted social encounter rather than in more intellectually demanding tasks--he does not want to work too hard. There is liking for excitement and stimulation, perhaps in sensual pleasures, and changing activities. Alteration in mood is possible with positive affect replaced by negative attitudes, especially toward other persons. This may imply a lack of long-term personal involvement; thus, immediate acquaintances are enjoyed but enduring friendships are not established.

A-II (high origence/high intellectence). This scale describes a person who tends to hold himself apart from other people on a personal and on a social basis. He is not really interested in others but is intensely self-concerned. This is apparent in his introspective involvement with his own thoughts rather than

TABLE VI-5.   SUMMARY OF GROUP-IDENTIFYING ITEM
              CLUSTERS ON SPECIAL ACL SCALES*

A-I HIGH ORIGENCE LOW INTELLECTENCE		A-II HIGH ORIGENCE HIGH INTELLECTENCE	
adventurous	fussy	aloof	leisurely
attractive	gloomy	complicated	original
charming	lazy	conceited	outspoken
clever	polished	cynical	quiet
confused	quarrelsome	disorderly	rebellious
cool	relaxed	dissatisfied	reflective
daring	sexy	dreamy	restless
dependent	sophisticated	egotistical	spunky
easy-going	unselfish	forceful	temperamental
flirtatious	worrying	forgetful	unconventional
frivolous		hostile	uninhibited
		imaginative	zany
		individualistic	

A-III LOW ORIGENCE LOW INTELLECTENCE		A-IV LOW ORIGENCE HIGH INTELLECTENCE	
appreciative	organized	alert	methodical
cheerful	pleasant	assertive	moderate
contented	pleasure-	autocratic	optimistic
good-natured	seeking	clear-thinking	painstaking
hasty	practical	conventional	persistent
humorous	touchy	deliberate	preoccupied
jolly	trusting	discreet	resourceful
kind	understanding	efficient	shy
mild	wholesome	enterprising	stable
		fair-minded	stubborn
		intelligent	thorough
		logical	tolerant

*Items from the Adjective Check List, copyright 1952 by
Harrison G. Gough, are used with permission. The ACL is distributed by the Consulting Psychologists Press.

with the ideas of others and leads to a poignantly personalized view of the world. He is not content with the *status quo* and wants to change things to suit himself. Rather than trying to ingratiate others and win them over to his ideas, he does not hesitate to express his views in a direct or even a blunt manner. Since he is unorthodox in his thinking and manner, his views may seem unusual or even "wild" to ordinary persons. He is determined in character and does not yield to others in matters of importance where he may be fiercely independent. Generally he seems slow in personal tempo but becomes active and incisive when necessary. His mood is somewhat melancholy although he does not appear to become dispirited; it is rather a realistic pessimism about himself, other people, and the world.

A-III (*low origence/low intellectence*). People seem to be a source of pleasure and enjoyment for the person that this scale characterizes. He genuinely likes them and wants to be around them as much as possible. His self-concept and his view of other people is a positive one--we are all good fellows, he seems to say, and there is no reason why we cannot be happy together. He does things for others and responds gratefully when they reciprocate. All is not sweetness and light, however, for he sometimes may become irritated. But generally his mood is optimistic and hopeful. He expects the world to treat him well and he invites such a favorable response by doing what is required of him without complaint.

A-IV (*low origence/high intellectence*). This scale represents an intellectualized approach to the world where problems can be solved by rational methods and by hard work. Such a person keeps his eyes open and pays attention to things so that he can discern difficulties and correct them in an orderly way by applying regular rules. This leads to a rather optimistic lifeview in which the efforts of the individual person count for something. Others must carry their share of the burden and responsibility, and they sometimes must be told what to do and how to do it. He is not completely at ease with other people, however, although he does not dislike them or withdraw from them. His manner is calm and he seems poised; perhaps he is sustained by a quiet self-confidence in his own ability and skill.

MINNESOTA MULTIPHASIC PERSONALITY INVENTORY

Interpretation of the four scales from the MMPI is complicated both by the large number of items for each scale, and also by the complex nature of the items themselves. Although the SVIB

scales discussed above could be arranged easily according to the
eight parts of the SVIB, the items of the MMPI are not divided
into categories in the test itself. The classification employed
is an arbitrary one based on what seem to be psychological similarities in the implications of the content of the items. The
interpretations offered are thus more speculative in nature and
a higher level of inference is involved than was true for the
SVIB and the ACL scales, where the connections seem much more direct. It must also be kept in mind that the items in the MMPI
were originally selected because of their potential relevance to
matters of ill health, maladjustment, and personality difficulties (Hathaway and McKinley, 1940). The content of the items is
necessarily biased in the direction of pathology although there
are, to be sure, some items that are positively oriented and refer to interests, attitudes, and other matters of a more "normal"
nature. Item numbers for the MMPI test booklet for all of the
items on each scale are given in Appendix C. Table VI-6 gives a
summary of the item clusters used in analyzing the scales for the
descriptive summary.

Descriptive Summary of MMPI Scales

M-I (*high origence/low intellectence*). The person described
by this scale may seem at first to manifest paradoxical or inconsistent attitudes or emotions, but they may be interpreted in
terms of lability or instability where one extreme replaces another. He seems to like people and to respond to their feelings,
but when crossed or threatened he rejects them and may deliberately shun them or bear petty grudges. Ordinarily he can take a
joke on himself if it is clever and can put up with kidding at
his own expense, but he tires of such behavior easily and may become resentful and vengeful. He likes important people until
they attempt to exert some authority or make demands on him, then
he resists and turns against them. Although he protests, perhaps
too loudly, that he is the equal of anyone, this may actually reflect deep-seated feelings of inferiority or inadequacy.

In mood, too, he shows wide swings from cheerful involvement in everyday affairs to dispirited withdrawal. Periods of
intense activity are followed by an inability to mobilize and get
things done. He shows a contradictory attitude toward symptoms
when he denies on the one hand physical aches and pains and minor
fears, but on the other admits many more serious and even bizarre
symptoms.

Many of his characteristics seem to reflect a superficiality
of interest and a shallowness of emotion. He likes frequent

TABLE VI-6.   SUMMARY OF GROUP-IDENTIFYING ITEM
CLUSTERS ON SPECIAL MMPI SCALES

M-I	M-II
HIGH ORIGENCE **LOW INTELLECTENCE**	**HIGH ORIGENCE** **HIGH INTELLECTENCE**
Misanthropic and negative attitude toward others	Asociality, lack of social interests
Tension and excitement	Introversive withdrawal, emotional subjectivity
Need for stimulation and change	
Variable energy level	Denial of physical, mental symptoms and fears
Worry, pessimism, indecision	Interest in serious matters, lack of interest in trivia
Impulsivity and compulsivity	
Lack of resentment of others, permissive morality	Permissive morality, attitudinal frankness
Family difficulties	Recognition and acceptance of basic id urges and impulses
Regressive attitude toward childhood	Rejection or denial of conventional religiosity
Lack of serious interests	Rejection of home and family

M-III	M-IV
LOW ORIGENCE **LOW INTELLECTENCE**	**LOW ORIGENCE** **HIGH INTELLECTENCE**
Sociable and gregarious, personal objectivity	Positive regard for others, philanthropic and altruistic attitudes
Conventional, orthodox, fundamentalistic religiosity	Denial of somatic symptoms, fears, and worries
Admission of symptoms, fears, and phobias	Decisive and self-confident
Mental alertness and practicality	Denial of basic id urges and impulses
Denial of basic id urges and impulses	Social ineptness, lack of social ease
Conventional and practical interests	Lack of aesthetic interests
Dependence on and acceptance of family	

*For additional information, see Appendix C

social encounters of a lighthearted nature rather than enduring
personal involvement. He shows irritation and situational anger
rather than deep-seated hostility. He is tense, on edge, ready
to travel, looking for a change of scene; he seems to become
bored easily and wants to move on before he has fully explored
his current engagements. He shows a lax attitude toward law and
order and is not above shading things in his own favor, nor does
he blame others for their remissions.

    In the family there seems to have been a maternal identi-
fication. There are difficulties and friction in the home. Perhaps demands were made there and he reacted against them. This
may be another example of his tendency to project and blame others for his own shortcomings. He is really not as competent and
as self-confident as he would like others to believe, or, more
importantly, as he himself would like to believe.

    M-II (high origence/high intellectence). An inlooking and
indwelling orientation characterizes this scale. The person described is introspective and more concerned with his own subjective feelings and his personal experiences than he is with the
outside world. He is asocial and does not like parties or dances
where there are crowds of people; he prefers the isolation of the
forest. At the same time, he is not unresponsive to others but
they must take the initiative first--he will not go out of his
way to seek them. Nor will he take responsibility for leadership or assume the direction of others. This does not seem to be
fear of failure (because he is candid in appraising his own abilities and disabilities), but rather a lack of interest in that
kind of role.

    His interests are in serious matters or of more intellectual
than social character. He ignores the trivial and unimportant
happenings of the moment to concentrate on long-term and enduring
problems. On personal problems of morality and ethics he is willing to take a position, again more intellectually oriented, and
to stand up for the rights of others to hold their own beliefs
and conduct their affairs as they see fit. In religious matters,
however, he does not seem so tolerant and he rejects the people
who hold conventional beliefs as well as dogma itself.

    An introspective attitude leads him to close contact with
his unconscious and he expresses interest and concern with dreams
and fantasy. He recognizes his own basic urges of aggression and
sexuality and does not fear that these drives will get out of
hand. Danger and excitement are sought perhaps because he is confident that he can handle such situations and likes the challenges
that they pose for him. He denies that he is fearful just as he
denies that he is troubled by physical symptoms or by phobias.

M-III (low origence/low intellectence). The person described by this scale seems to be a complete social animal and
genuinely interested in other people. He makes friends easily
and enjoys their company at all times whether for a brief chit-
chat or a more formal social gathering. Initiative for interaction comes directly from him and he seeks people out and goes out
of his way to speak to them. He is tolerant of their shortcomings and does not become impatient even if they do something
wrong.

This social orientation may account in part for his interest in religious matters; perhaps church attendance in the company of other people is as important as matters of belief. His
views in such matters are conventional too and follow popular,
pragmatic, or social direction.

In general, he is practically motivated and pays attention
to what he is doing without being distracted by inner musings;
he will not allow his mind to wander. Perhaps he fears recognizing his own fantasy or the promptings of his unconscious that
may lead him into some unseemly behavior. He seems to need and
to respond to external control and feels that others also do--
keep temptation away because we may yield.

His mood seems to be good and he denies that he feels out
of sorts. However he does seem to be somewhat squeamish about
accidents or injuries and he is afraid of bugs and animals.

His family life reflects his interest in people and he gets
along well at home admitting his involvement and dependency on
parents and relatives.

M-IV (low origence/high intellectence). This scale describes
a person who respects people and expects in turn to be respected
by them. He holds high standards of conduct and behavior for himself and for others. Truth, honesty, probity, and integrity should
be displayed in all situations. One does not shirk responsibili-
ties or refuse to face problems because they are difficult or unpleasant. One does not take advantage of others to gain some personal benefit. Determined adherence to truth and logic will lead
to equal justice for all. Once a rational decision has been made,
one should stick to it and not reflect on it with misgiving and
doubt.

This person is self-confident and rather sure of his abilities; he can defend himself intellectually and convince others
because he knows that he is right. Criticism does not upset him
unduly since he feels that he generally shows good judgment. He

does not disparage himself any more than he would deprecate others. He feels good and has no physical complaints nor does he feel nervous or worried.

He does, however, feel the need to keep a tight control over impulses particularly of a sexual nature. High standards of moral conduct may help to maintain such strivings and channel them into acceptable expression that is socially approved.

His one admitted shortcoming is that he is not socially at ease and is not completely confident of himself in social situations. He cannot make small talk and it is difficult for him to take the initiative in social encounter. Apparently he is not sure of his appearance or looks and may fear that he will be judged on a superficial basis rather than in terms of his ideas and abilities. The scale does not give any hint as to what his interests are but does show a lack of interest in flowers and the theater reflecting, perhaps, a lack of aesthetic or artistic sensitivity.

TYPOLOGICAL SUMMARY

In discussing the four personality types inferred from the scales of the three tests, an effort was made to stick fairly close to the content of the items themselves and to be basically descriptive. It is, of course, inevitable that some interpretation occur even though an effort was made to minimize this aspect in the analyses given above; this seems consistent with the spirit of the psychometric and psychological implications of the operational approach.

These descriptive discussions, however, should result in further inferences and should lead to hypotheses for future research. A number of them will be outlined in Chapter XI and will be set in a more general theoretical structure at that time. For the present, general summaries of the four types will be offered with a few speculative elements included that do not follow quite so directly from examination of the individual items in the particular scales.

Group I

The first personality type which is high on origence and low on intellectence seems to be generally extroversive in temperament rather than introversive. He tends to respond to obvious events in the world around him and to the overt actions of others with whom he has contact either personally, socially, or vocationally. His reactions to people are influenced by his feelings of the moment rather than by a studied or calculated analysis either of his own emotions or those of other persons. He is not introspective by nature and does not appreciate this characteristic in others. He likes to have lively and stimulating people around him, particularly those who will feed his self-centered drive for attention. When they praise him or amuse him, he readily accepts them and seeks them out, but when they impose some standards of performance or criticize his behavior, he rejects them and may even turn against them.

In many ways he seems immature both emotionally and intellectually. He needs immediate gratification and cannot endure the delay of working toward long-term goals nor does he enjoy work or other activity just for its own sake. He needs to be flattered and praised for what he does right now and cannot imagine waiting for some distant reward. He is thus more at home in vocations such as dramatics and selling where he gets immediate applause and quick results from histrionic performance. He seeks to persuade others by his own efforts and personal charm rather than by rational or logical arguments. In turn, he is more easily influenced by superficial appearance and short-term outcomes than by reasoned evaluation of remote consequences.

He inclines toward rebellion for its own sake rather than for an ideological principle and rejects authority both personally and in terms of formal social values. He has his own moral code and makes judgments here in the same manner as he does in other areas, by personal and emotional reaction. These attitudes may stem from an identification with the mother and a rejection of the father in the family constellation which then generalizes to the entire social situation. The mother who gratified his wants immediately when he cried or had a temper tantrum is represented by a society that responds in a similar way and praises him for what he accomplishes but does not require him to work unselfishly for others. The demands of the father that he learn perseverance and orderly procedures have a counterpart to which he reacts in a parallel way.

Group II

The second personality type, high on orience and on intellectence, is contrastingly introversive in temperament and introspective by nature. Where the first type looked outward he looks inward and responds to his own subjective feelings and attitudes, rejecting at the same time the views and opinions of others.

Although he may have a few intimate friends, he is generally asocial and is uninterested in having people around him. He is more inclined to act impersonally and to express his views indirectly by writing than by face-to-face interaction; likewise he would rather read what someone has to say than to hear it directly from the person himself. There is an isolative and withdrawing tendency that leaves him to his own devices intellectually and emotionally.

He is planful and persistent and can work toward his own distant goal independently. He rejects the help of others just as he is so preoccupied with his own views that he cannot accept ordinary social values and conventional morality. He would rather do things his own way than to yield to others although he may respond to rational and logical argument of an intellectual kind. He is not affected by emotional appeals unless they coincide with his own values and attitudes. Similarly, he cannot understand why others do not accept his views and ideas and he fails to recognize the need for emotional or social appeals to other persons. He may appear tactless and stubborn because he expects others to recognize as obvious the conclusions that he has arrived at by his own insights which seem so compelling to him. This leads to further estrangement from the social world around him and to greater self-involvement. He becomes convinced of the correctness of his own views and is not afraid to take risks because he has confidence in his own ability. If he fails, it is others who do not understand him or appreciate what he is trying to do--they should change, not he.

Perhaps he was unable to accept his mother's love or his father's discipline and reacted by withdrawal from both of them and by a retreat into fantasy, a world in which he controls and directs the family and himself, and which he now seeks to impose on society at large.

Group III

The third personality type, low on both dimensions, is extroversive like the first and turns outward to the world and to the people around him. But, where the first type seeks others because of the value they have for his self-seeking needs, the third type genuinely likes people for their own sake and is willing to work as hard for them as he is for himself. He accepts them for what they are just as he is self-accepting and can acknowledge his weaknesses and shortcomings without apology. His self-acceptance stems from a lack of interest in, or an inability for, introspection--making him less critical than he might be.

This does not lead to smugness, however, merely to a bland conformance and conventionality. He does not recognize the extent
to which his attitudes have been formed by those around him, nor
to his dependency on externally-imposed rules and regulations.
He is a follower and is willing to accept the leadership of
others in personal and intellectual matters.

A well organized and well structured existence is congenial to his temperament and he exhibits a practical orientation
to his work and his leisure. He is cautious and skeptical of
anything new or unproven unless some authority figure urges it
on him; his predilection is for the tried and true. He seeks a
stable world and seems to find it in the kinds of occupations he
chooses as well as in the social milieu in which he establishes
himself.

His family background seems to have been a settled and a
protective one in which he accepted the emotional warmth of the
mother and learned to reply in kind. Likewise, he accepted the
authority of the father and was able to follow directions without
having to assert his independence. He becomes a sincere and loy-
al citizen who does his duty for his community cheerfully and with
conviction.

Group IV

The fourth personality type which is high on intellectence
but low on origence is somewhat introversive like the second,
but does not seem quite so withdrawn and asocial in orientation,
nor is he so introspective by nature. He is much more objective
in outlook and responds to people in the world around him and to
their attitudes and ideas, although he tends to maintain some social and personal distance from them. Most of his responses are
intellectualized or rationalized and he seldom acts impulsively
as the first type often does. He seems to believe that the world
is an orderly place and that there are rules and regulations to
be followed both in daily conduct and in solving problems that
may appear. For this reason he finds mathematics and the physical
sciences congenial since they are impersonal in nature but challenging intellectually.

He respects his own accomplishments as well as those of
other persons but expects them to follow protocol strictly and
is resistant to the flashes of insight or the intuitive solutions
that the second type may achieve. The nonlogical does not fit
into his systematic approach to problems. He follows a well specified code of ethics and expects others to act in the same manner;

perhaps he may sometimes seem to be overly strict in his interpretation of moral behavior. He seems to be more optimistic in
outlook than the second type, possibly because of a belief that
a desirable and worthwhile outcome may be achieved through hard
work and the application of comprehensible principles.

It may be that an identification with the father and his
role in the family has led him away from the emotional and toward
the rational orientation that he characteristically displays.
Rather than remain a follower, he becomes a leader as an adult
who seeks to persuade others by rational argument and by setting
a good example.

THE CREATIVE PERSON

In Chapter I an approach to the study of creativity through
different perspectives was outlined. In this discussion an article by Dellas and Gaier (1970) was cited in which the authors summarized thirteen personality characteristics of the creative person consistently found in research that they reviewed. We now
ask whether any of these traits appear in the typology summarized
above and, further, to see whether any one of the four types described in the present study comprises many of these characteristics.

For one of their traits, "flexibility," there seems to be
no evidence in our summary of any clear-cut relationship, although
some of the features of the first type may possibly be construed
as similar in some ways to the concept of flexibility. Another
trait is not markedly congruent with any of the types, "social
presence and poise." In fact, the implications of this trait
seem contrary to some characteristics of the fourth type.

The remaining eleven traits, however, are clearly evident
in the summary for the second type: independence in attitude and
social behavior, dominance, introversion, openness to stimuli,
wide interests, self-acceptance, intuitiveness, asocial attitude,
unconcern for social norms, radicalism, and rejection of external
controls. This degree of agreement can hardly be considered fortuitous and two major conclusions seem warranted.

First, the assumption of the present study that the traits
summarized by Dellas and Gaier are susceptible to measurement by
objective personality tests seems to have been demonstrated. Item
analyses of standard tests resulted in clusters of terms that had
psychometric characteristics of useful measurement scales as
shown in Chapter V. In the present chapter, interpretation of

the items in these scales resulted in a psychologically meaningful typology.

Second, some credence must be given to the argument advanced that a subgroup of Governor's School subjects is more
likely to be creative than the others. Those who fall into type
two, high origence/high intellectence, resemble to a striking
degree the composite picture of the creative person inferred from
the thirteen-trait summary. The prediction seems justified that
Governor's School students of this type can be considered to be
potentially creative from the standpoint of personality.

A further implication for which evidence will be presented
later is that creativity requires both origence and intellectence,
and that a person who is high on both dimensions is more likely
to demonstrate creative behavior than one who is not. In contrast, a person who is low on both dimensions is less likely to
be creative.

Chapter VII

PERSONALITY AND INTEREST TEST CORRELATES
OF DIMENSIONAL SCORES

The last chapter discussed at some length the items on the four special scales for the three tests used in explicating the two basic dimensions hypothesized earlier. This chapter turns to the correlates of the composite scores for intellectence and origence, INT and ORIG, with regular scales* of the Strong Vocational Interest Blank, the Adjective Check List, and the Minnesota Multiphasic Personality Inventory.

Since many psychological implications of the regular scales of these tests are known, it will help in the interpretation of the dimensions proposed to examine them in this context. That is, some insight into the psychological nature of origence and intellectence may be gained by a scrutiny of their correlational patterns with scales of the three tests. Correlation coefficients were calculated between the two composite scores and all of the regular scales on the three tests; correlations were also run on the special group scales described in the last chapter. These data have been presented in graphic form rather than by merely listing the values in tabular form in the hope that their relationships may be more easily grasped. Each of the three tests is given separately and will be discussed in turn. Data for the SVIB are given in Figure VII-1, for the ACL in Figure VII-2, and for the MMPI in Figure VII-3.

The following method was used to construct the figures: Two orthogonal (right-angled) axes were drawn to represent the two independent dimensions and distances marked off to represent the magnitude of the correlation coefficents. The vertical axis

---

*Use of the term "regular" scales here implies the scales that are generally (and for the most part ordinarily) routinely scored and profiled by most persons using the test, although it must be noted that there are exceptions to this regularity. That is, some psychologists do not always score all of the usual scales and some routinely score in addition various "special" scales for particular purposes. In the present research we have employed for the ACL some special scales developed in the course of the Governor's School Study in addition to the origence/intellectence scales already described.

was used for origence score correlations and the horizontal for intellectence score correlations. Positive correlations are given on the upper and right-hand halves of the axes; negative values fall on the lower and left-hand halves of the axes. Correlations were calculated separately for the sexes and each scale is represented by two points, a filled circle for boys and an open circle for girls; these points have been connected with a light line.

It will help in understanding the graphic method of display to look at the figure first and then to follow the explanation of the entries.

STRONG VOCATIONAL INTEREST BLANK

Correlates of the regular SVIB scales are shown in Figure VII-1. It is apparent, for example, that Advertising Man had high positive correlations with origence but was essentially uncorrelated with intellectence. The actual values of the correlations for the Governor's School boys and girls, respectively, are .58 and .48 for origence, and .07 and .03 for intellectence. Thus, Governor's School students who had high scores on ORIG tended also to have high scores on Advertising Man, while there was no systematic relationship between the SVIB scale and INT (*i.e.*, a high score on one could as easily accompany a low score on the other as vice versa).

On the other hand, students who scored high on the SVIB scale for Math-Science Teacher tended to have *low* scores on ORIG or, conversely, high ORIG scores accompanied a tendency to obtain low scores on Math-Science Teacher.

The Architect scale shows positive correlations with both dimensional scores, .25 and .41 for the ORIG and INT correlations, respectively, for the boys, and .22 and .41 for the girls. The location of this scale in the upper right portion of the figure indicates a tendency for high Architect scores to accompany high scores on both ORIG and INT.

Low scores on ORIG with high scores on INT are implied by the lower right hand location of Engineer while an opposite trend for Real Estate Salesman may be seen in its location indicating high ORIG and low INT scores.

Finally, it may be noted that the special group SVIB scales described in the last chapter fall in appropriate locations: S-I, upper left; S-II, upper right; S-III, lower left, and S-IV, lower right.

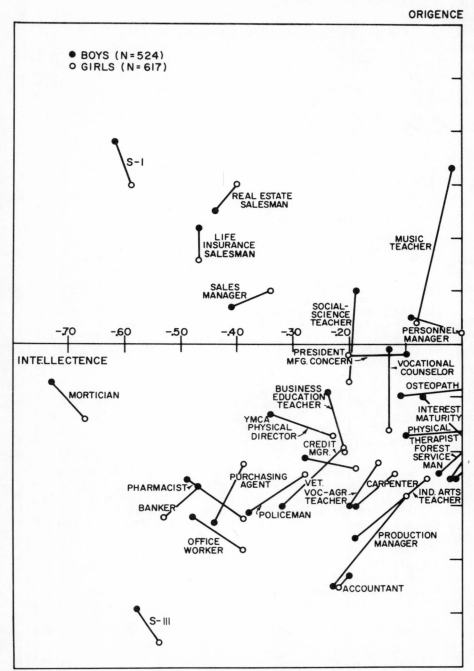

Figure VII - 1

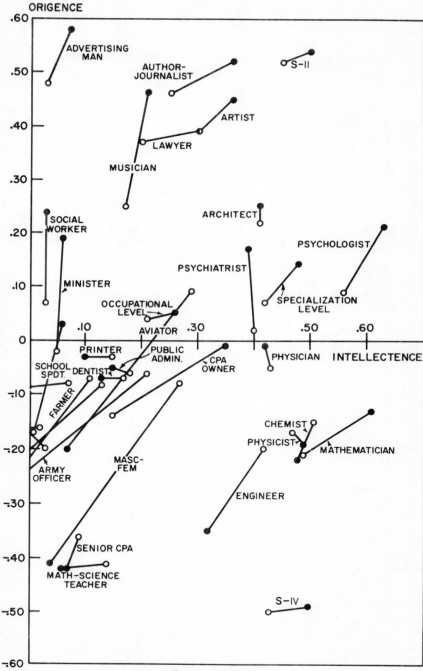

Figure VII - 1

Intellectence

        Some inferences about the dimension of intellectence may
be made by considering scales showing the highest positive and
the highest negative correlations with INT scores. For the present, correlational differences between the Governor's School
boys and girls will be passed over since sex differences will be
discussed later.

        It is apparent from Figure VII-1 that there are differences
in the amount and degree of education and training for the scales
lying at the extremes of the intellectence dimension. Scales
with high positive correlations are all characterized by requirements of graduate or professional degrees and by specialized
training. The average educational achievement of subjects used
in standardizing SVIB scales has been reported by Strong (1959:
25-28) in terms of grades completed.

        A comparison of vocational scales falling at the extremes
in positive and negative correlations on the horizontal dimension
may be made with relation to educational attainment. Names of
the scales followed by degree or grades completed are given in
Table VII-1.

TABLE VII-1.   EDUCATIONAL ATTAINMENT OF VOCATIONAL
                SCALES FOR INTELLECTENCE

Negative Correlation (low INT)		*Positive Correlation* (high INT)	
Mortician	13.0*	Psychologist	Ph.D.
Banker	12.2	Mathematician	18.8
Life Insurance		Chemist	16.8
Salesman	13.6	Physicist	18.5
Pharmacist	Not reported	Specialization	
Office Worker	11.5	Level	M.D.+**
Real Estate		Physician	M.D.
Salesman	12.1	Architect	14.4
Purchasing Agent	11.8	Psychiatrist	M.D.+
Sales Manager	13.0		

---

        *Graduation from high school is signified by 12 and gradu-
ation from college by 16.
        **The + sign following psychiatrist and specialization level
indicates that advanced training beyond the basic degree is required.

It is necessary to comment on the Specialization Level scale since it is not strictly an occupational scale. Derivation of this scale and its implications are given by Strong (1959:28):

> Responses of 400 internists, surgeons, psychiatrists and 300 pathologists were averaged and contrasted with the responses of 500 physicians in general.... On theoretical grounds the scale may differentiate specialists from non-specialists in other areas than medicine; actually it does differentiate Ph.D. chemists from M.S. and A.B. chemists.

Scales at the lower end of the intellectence dimension are obviously much lower in average educational attainment and even the one with most education, Life Insurance Salesman, does not reach the level of Architect, which is the only high intellectence scale not surpassing the B.A. level. Since the average education for Pharmacist was not reported, there is no way of knowing whether or not it might have been equal to Architect. It must be pointed out, however, that Pharmacist does require specialized training, although at the time the scale was developed, 1949, it was at an undergraduate level.

Superior social status and prestige accompany the educational achievement of high intellectence. Only one scale at the lower end, Banker, is ordinarily thought of as high status--but even here there is evidence (Baughman and Welsh, 1962:209; Gilbert, 1970:148) that it has slipped from preeminence in this regard.

Although the last three occupations at the upper end offer services to the public, it is not of the same nature as that at the lower end. Indeed, it is against the ethics of medicine and architecture to advertise commercially.

The four scales at the head of the high intellectence list are all scientific and intellectual in character; at times they may be academically oriented, but professional services are frequently offered to the public as well. Often theoretical interests are at the core of the occupation and even practical application of skills is more often conceptual in nature than the concrete pragmatics of those low in intellectence.

Crucial to the contrast of the ends of the dimension is the attitude and orientation of the practitioner. At the lower end the public must be sought out and service sold; direct personal and social relationships are frequently sought for this purpose.

The upper end is more often impersonal and, at times, asocial since practitioners are sought by the public and may be in much demand for their specialized talents and skills. They are not necessarily unsocial in personal relationships, but they can practice their profession by waiting for the public to come to them.

Origence

Scales falling at the extremes of the origence dimension do not show any differences in average educational achievement and are quite similar in this characteristic, as can be seen in the following table.

TABLE VII-2.   EDUCATIONAL ATTAINMENT OF VOCATIONAL
              SCALES FOR ORIGENCE

Negative Correlation (low ORIG)		*Positive Correlation* (high ORIG)	
Accountant	12.3	Advertising Man	14.0
Math-Science Teacher		Author-Journalist	14.3
Teacher	16.4	Artist	11.9
Senior CPA	14.4	Lawyer	17.0
Production Manager	13.3	Musician	13.6
Office Worker	11.5	Real Estate Salesman	12.1
Banker	12.2	Architect	14.4
Pharmacist	Not reported		

The mean of the averages is 13.4 at the lower end and 13.9 at the upper; these values might be even closer together were data for the Pharmacist scale available.

There are no gross differences in socioeconomic status or prestige between these extreme scales, although Lawyer may have a slight advantage in this regard over Banker, and Office Worker may be somewhat lower than counterpart scales at the upper ORIG end.

Obvious differences appear when the specific nature of the content of the occupations is examined. At the lower end the emphasis is on figures and things, at the upper end it is on verbal and visual forms. Advertising Man, Author-Journalist, and

Lawyer are all concerned with the written word and, to some extent, the spoken word.

All of the low ORIG scales deal with facts, figures, and quantities; this is true whether the orientation is pedagogical as for Math-Science Teacher, or a professional service related to the area of health as represented by Pharmacists.

Artist and Architect, while not verbal in nature, deal with visual forms, shapes, and spatial relationships. None of the scales at the lower origence end have this concern. These two scales, plus Musician, also are directly involved in aesthetic matters while Advertising Man and Author-Journalist scales are, indirectly at least, related to problems of taste if not aesthetics.

At the lower end, Production Manager and Officer Worker are directly concerned with business detail; Banker, Accountant, and Senior CPA are very close to them in this regard.

Perhaps the most characteristic difference between the scales at the ends of the origence dimension may be seen in the manner of procedure or product. At the lower end activities are, for the most part, regular and orderly, following standard rules and principles; to this extent the scales may be impersonal as well. Impersonality is also implied by the fact that anyone who is able and motivated may learn rules and apply them more or less routinely.

At the upper end, however, emphasis is on personal interpretation with more flexibility and spontaneity required for the solution of problems. Guiding principles of conduct are much looser and more general in nature. Zestful inspiration rather than dogged determination seems to be a feature of high ORIG.

Sex Differences

There are some differences between the locations of the SVIB scales for the Governor's School boys and girls, reflecting meaningful inferences that may be drawn from the correlational display. Many scales, however, are extremely close in location and show remarkable consistency: Physicist, Physician, Public Administrator, Dentist, Printer, Accountant, Senior CPA, Math-Science Teacher, Architect, and Occupational Level.

Occupational Level is another nonvocational scale which "was developed by identifying items which differentiate unskilled workers from the men-in-general group. A low score thus indicates

interests similar to those of manual laborers; a high score means
the person has responded to the items the way most business and
professional men do" (Strong, 1959:10). For the boys and girls
alike, Occupational Level is unrelated to the dimension of origence but falls moderately high on intellectence, which seems consistent with its derivation.

The most extreme difference in location is shown by the
Masculinity-Femininity scale which is scored in the masculine
direction. That is, a high score indicates masculinity for both
males and females. For girls, it is related to high intellectence,
while for boys it is related to low origence. This is particularly intriguing since it is consistent with the finding of
feminine interest patterns among creative males (see pp. 152 & 168).
A similar relationship is also shown by Aviator, Army Officer,
Farmer, Engineer, and Forest Service Man. High scores on these
scales accompany high intellectence for the girls but low origence for the boys. An opposite trend is shown by CPA Owner, and
to some extent Mathematician, where for boys the scales are more
highly related to intellectence than they are for the girls.

Several scales are unrelated to intellectence but show
marked sex differences along origence. Music Teacher, Social
Worker, and Minister are characteristic of high ORIG scores for
boys but are essentially unrelated to these scores for the girls.
Musician shows a similar trend for origence but is, in addition,
positively related to intellectence for both sexes.

Other less striking sex differences in the patterned relationship of scales can be seen in Figure VII-1 but may, perhaps,
be written off as fluctuations to be expected in any extensive
statistical analysis. What is truly remarkable is the amount of
consistency displayed which offers further support for the use
of the Men's Form of the SVIB for both sexes at the Governor's
School.

Relative Position on Origence and Intellectence

One of the implications of the origence/intellectence model
is that personality characteristics related to both dimensions
are necessary for creativity and some evidence has been presented
in support of this argument. At the same time, it is apparent
that vocations may differ markedly in their locations along these
dimensions as may be inferred from the correlational display of
the Strong Vocational Interest Blank scales (Figure VII-1, pp. 110-
111) and is suggested by the summary of occupational preferences
offered in the Afterword (Table A-1, page 200).

What can be said of occupations and professions that do not fall in the high orient/high intellectent area of the two-dimensional space? Are these vocations to be characterized as "noncreative" and attractive only to persons who are themselves noncreative? Is it possible for an individual to be creative if he is engaged in an occupation that lies low on either origence or intellectence?

For the individual person a resolution is possible by divorcing the creative endeavor from the manner of earning a living. One thinks of Herman Melville and Walt Whitman working as government clerks to sustain themselves, or of the modern poet, Wallace Stevens, successfully employed as an insurance company executive. What is needed, however, is a general principle to cover all persons and occupations, not just the exceptional individual.

One of the difficulties in approaching this problem stems from the tendency to consider creativity in absolute terms and to conceptualize it in a quantitative framework along a single dimension. This is one of the consequences of the cognitive approach favored by many researchers as discussed in Chapter III. Creativity is construed by them as an ability like intelligence and, just as a high IQ score is considered to be a *sine qua non* for intelligence, so must a person give the correct answers on some "creative thinking" test to be seen as creative. A clear implication of this approach is that a person scoring low in this kind of cognitive performance lacks creativity.

However, if creativity is construed as a multidimensional concept requiring a combination of ability and personality traits, as discussed in Chap. I, the appropriateness of the configuration of abilities and traits for the requirements of a specific task can be gauged. Likewise, the particular demands of a situation can be related to both the person and the context in a qualitative and a relative manner instead of restricting the evaluation to the quantitative and absolute judgments inherent in the cognitive approach. Is there any reason to differentiate the creativity of a kindergarten child's spontaneous drawing or the free verse of an adolescent from the painting of an artist or the sonnets of a poet?

In the framework of origence and intellectence the following hypothesis is proposed to account for differential evaluation of creativity: A person is likely to be judged as creative if he falls high on origence and intellectence *relative* to the central tendency of his own peer group.

For example, say banking falls in the low origence/low intellectence quadrant and painting in the high origence/high intellectence quadrant. A specific artist might be absolutely higher on both dimensions than a specific banker, but this artist
would not be seen as creative if he fell below the dimensional
averages for his occupational group. A banker, on the other
hand, falling above his fellow financiers would be seen as creative or, if the term creative is not appropriate in the circumstances, he might be called original, clever, innovative, imaginative, or some related term.

However, if a banker fell too far above the average for his
occupation, he would be inclined to seek another type of occupation more congruent with his origence/intellectence characteristics unless, as discussed earlier, he can express his creativity
in a non-banking related avocation such as poetry or painting.

It may be speculated, further, that some occupations have
a narrow range on origence and intellectence within which an individual must fall to remain on the job. That is, specialized
requirements within a vocational field may impose a low thresh-
hold for departure and make a particular occupation vulnerable
to the loss of potentially creative employees.*

Another implication of this formulation is that in some
occupations differences between more creative and less creative
members of the occupation may not be very great. This interpretation would account for the fact that the IPAR scientists were
less well differentiated in creativity than the architects
(Chap. VIII). The principle could also be invoked to explain the
results of Schaefer's study mentioned in Chapter IV (p. 65),
see Appendix A for details. He found in high school subjects
that artistic boys were better differentiated by the art scale
than scientific boys. It may be noted, incidentally, that if
these scientific boys fell relatively low on origence it would
account also for their high scores on the ACL order scale as contrasted with the low scores on this scale for artistic boys and
artistic girls.

ADJECTIVE CHECK LIST

Figure VII-2 shows the correlations of ACL scales with the
dimensions of origence and intellectence. The graphic display

---

*This view would be consistent with the theoretical analy-
sis of conflict by Kurt Lewin in which one of the resolutions is
"leaving the field" (Lewin, 1935).

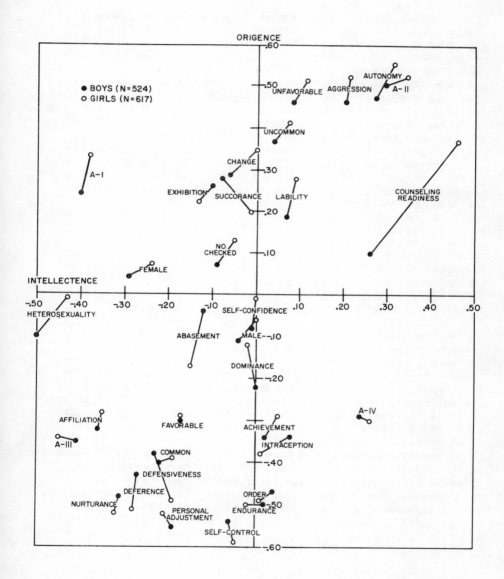

Figure VII - 2

is less completely filled out than that for the SVIB, in part
because there are many fewer scales for the ACL, but also because these scales tend to cluster in a diagonal from lower left
to upper right. It may be seen that the lower right hand quadrant, low ORIG/high INT, is practically empty except for A-IV--
and even this special ACL scale seems to be somewhat less effective than the other three in terms of correlation.

Most of the scale locations fall fairly close together for
the boys and the girls and indicate similarity for the sexes in
dimensional relationships. There is one marked exception, however, and that is Counseling Readiness. Difference between the
sexes is to be expected on this scale since there are actually
two separate forms of the scale, with different items, one form
for males and one for females (Gough and Heilbrun, 1965:9).
Counseling Readiness shows higher correlations for the girls on
both dimensions.

There are four extra scales in Figure VII-2 that are not
described in the ACL manual (Gough and Heilbrun, 1965), since
they were developed in the course of analyses of the Governor's
School data (Welsh, 1967b). These scales are: Common Response,
Uncommon Response, Male Response, and Female Response.

The Common Response and Uncommon Response scales were developed by locating in an item analysis those adjectives very
frequently or very infrequently checked by all subjects. These
scales are intended to be analogous to the F scale of the MMPI
(Dahlstrom and Welsh, 1960:134-42) and the Communality scale of
the California Psychological Inventory (Gough, 1964), and to reflect typicality or atypicality of general response to the ACL
test.

The Male Response and Female Response scales were developed
by locating in an item analysis those adjectives showing the
greatest difference in frequency of endorsement by the sexes.
Those checked more often by the boys form the Male response scale
and those more often checked by the girls, the Female response
scale.   They were developed to pursue sex differences in general
and also because of the oft-noted relationship of feminine interest patterns to creativity.

Intellectence

Only one of the standard ACL scales, Heterosexuality, has
a clear-cut correlation with this dimension alone. The other
ACL scales with significant negative correlation (indicating low

INT) such as Affiliation, Nurturance, and Deference, all have significant negative correlations with origence at the same time. Likewise, none of the scales having high positive correlations with intellectence are free from positive correlations on origence as well.

It is informative to read the description of the Heterosexuality scale from the ACL manual (p. 8) in terms of intellectence. It states that a person low on the Heterosexuality scale (who would be high on INT), "thinks too much, as it were, and dampens his vitality; he tends to be dispirited, inhibited, shrewd and calculating in his personal relationships."

At the opposite end, the low INT, high heterosexual person, "is interested in the opposite sex as he is interested in life, experience, and most things around him in a healthy, direct, and outgoing manner. He may even be a bit naive in the friendly ingenuousness in which he approaches others."

Such descriptive material is, of course, not available for the newly devised Female Response scale, but it may give some insight into the nature of the dimension to look at a cluster of ten adjectives that are common to Heterosexuality and the Female scales. These adjectives are:

affectionate	feminine
attractive	flirtatious
charming	natural
emotional	outgoing
excitable	warm

These terms all contain a common concern with more or less superficial appearance and socially-oriented behavior.

Positive social interest for the lower end of intellectence may be inferred also from the description in the manual of the other scales with negative correlations. As implied above, allowance must be made for relationship with the other dimension. By implication, then, the upper end of intellectence is lacking in concern for warm human social relations and there may well be some self-centered asociality.

Origence

This dimension is more clearly defined in terms of the ACL scales since there are a number with significant positive or negative correlations on origence but with little or no correlation

on intellectence. One of the new scales, Uncommon Response, also appears on this dimension. These scales are:

Low Origence	*High Origence*
Self-Control	Unfavorable
Endurance	Change
Order	Succorance
Intraception	Uncommon
Achievement	Lability
	Exhibition

By reading the descriptions of these scales in the ACL
manual it is possible to infer the nature of the characteristics
of persons falling either high or low on origence and form composite pictures of those at the two extremes of the dimensions.

Low origence seems to reflect self-control and even over-
control with an accompanying loss of spontaneity and a submergence
of individuality. Such a person is conventional and conforming
which leads to diligence and a sense of responsibility and rec-
titude on the one hand, but also to caution, placidity, deliberate
slowness, and apprehension about risktaking. He may be overly concerned with his obligations and the methods required to achieve
goals to such an extent that he is self-denying and inhibited.
His achievements are accomplished more because of dutiful application than by zest and imagination. He seeks stability and con-
tinuity in his life and is more at home in simple, well structured situations where clear-cut solutions are possible.

The person high on origence seems to thrive in an aura of
uncertainty where he can abandon conventional guidelines and regulations. He seems disorderly at times and prefers complexity.
His quick and spontaneous manner may often lead to impulsive
judgments and a self-centered, headstrong approach to problems.
Need for variety and change may take the form of impatience and
inability to tolerate prolonged effort. Nonconformity and unconventionality are marked features of the upper end of his dimension.

MINNESOTA MULTIPHASIC PERSONALITY INVENTORY

The configuration of the standard MMPI scales* shown in
Figure VII-3 follows a direction opposite to that seen in the
ACL. The MMPI scales all fall in a band from upper left (high
ORIG/low INT) to lower right (low ORIG/high INT). The lower left

---

*Clinical scales were not modified by the so-called K cor-
rection in this analysis.

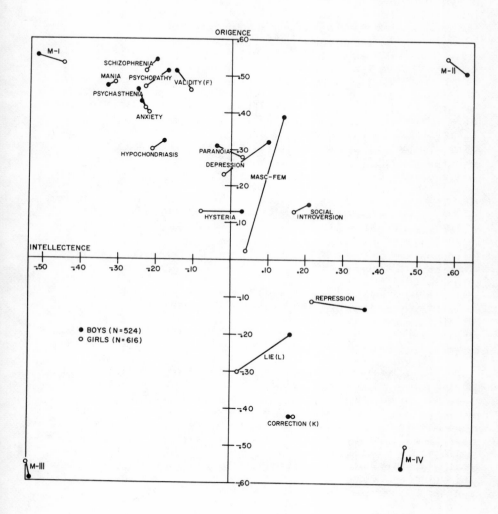

Figure VII - 3

quadrant, so well filled out in the ACL, is completely devoid of
MMPI scales except for the special group M-III scale, which falls
nicely into its expected corner. The other special group MMPI
scales likewise are located in appropriate positions.

The locations are quite similar for the sexes with the exception of the Masculinity-Femininity scale, Mf. This scale is
complicated both by different scoring directions for the sexes
and also by a subset of items that are scored oppositely (Dahlstrom and Welsh, 1960:63-66). Although Mf is unrelated to the
dimensions for the girls, it shows a significant positive correlation with origence for the boys. Once again the relationship of creativity and femininity of test scores must be pointed
out.

Also to be remarked is the location of the clinical scales
of the MMPI (see Fig.VII-3, p.123); this is consistent with reports by the IPAR groups of elevated scores on many of these
scales in their creative subjects (MacKinnon, *et al.*, 1961).

Intellectence

None of the MMPI scales show a clear-cut correlation with
intellectence free of attendant correlation with the other dimension. Two scales, however, falling at opposite points on
origence show significant positive correlations with intellectence. These are Social Introversion (Si) and Repression (R).

The R scale was especially developed to afford a direct
measure of a major factor dimension of the MMPI (Welsh, 1956).
High scores on this scale reflect mechanisms of repression,
denial, and rationalization, and some writers have also made an
interpretation of this factor as inhibition or introversion
(Kassenbaum, Couch, and Slater, 1959). The implications of the
positive correlations of both Si and R with intellectence are
that high INT scores are associated with an introversive tendency;
this finding is consistent with observations that have been made
earlier.

In an extensive study of undergraduate college students
seen in a counseling center, L.E. Drake and E.R. Oetting (1959)
reported that males with peak scores on Si were "introverted,
self-conscious, or socially insecure" (p. 40), while females were
"socially shy" (p. 73).

Although in the present study no scale is negatively correlated with intellectence alone, it may be of interest to

consider Mania (Ma), the scale with the largest coefficient in
this direction on the dimension. In the Drake and Oetting study
male cases having peak scores on Ma and low scores on Si were described as "aggressive or belligerent" and they report that, "This
pattern was infrequently associated with introversion or self-
consciousness or social insecurity, shyness in the interview,
being nonresponsive or nonverbal or a nonrelator, indecisiveness"
(p. 72). Females were described as "marriage oriented, socially extroverted, verbal" (p. 123). Low INT scores, then, are
likely to be related to social extroversion in contrast to the
social introversion noted for high INT scores.

The R scale was used in another study of college undergraduates (Stix, 1967). When students were matched for ability on the
Scholastic Aptitude Test, males high on R tended to show significantly higher academic achievement, although the relationship
did not hold for females. It may be noted in the present study
that the correlation of R and intellectence is higher for the
Governor's School boys (.36) than it is for the girls (.22).

Origence

There is no clear-cut relationship on this dimension since
the scales having the highest correlations also tend to have correlations on intellectence as well. In understanding the MMPI
correlates of origence, allowance has to be made for the possible
interactive effect of the dual nature of the scales' relationship.

It may be well to look first at the three *validity* scales
of the MMPI which are ordinarily referred to by letter alone--
L, F, and K. These scales were developed to afford an index of
the general test-taking attitude of a subject so that the profile of *clinical* scales could be more adequately interpreted.

The L scale (referred to as "Lie" in Figure VII-3) comprises a series of items of obvious psychological and social significance scored in such a way that a high score on L is earned
by a subject who denies or tries to cover up minor personal
faults. While most people are willing to admit that they sometimes put off until tomorrow what they ought to do today, the
high L subject denies it. He is thus frequently found to be
defensive, rigid, naive, lacking in insight, sometimes low in
intelligence, and often overly conventional (Dahlstrom and Welsh,
1960:47-50, 126-33).

The K scale ("Correction" in Figure VII-3) is a more sophisticated and psychometrically complicated way of getting at the defensiveness characteristic of L. It is actually used to correct statistically certain clinical scales for the defensive tendency it reveals, but of concern here is only the meaning of K in the Governor's School correlational analysis. In better educated subjects K may reflect high self-acceptance; the subject says favorable things about himself because he is truly satisfied with himself (Dahlstrom and Welsh, 1960:50-53, 142-54).

The third validity scale, F, has no conventional term and thus is referred to in Figure VII-3 as "Validity" for convenience. This scale was developed by finding items very infrequently endorsed by the normative group of Minnesota subjects. A low score indicates response conformity, and a high score, lack of conformity. High scores are also earned by subjects of limited intelligence or those who do not understand the items or mark their answer sheet in a careless fashion. They may also be overly candid or psychologically exhibitionistic in displaying their faults or shortcomings; this is often a kind of rebellious nonconformity (Dahlstrom and Welsh, 1960:49-50, 134-42).

It is clear from Figure VII-3 that F falls at the upper ORIG end of the dimension while L and K fall at the lower ORIG end. This is consistent with the placement of similar ACL scales where Unfavorable and Uncommon Response are at the upper end of Origence with Favorable and Common Response at the lower end.

The implication for the dimension may be seen in terms of attitude toward the self. Low origence may reflect guarded defensiveness or smug satisfaction and conforming conventionality. High origence may reflect intemperate expressiveness or exaggerated dissatisfaction and nonconforming unconventionality.

Only two of the clinical scales have significant positive correlations on origence without correlation on intellectence, Paranoia (Pa) and Depression (D). These two scales did not appear together in the Drake and Oetting study, but they do report Pa to be associated with personal sensitivity and concern about the reaction of others (1959:25-26). The combination of peak scores on D and Pa did occur in a study of medical patients by Guthrie and they were found to be sensitive, resentful, aggressive, hostile, worried, and depressed (Dahlstrom and Welsh, 1960: 178-97).

Most of the clinical scales, however, fall clearly into the high ORIG/low INT quadrant so that the implication for origence alone cannot be clearly seen. One common feature of these scales

is a willingness to admit complaints of various kinds; this
would be consistent with the interpretation previously placed on
the validity scale F, discussed above.

It should be noted that the factor scale for Anxiety (A)
also falls into this cluster. The A scale, like R, was especially developed to assess a major factor dimension of the MMPI
(Welsh, 1956). This factor, A, has been related to anxiety or
general emotional upset and distress and is often associated
with personal inefficiency. Daniel L. Stix, in the study of
undergraduates, referred to the above in the discussion of Repression, found that the A scale showed a complex relationship
to academic achievement with different patterns for the sexes.

SUMMARY OF ORIGENCE AND INTELLECTENCE

Intellectence seems to be related to personality characteristics, temperamental dispositions, and interests associated with
a dimension that has been conceptualized as one extending from
the concrete to the abstract. That is, at the lower end of intellectence, emphasis is placed on literal and specific events
which may be expressed in concrete terms and may have practical
or pragmatic applications for the experiences of everyday life.

At the upper end of intellectence, on the other hand, an
abstract attitude may be seen that leads to concern with figura-
tive or symbolic expression and generalized principles of comprehension. This attitude finds expression also in differences between the ends of the dimension regarding social behavior; while
the upper end seems more impersonal and even unsocial, the lower
end is much more directly personal in outlook and more socially
participative.

This dimension may also be related to academic achievement,
to vocational level, and educational attainment because of the
concrete/abstract differentiation. That is, an interest, aptitude, and predilection for abstraction is a requisite for success
in school and those who do not find this kind of experience congenial drop out sooner, rather than later. Thus, occupations
and professions requiring more education are likely to recruit
those higher on intellectence.

It must be stressed that this personality dimension has to
be kept separate from the concept of intelligence. Persons at
the lower end of intellectence may be just as intelligent as
those at the upper end and may, in many cases, be more success-
ful in dealing with ordinary problems of life. In fact, as

measured by salary and financial reward, those at the lower end
often exceed those at the upper end.

It is likely that there is a systematic relationship between scores on conventional intelligence tests and the dimension of intellectence because the tests are loaded with the kind
of content that requires abstractions for correct response. The
tests are biased against the person who expresses his intelligence
and ability in practical ways. Also, conventional tests of intelligence have been developed, for the most part, to predict
academic achievement rather than success in the pragmatic world
of everyday affairs.

Origence, by contrast, is not directly related to intellectual performance either in terms of conventional intelligence
tests or of academic achievement. The dimension seems to distinguish those at the lower end who prefer, and are more at home
in, an explicit and well-defined world which can be grasped by
the application of impersonal rules, from those at the upper end
who find congenial an implicit and open universe which they can
structure and order in their own personal way.

The high origent person resists conventional approaches
that have been determined by others and would rather "do his own
thing," even if it is unpopular or seems to be rebellious or nonconforming. He is more interested in artistic, literary, and
aesthetic matters that do not have a "correct" answer agreed upon
by consensus and that allow more individualized interpretation
and expression.

At the lower end of origence are those who are more at
ease in an orderly, structured, and regular environment where
problems can be solved by conventional methods and by conforming
to the *status quo*. In academic settings that stress rote memory
and course content which is oriented to facts and figures, they
may seem to achieve more than those at the upper end of the dimension. Some success may also accrue because of stylistic features related to persistence and planfulness as well as to personal characteristics of deference to authority and self-efface-
ment.

EXTENSION OF ORIGENCE AND INTELLECTENCE

To put origence and intellectence into a format that af-
fords an overview of the material presented in this study and to
extend their implications further, a speculative and elaborated
summary of each dimension appears in Tables VII-3 and VII-4.

TABLE VII-3.   SPECULATIVE SUMMARY OF TERMS RELATED TO THE ORIGENCE DIMENSION

Lower Pole	Upper Pole	Lower Pole	Upper Pole
banal	original	obedient	rebellious
careful	careless	other-oriented	self-oriented
causal	contingent	orderly	disorderly
cautious	adventurous	optimistic	pessimistic
certainty	uncertainty	planned	spontaneous
circumscribed	extended	plodding	facile
confined	open	practical	impractical
conformity	nonconformity	prosaic	interesting
conservative	liberal	prohibitive	permissive
contrived	accidental	proscribe	prescribe
conventional	nonconventional	puritanical	sensual
compulsive	impulsive	quantities	qualities
cooperative	noncooperative	reactionary	radical
concordant	discordant	regular	irregular
definite	vague	responsible	irresponsible
direct	indirect	restrained	unrestrained
discover	invent	restrictive	expansive
discrete	relational	rigid	flexible
duty	pleasure	routine	ingenuity
defensive	unguarded	self-controlled	uncontrolled
even	uneven	self-effacing	self-seeking
explicit	implicit	simple	complex
factual	interpretive	slow	quick
follow rules	reject rules	sobriety	inebriety
finicky	casual	stable	unstable
gauche	sophisticated	stringent	lax
gravity	levity	structured	unstructured
gross	refined	symmetry	asymmetry
insensitive	sensitive	tactful	tactless
intolerant	tolerant	tangible	ineffable
literal	imaginative	temperate	intemperate
matter-of-fact	far-fetched	things	fantasies
monotony	variety	tight	loose
naive	candid	unartistic	artistic
numerals	words	vulgarian	aesthete
objects	relationships	work	play
obvious	subtle	withheld	released

Terms related to the empirical results of the present study were used as a starting point and to these findings were added other terms that seemed to follow either logically or psychologically.

TABLE VII-4.   SPECULATIVE SUMMARY OF TERMS RELATED TO
               THE INTELLECTENCE DIMENSION

Lower Pole	Upper Pole	Lower Pole	Upper Pole
accepting	assertive	manifest	recondite
active	latent	material	spiritual
actual	hypothetic	mollifying	incisive
admitting	denying	objective	subjective
affectionate	rational	open	guarded
aggressive	unpresuming	ordinary	exceptional
amiable	unamiable	outgoing	indwelling
application	conceptualization	participate	withdraw
brash	shy	particular	universal
charm	convince	personal	impersonal
circumstantial	categorical	physical	mental
close	distant	please	displease
concern with status	attained status	practical	theoretical
concrete	abstract	pragmatic	cognitive
content	discontent	prepossessing	uninviting
corporeal	psychic	productive	interpretive
cordial	cold	prolix	succinct
easy	difficult	proximate	ultimate
emotion	cognition	real	ideal
examples	principles	relative	absolute
exhibition	inhibition	representational	figurative
experiencing	calculating	social	intellectual
expression	repression	socially secure	socially insecure
extroversive	introversive	self-accepting	self-critical
evoluted	involuted	self-assured	self-conscious
friendly	unfriendly	soft	hard
immediate	delayed	specific	general
include	exclude	striving	achieving
involved	detached	superficiality	profundity
irresolute	persevering	thoughtless	reflective
literal	symbolic	tyro	expert
loud	quiet	warm	cool
love	respect		

They are presented in pairs with opposite and contrasting terms
having been supplied freely to indicate the nature of the antonymy
implied by one member of the pair. "Lower pole" terms represent
the lower end of the dimensions, "upper pole" terms, the upper
end of the dimension. It is explicitly assumed that all of the
terms at one end of a dimension will show some degree of positive

intercorrelation with each other but will be negatively related
to terms at the opposite pole. Across dimensions, however,
there should be relative independence of the terms correlational-
ly, at least in general, although in some specific cases, terms
on different dimensions seem to be related. The terms have been
listed in alphabetic order for the lower pole of each dimension.
This is a natural way of ordering them rather than imposing in
advance some kind of categorical organization.

It is contended, then, that the concepts of origence and
intellectence, although developed in the context of studying
creativity and intelligence, have implications for many other
aspects of human behavior as well. The speculative lists suggest that the dimensions can be utilized to investigate problems in personal and interpersonal relations, vocational satisfaction and occupational efficiency, educational selection and
response to training, and other phenomena of interest to psychological research. The dimensions offer a practical method of
determining the degree of similarity or dissimilarity between
persons and may be extended to the contextual or environmental
factors that affect the individual person.

Chapter VIII

CROSS-VALIDATIONAL STUDIES

It is necessary to show that the special group scales described above will work as expected when applied to other groups of subjects. The results obtained from the analyses of the Governor's School data must be verified by replication on a different group of subjects who were unrelated to the original item selection and derivation of the scales. This procedure is technically called *cross-validation* (Anastasi, 1968:181-84).

Problems and designs of cross-validation have been studied by Mosier (1951). He points out that a certain amount of validity shrinkage is to be expected in terms of statistics so that correlation coefficients, for example, are usually not of the same magnitude as those in the original derivational group. Items that significantly discriminated in one group may not do so in a new group.

In part this can be accounted for by the random or chance fluctuations that occur in any sampling procedure. Suppose that 60% of a sample of adults reply "True" to an item such as, "It takes a lot of argument to convince most people of the truth." How likely is this same percentage to occur in a new and different sample? If the original sample had only ten subjects, it would not be surprising at all to find the percentage rising to 90 or dropping to 20 in another small sample. On the other hand, if the original derivational group had a thousand subjects and the cross-validational group were equally large, the percentage in the latter would almost certainly be much closer to the original value. Most statistics, such as percentages and correlation coefficients, are more stable psychometrically when derived from large groups.

Another source of fluctuation may be found in the nature of the derivational group. If the original group was male and the cross-validational group is female, there may well be differences related to the shift from one sex to the other. Age, education, occupation, socioeconomic status, and many other characteristics may be related to the criterion behavior being studied and may affect the frequency of response to test items.

Among the Governor's School subjects, 44% of the boys replied "True" to the item, "I very much like hunting," while only 15% of the girls did so. On the other hand, "True" percentages to "I work under a great deal of tension" are the same for both sexes, 31 and 32; for a representative group of Minnesota adolescents, however, the percentages are only 10 and 9 (Hathaway and Monachesi, 1963:122). Thus, there is evidence that the Governor's School subjects may differ from other adolescent groups in response to this item.

Further indication of the complexities of item analysis may be found in a study by Pearson, Swenson, and Rome (1965). For the specific item cited above--working under tension--they report a curvilinear relation to age so that middle-aged subjects in their sample gave more "True" responses than either younger or older groups; further, the middle-age peak was greater for males than females.

Sampling fluctuations and changes in group characteristics work against the likelihood of obtaining the same statistical results upon cross-validation of a scale. Thus, if it can be shown on cross-validation that the origence/intellectence scales do behave psychometrically in the same way as they did for the original Governor's School analyses reported in Chapter V, some confidence can be held in the psychometric properties of these scales. If the scales are statistically stable, interpretation of the psychological meaning of the scales will be more justifiable.

IPAR GROUPS

The Institute of Personality Assessment and Research (IPAR) has been discussed above and their studies of creative adults have been outlined. Many of the tests used in IPAR assessment procedures were employed at the Governor's School for the express purpose of making comparisons possible between the gifted adolescents and creative adults (Welsh, 1969a). Three tests employed at IPAR as well as at the Governor's School were the Strong Vocational Interest Blank (SVIB), the Adjective Check List (ACL), and the Minnesota Multiphasic Personality Inventory (MMPI). It was possible, then, to score the origence/intellectence scales on IPAR subjects. Two groups were made available for the scoring procedure, a relatively large sample of architects (N = 124) and a smaller group of research scientists (N =45).*

*I am indebted to Drs. Donald W. MacKinnon, Harrison G. Gough, and Wallace B. Hall for these data.

These subjects differed markedly from the Governor's School boys and girls in age, education, experience, and geographical locus. Both of the IPAR groups were male, reducing to some extent fluctuations stemming from sex differences, although it will be recalled that an attempt was made to control for this variable by including equal numbers of males and females in the original scale derivation (p.76). Even so, minor sex differences did appear in some of the analyses.

The success of the cross-validation tests on IPAR subjects can be judged from the matrix of intercorrelations shown in Table VIII-1, where the twelve scales are correlated with each other for the architects and for the scientists. A similar format was employed here as for the Governor's School analysis (see Table V-III, p. 83), except that a less stringent level of significance, .05 rather than .01, was employed.

On the diagonals, where negative correlations were expected (Group I scales opposite IV, II opposite III), 30 of the 36 entries were in the predicted direction. On the positive diagonals (I compared with I, II with II, etc.) 23 out of 24 correlations were in the expected direction. For adjacent scales, where no intercorrelation was predicted (I and II, I and III, II and IV, III and IV), 62 of the 72 correlations did not differ significantly from zero. Of the 132 entries in the correlational matrix, 114 or 86% were in the expected direction.

In terms of magnitude of correlation, 26 correlations of the 114 failed to reach the .05 significance level, yielding 77% of those in the predicted direction that did achieve the called-for statistical level. If the findings for direction and for magnitude are combined, 88 out of 132 correlation coefficients-- exactly two-thirds--fell as predicted.

Considering the hazards of item fluctuation and scale instability, these findings would be reassuring evidence for the statistical integrity of the scales even if they had occurred with another sample of adolescents. Since these results were actually obtained in a much different kind of sample, some degree of confidence can be placed in the origence/intellectence scales as psychometric instruments.

The next step parallels that taken with the Governor's School subjects, namely that composite scores (ORIG and INT) were computed for the two dimensions following the same method outlined above (pp. 85-86). The sets of T scores previously generated for the boys were employed for the IPAR subjects and thus the composite scores can be interpreted in the same way. A score

TABLE VIII-1. MATRIX OF INTERCORRELATIONS FOR ORIGENCE/INTELLECTENCE SCALES ON IPAR SUBJECTS

	SVIB				ACL				MMPI			
	S-I	S-II	S-III	S-IV	A-I	A-II	A-III	A-IV	M-I	M-II	M-III	M-IV
S-I	_S-I_	(.10)	(.07)	-.33	(.01)	(-.02)	(.09)	(-.07)	(.10)	(-.03)	(.05)	(-.10)
S-II	(.03)	_S-II_	-.45	(.07)	(.14)	.34	(-.12)	(-.11)	(-.05)	.40	-.26	(-.13)
S-III	(.14)	(-.18)	_S-III_	(.04)	(.09)	(-.16)	(.13)	.18	(.10)	-.33	.28	(-.06)
S-IV	(-.14)	(-.20)	(-.28)	_S-IV_	(.07)	(.02)	(-.05)	(.08)	(-.16)	(-.05)	(.01)	(.10)
A-I	.32	(-.04)	(-.16)	(.05)	_A-I_	.26	(.07)	-.21	.27	.19	(.00)	(-.10)
A-II	(.03)	(.18)	(-.22)	(.00)	(.07)	_A-II_	-.44	-.45	(-.02)	.29	-.33	(-.12)
A-III	(.03)	(.00)	(.28)	(-.07)	(-.08)	-.35	_A-III_	.23	(.04)	-.23	.27	(.14)
A-IV	(.04)	(-.16)	.35	(.03)	-.34	-.37	(-.10)	_A-IV_	-.32	-.23	(.11)	.24
M-I	(.26)	(.11)	(.21)	(-.28)	(.12)	(.15)	(.18)	(.17)	_M-I_	(-.03)	(.12)	-.55
M-II	(-.05)	.31	(-.14)	(.05)	(.11)	.34	(-.03)	(.17)	(.05)	_M-II_	-.49	(-.16)
M-III	.34	(-.14)	.57	(-.07)	(.16)	(-.05)	.37	(.26)	(.01)	-.40	_M-III_	(.04)
M-IV	(.19)	(-.23)	(.08)	(.28)	(-.07)	-.36	(-.11)	(-.14)	-.37	(-.20)	(.12)	_M-IV_

NOTE: Architects above diagonal, $N = 124$; Scientists below diagonal, $N = 45$. Correlations not significantly different from zero at .05 level or beyond are enclosed in parentheses (r). ACL intratest correlations are partial r's.

of 50 falls at the boys' average, 60 is above, and 70 far above
average; the standard deviation for T scores is set at 10 in a
normative group.

The interpretation placed on intellectence in Chapter VII
clearly suggests that both IPAR groups should fall relatively
high on this dimension because of the level of professional training and educational requirements associated with intellectence.
For origence it is, perhaps, less obvious where they should fall
although the placement of the occupational scales of the SVIB
shown in Figure VII-1 (p. 111) suggests that architects might lie
above the mean and scientists somewhat below.

Table VIII-2 gives the appropriate statistics for the IPAR
groups. As expected, both architects and scientists fall well

TABLE VIII-2. SUMMARY OF COMPOSITE SCORES INT AND
ORIG FOR IPAR SUBJECTS BASED ON T
SCORES FROM GOVERNOR'S SCHOOL BOYS*

GROUP	ORIGENCE		INTELLECTENCE		
	M	SD	M	SD	N
Architects					
I	56.90	5.73	59.98	4.99	40
II	50.70	6.97	56.65	5.38	43
III	47.71	5.36	55.59	6.42	41
Total	51.71	7.16	57.37	5.92	124
Scientists					
I	49.47	4.77	62.60	4.18	15
II	45.13	4.49	63.53	3.88	15
III	48.40	7.48	61.27	5.82	15
Total	47.67	6.03	62.47	4.79	45

NOTE: N = number; M = mean; SD = standard deviation.
*The mean for boys in T-score terms is 50, with a standard
deviation of 10.

above the mean of the Governor's School boys (50) on intellectence with averages of 57.36 and 62.47, respectively. It may be noted that the standard deviations are only 5.92 and 4.79, compared to 10 for the original norm group's *SD*. This is, of course, in part a function of the reduced size of the cross-validating groups and it also reflects the restriction in the range of scores for the IPAR subjects.

The IPAR means are significantly above the Governor's School values as shown by t tests. These statistics are 7.5 for the architects and 11.6 for the scientists; both t's fall well beyond the .0001 level of statistical significance.

On origence, however, the IPAR groups fall much closer to the boys, with architects slightly above their mean at 51.71 and scientists somewhat below with 47.67. The t-test value is non-significant for architects (1.51), but that for scientists (2.0) is significant at the .05 level. Thus, it can be said that the scientists had a lower average than the boys on origence although the architects did not differ from them.

It is of interest to compare the IPAR groups with each other as well. The scientists are significantly higher on intellectence ($t = 4.2$, $p < .001$) while the architects are significantly higher on origence ($t = 3.3$, $p < .01$).

Architects and Creativity

The architects assessed at IPAR were not an unselected and homogeneous sample, but were instead, three distinct groups specifically chosen to tap a wide range of creative talent in their profession. The specific procedures employed have been summarized in Appendix A. The most creative were designated Group I, those having had some working experience with the top group were Group II, while a group representative of architects-in-general were called Group III.

A good deal of material has been presented by McKinnon (1962, 1965) indicating that the three groups of architects do represent different levels of creativity. Thus, any scales that may be related to creativity should differentiate these groups. It has already been seen that the original art scale does so. The question now is whether the composite scores for origence and intellectence (ORIG and INT) will distinguish the levels of architects.

Table VIII-2 shows that the average scores for ORIG and INT fall in the predicted direction with Architects I highest and Architects III lowest on both dimensions. The effectiveness of the separation is indicated by an analysis of variance which yields an F value of 6.5 on INT, significant at the .005 level, while the F for ORIG of 23.5 exceeds the .00001 level of significance. The most creative group of IPAR architects, Architects I, is clearly higher on origence and on intellectence.

It may be noted also in Table VIII-2 that all three groups have higher averages than the Governor's School boys on INT-- 59.98, 56.65, and 55.59. On ORIG, however, only Architects I with 56.90 exceed the boys. Architects II fall at the boy's average with 50.70 and Architects III lie below it with 47.71. These results are consistent with the argument advanced above that creative persons are both origent and intellectent.

A correlational analysis sustains the argument further. The overall mean creativity ratings for the individual architects was significantly correlated with ORIG scores, r = .47 (p < .001) and, though somewhat lower in absolute value, INT showed an r = .30, significant at the .005 level, for the creativity ratings.

Scientists and Creativity

The 45 scientists studied at IPAR did not represent three distinct groups comparable to the architects in levels of creativity, but were instead relatively homogeneous in this characteristic. As has been mentioned previously, these subjects were all industrial research workers--mostly physicists, mathematicians, and electronic engineers employed in "positions giving opportunity for creative effort, and each man was nominated by a department head or by a supervising scientist aware of our interest in the creativity problem" (Gough, 1961:III-6).

It was the intention of the IPAR psychologists to locate a representative sample of research scientists in industrial laboratories that would be typical of this type of employment. "The search was not for men of renowned or outstanding creativity. To use an analogy from athletics, the sample was one of varsity players rather than all-Americans" (p. III-7).

On the basis of modified ratings, the 45 scientists were divided more or less arbitrarily into three equal subgroups of 15 subjects each. The method of selection as well as the division into such small subgroups all work against the possibility of finding differences on the two personality dimensions. At the same time, it must be noted that the art scale did show differences in mean scores in the expected direction,* although Scientists I, II, and III averaged much lower than the three groups of architects.

Table VIII-2 shows the appropriate statistics for the scientists. The mean scores do not fall into the expected hierarchy and there are inversions in the order. Scientists II are highest on INT although they are lowest on ORIG; the subgroup highest on ORIG is Scientists I, and it lies in second place on INT. Perhaps not too much should be made of these findings since the analysis of variance shows nonsignificant F values, only 2.2 for ORIG and .8 for INT, even though the former lies close to the .10 level of significance. It should be noted in Table VIII-2 that Scientists III are more variable along both dimensions as indicated by larger standard deviations, particularly that for ORIG which is 7.48.

Although the composite scores for origence and intellectence placed the total sample of scientists in an appropriate location on the two-dimensional space, it must be concluded that the scores did not effectively differentiate the three subgroups according to their rated creative originality.

A correlational analysis likewise failed to show a significant relationship: Overall mean creativity ratings yielded a correlation of .05 for ORIG and .17 for INT.

Analysis by Combined Origence and Intellectence Scores

It is of interest to see how effective the composite scores for origence and intellectence would be in identifying the most creative groups of architects and scientists. That is, could ORIG and INT scores be used to pre-select persons in these fields who would prove to be creative?

If a cutting score of 55 on both ORIG and INT is employed, a majority of Architects I, 52.5%, will fall above these values while only 14% of Architects II and 4.9% of Architects III do so. Maintaining the cutting score of 55 on ORIG but lowering the score on INT to 45 would successfully identify 62.5% of the most creative architects at the expense of misclassifying 20.9% of the middle group and 7.3% of the bottom group. This is consistent with the correlational data reported above--that while both

---

*That is, Scientists I had a higher score on the art scale than Scientists II and III (see Appendix A).

origence and intellectence are important for creativity, the
former seems to be more salient for architects.

For scientists, although the correlational analysis did
not reach statistical significance, the direction and magnitude
suggests that intellectence may be more important than origence.
If cutting scores of 45 on ORIG and 55 on INT are employed, the
number of cases for each level of rated creative originality are:
Scientists I, 80%; Scientists II and III combined, 53.3%. This
may be construed as further support for the origence/intellectence
argument, although it must be acknowledged that it is not as
striking a case as that shown for the architects. Had the subgroups of scientists been larger (which would lead to more stable
statistics) and had the levels of creativeness been more widely
separated, perhaps more clear-cut results would have been evidenced.

SVIB SCALES IN A COMMUNITY COLLEGE

A direct cross-validation of the four special Strong Vocational Interest Blank scales was carried out by Minta Saunders.
Her subjects, 126 males and 110 females, were volunteers from the
first year entering class of a community college "whose sole criterion for admission is graduation from high school. In fact,
some students are conditionally admitted and are permitted to
make up high school deficits while pursuing college work" (Saunders, 1968:11).

These subjects were administered the Concept Mastery Test,
the Welsh Figure Preference Test, and the current form of the
Strong Vocational Interest Blank for Men, Form T 399. It must
be pointed out that these SVIB scales are not exactly the same as
the ones originally developed from the earlier form of the test,
since many of the old items have been deleted in the new version
(see Appendix C, p. 234). This results in some reduction in
the length of the SVIB scales for origence/intellectence as follows: S-I from 32 to 26 items, S-II from 56 to 42, S-III from 35
to 28, and S-IV from 33 to 29.

In general, longer scales are more stable statistically and
give more consistently reliable results so that the reduction in
the length of the four scales works toward attenuation of relationship. Revised S-II, for example, is only 75% as long as the original scale.

The change in the character of the subjects also poses a
challenge to the establishment of cross-validation. Although the

community college subjects did not differ from the Governor's School subjects on the Revised Art Scale (M = 29.26, SD = 14.16), they scored significantly lower (t = 22.4, p < .0001) on the intelligence test. The CMT showed a mean of 21.99 and a standard deviation of 23.57. The range of scores, however, was almost as great, from -26 to 124 compared to -32 to 161 for the Governor's School subjects (see Table II-1, p. 36).

Scores on the RA and CMT were uncorrelated with a correlation of only .04 as previously noted. Thus it was possible to divide the college students into four groups similar to that employed with the Governor's School analysis. That is, Saunders' subjects who fell high on RA but low on the CMT formed Quadrant I; those high on both, Quadrant II; low on both, III; and low on RA but high on the CMT constituted Quadrant IV.

Saunders next considered the pattern of scores for the SVIB scales when the raw scores were converted to standard scores. Her reasoning was that subjects in Quadrant I should have T scores relatively higher on S-I than on the other three scales; Quadrant II should show peak scores on S-II, and so on. There were 117 subjects who had patterns that placed them clearly into quadrants and by means of a chi-square analysis she demonstrated that they tended to show the appropriate pattern for the special SVIB scales.

With a group of subjects quite different from the Governor's School, using somewhat different SVIB scales and employing a different type of statistical analysis, Saunders was able to demonstrate a significant relationship between these scales and the original criterion measures, CMT and RA scores.

She reported some additional findings that are of considerable interest because they bear on a problem of great concern to education, namely academic achievement. The question raised here was whether the SVIB would show any relation to this variable as indicated by grade point average (GPA).

On a sample of 138 subjects from her college group, the GPA based on a 4.0 scale shows significant differences for the quadrants as given in Table VIII-3. Students with peak scores on S-III (low origence/low intellectence) averaged lowest on GPA, .94, while those with an S-II (high/high) pattern obtained the highest average GPA of 3.11. An analysis of variance was significant, and a Scheffé test indicated that the high intellectent scale pattern groups, S-II and S-IV, yielded higher GPA's despite the small number of subjects.

TABLE VIII-3.   MEAN GRADE POINT AVERAGE FOR COMMUNITY
                 COLLEGE SUBJECTS CLASSIFIED BY
                 QUADRANTS ON SPECIAL SVIB SCALES

INTELLECTENCE

	Low	High	Total		
	S-I	S-II			O
Number	78	11	89		R
				High	I
Mean	1.78	3.11	1.94		G
					E
	S-III	S-IV			N
					C
Number	42	7	49		E
				Low	
Mean	.94	2.14	1.11		
Total Number	120	18	138		
Total Mean	1.49	2.73	1.64		

    It is worthwhile to note an incidental relationship in Ta-
ble VIII-3. A majority of the community college subjects, 88%,
showed low intellectent scale patterns; somewhat more subjects
fall in the high origent quadrant (57%) than in the low/low S-III
corner (31%). Although determined by different procedures, these
distributions are congruent with the results of the IPAR scores
given above, which clustered at the upper end of intellectence.
There seems to be a consistent positive relationship between
this dimension and advanced education.

UNDERGRADUATE ACHIEVEMENT

    Another test of the effectiveness of the special SVIB
scales in predicting academic achievement was carried out on
data obtained in a large Midwestern university. Two groups of
undergraduate students were selected on the basis of their

predicted grade point average and their actual GPA. The first,
a group of 26 "achievers," had obtained GPA's concomitant with
those predicted from their scores on the Scholastic Aptitude
Test (SAT) of the College Entrance Examination Board. A second
group of 28 students were "non-achievers" in the sense that their
actual GPA's were lower than those expected on the basis of their
entering SAT scores. The groups were equated for SAT score itself so that they were alike in intelligence.

Since the SVIB had been used in the study, it was possible
to score the four special scales for these subjects.* To the extent that college achievement requires some degree of intellectence as we have described it, the achieving group should fall
higher on S-II and S-IV, but should be relatively lower on S-I
and S-III. Table VIII-4 gives the appropriate statistics for
the two groups.

TABLE VIII-4.   COMPARISON OF UNDERGRADUATE GROUPS ON
                SPECIAL SVIB SCALES

SVIB SCALE	ACHIEVERS (N = 26)		T SCORE	NON-ACHIEVERS (N = 28)		T SCORE	SIGNIFICANCE OF DIFFERENCE	
	M	SD		M	SD		t	p
S-I	8.35	4.33	(46)*	11.29	3.79	(53)	2.64	.01
S-II	27.92	8.20	(52)	23.61	7.69	(46)	1.96	.03
S-III	10.85	4.66	(47)	11.61	4.34	(48)	.61	ns
S-IV	13.88	2.98	(48)	12.18	3.77	(43)	1.80	.05

*T-score equivalent of raw score mean using Governor's
School boys as norm, *i.e.*, M = 50, SD = 10.

It can be seen that all of the scale means fall in the expected direction and that three of the differences are statistically significant. Expressed in terms of T scores derived from
Governor's School boys, the achieving group falls 6 points higher on S-II and 5 points higher on S-IV, while S-I is 7 points
lower, and S-III is 1 point lower, although it did not reach
statistical significance.

*I am indebted to Dr. David Galinsky for making the test
protocols available and for the other data on these subjects.

Composite scores for orience and intellectence were obtained using the computational method described above (p.86) for the Governor's School subjects and also used in the analysis of IPAR subjects. It must be kept in mind that these data are not directly comparable since only one of the three tests was available for the university undergraduates. Thus, the differences between the sums could not be converted to the same standard scores and are expressed here merely in raw score form as calculated. As shown in Table VIII-5, the achieving group had significantly higher INT scores but the ORIG scores did not differentiate the two groups.

TABLE VIII-5.   COMPARISON OF UNDERGRADUATE GROUPS ON COMPOSITE SCORES OF SVIB FOR ORIGENCE AND INTELLECTENCE

	ACHIEVERS ($N = 26$)		NON-ACHIEVERS ($N = 28$)		SIGNIFICANCE OF DIFFERENCE	
	M	SD	M	SD	t	p
INT*	6.46	27.41	-11.68	23.27	2.58	.01**
ORIG*	4.46	20.38	8.04	22.01	.61	*ns*

*Values are partial composite scores based on SVIB scales only and expressed in raw score form.
**Because of directional hypothesis, one-tail test used.

These findings are consistent with those reported above for community college students and support the argument that traits comprised by intellectence are necessary for academic achievement as measured by grade point average, while origence *per se* does not seem to be related to this aspect of collegiate endeavor.

ACL AND LEADERSHIP

Leadership is as complicated a concept as creativity although it may be easier in some ways to identify a leader than a creative person by overt behavior. Leadership, as it is ordinarily understood, is a publicly observable behavior in the sense that there must be followers who acknowledge in some way the leader's role in directing, guiding, or influencing their behavior. A creative person *can* work by himself--a leader must work with others.

A leader does not necessarily have to like other persons; biographies of famous leaders in history show that many leaders actually held their followers in low regard. What seems to be common to most leaders is a wish to control and to direct others --often with a view of imposing some kind of order on their be- havior and altering the course of events in some way.

Is the phrase "creative leadership" a contradiction in terms? Can it be asserted meaningfully that some leaders are more creative than others? It is relatively easy for the histori- an, after the fact, to evaluate leaders in terms of the amount of influence they had on their followers or in changing the course of history. Indeed, from a practical point of view, men who were unsuccessful or had no influence on others were not actual leaders by this kind of definition. Even so, the descriptions of leaders and their need for direct control of others, power, *etc*., do not resemble the descriptions of creative persons that are usually set forth.

We can put this abstract and conceptual question in con- crete terms, however, as we have done in the case of intelli- gence and creativity and ask where undergraduate students who have been selected as campus leaders fall on origence and intel- lectence scales.

The Adjective Check List was administered to a group of university undergraduate students who had survived an initial screening for a program designed to identify a highly selected subgroup of campus leaders who would be awarded fellowships and be given opportunities for special experiences in leadership settings. Voluntary applications were received from several hun- dred students from which 54 were selected for further evaluation based on the number and quality of extracurricular activites, election to posts in organizations, participation in community and campus activities, and overall academic achievement. These 54 students were interviewed by two faculty members and about half, 23, retained for a final interview conducted some time later. Thirteen of these students were then selected as fellows in the program after an intensive weekend assessment away from the campus.

Since all 54 students considered had outstanding academic records it might be expected that they would be relatively high on the two intellectence scales, A-II and A-IV. The question of interest was whether the fellows would show any difference from the finalists and semi-finalists on the scales. It should be noted that none of the dozen staff members who did the selecting had any knowledge of the ACL results.

Table VIII-6 gives a summary in terms of the highest scale in the four-scale profile of scores; T scores based on the Governor's School scores were used for the appropriate sex since females as well as males had applied.

TABLE VIII-6.   PATTERNS OF SPECIAL ACL SCALES FOR STUDENTS IN LEADERSHIP STUDY

GROUPS	NUMBER	SPECIAL SCALES			
		A-I	A-II	A-III	A-IV
Fellows	13	1	3	0	9
Finalists	13	3	0	2	8
Semi-finalists	28	1	8.5	2	16.5
Totals	54	5	11.5	4	33.5
		9.3%	21.3%	7.4%	62.0%

NOTE: One semi-finalist tied on A-II and A-IV counted as .5 in each column.

It is apparent that this group of subjects is similar to the achieving group of students discussed above. Almost two-thirds of the high scales were A-IV and about a fifth were A-II; thus, the expectation that the group would be characterized by high intellectence is supported. More than 83% of the total group can be identified as intellectent by these peak scores in the ACL profile.

At the same time, it is clear that the subgroups do not differ very much in frequencies of high scales. There were no statistically significant differences between the fellows and the other two subgroups either as determined by analysis of variance of the scores or a chi-square analysis of the frequencies. There is, however, some suggestive evidence that may be of interest.

In the spring following their selection, the 13 fellows were evaluated by the program staff as to their activities and the contribution they had made to the program. The three fellows who ranked lowest in this regard were the three who had peak scores on A-II in the ACL profile. While this may be judged fortuitous in such a small sample, it is nonetheless consistent with the behavior of the high origent person given above and particularly with the description of the high origent/high intellectent type described earlier (pp. 103-04).

One implication of this observation is that effective leaders may fall relatively low on origence if they are high on intellectence. In this regard, it is of interest to recall that one of the "Like" responses for the S-IV scale (Table VI-4, p. 93) is "Politician."

Creative leadership may not be a contradiction in terms perhaps, but to the extent that leaders are found to be high on intellectence only, they are less likely to be seen as creative than persons high on both dimensions.

AN ACL CREATIVITY SCALE

George Domino (1970) has developed a collegiate creativity scale (Cr) for the Adjective Check List by contrasting faculty ratings made with the ACL on two groups of male college undergraduate students. One, an experimental group of subjects, had been nominated as freshmen by faculty members on the basis of MacKinnon's concept of creativity (see p. 57 above). They had also been identified subsequently during their second and third college years; the final N was 59. A control group of 82 subjects was matched for sex, age, and intellectual ability as measured by the Ohio University Psychological Test.

As to the question of whether these nominated students were actually creative, Domino comments: "The longitudinal experimental procedure was purposely used to select individuals who would be in fact independently characterized as creative on the basis of real-life achievement. That different groups of faculty members agreed closely in their independent ratings supports this contention" (1970:49). The groups differed significantly in the expected direction on Mednick's Remote Associates Test (p. 50 above), on Guilford's Alternate Uses (p. 49), and on the Revised Art Scale. It must be noted that both groups fell relatively low on the RA as compared to the Governor's School boys; the creatives had a mean of only 19.7 and standard deviation of 8.4, while the controls' mean was 16.3 and standard deviation of 9.6.

Rather than using self-descriptive ACL data, the test was employed by the faculty to rate students after they had been observed during a semester. Then composite ACL descriptions by faculty were made for each student, a procedure similar to that employed by the IPAR assessors in describing their subjects (Gough, McKee, and Yandell, 1955).

Fifty-nine items were used more often in describing creative subjects and nine terms were characteristic of the controls; the latter were discarded in the final scale to avoid negatively scored items.

A cross-validation was carried out on *self-description* by high school subjects utilized in another research project (Schaefer, 1968, see Appendix A, p. 205). It is important to note here that Domino's Cr scale effectively separated the creative from the control adolescents, that it worked as well for females as for males, and, further, that scores were not affected by type of creativity--artistic, literary, or scientific.

It is of interest to compare the Cr scale with the Governor's School special ACL scales for origence/intellectence. We find a total of 87 items appear on these four scales and 23 of them overlap with Domino's scale. Of these overlapping items, 16 fall on the high origence scales and only 7 on scales low on this dimension; 20 appear on the high intellectence scales and only 3 on low scales. A majority of the overlapping items (14) are on A-II, the high origence/high intellectence scale. The overlapping Cr items are listed below in the special scales format.

A-1		A-II	
adventurous	aloof	egotistical	rebellious
clever	complicated	imaginative	reflective
	cynical	individualistic	restless
	disorderly	original	unconventional
	dissatisifed	outspoken	

A-III		A-IV	
humorous	alert	autocratic	logical
	assertive	clear-thinking	resourceful

It may be noted that only one of the items falls in a completely "wrong" place; that is, the term *humorous* of Domino's Cr scale appears on A-III, the low origence/low intellectence scale, which characterizes the least creative group according to the hypotheses of the present study.*

That a significantly greater number of items fall into the high/high creative corner of A-II is shown by chi-square analysis when the overlapping items are arranged as follows:

	A-II	A-I, A-III, A-IV	Total
Overlap on Cr	14	9	23
No overlap	11	53	64
Total	25	62	87

This fourfold table generates a chi-square value of 16.05 which is significant at the .0005 level for one degree of freedom. Thus, A-II and Cr share psychometric similarity at the item level and reflect common psychological implications as a perusal of the overlapping items will reveal.

Another creativity scale for the ACL has been developed by James M. Smith and Charles E. Schaefer (1969) from analyses of the groups used by Domino in his cross-validation with Schaefer's high school subjects. It should be noted that these students, creative and control alike, fell rather high on the art scale (see Appendix A).

Smith and Schaefer carried out separate item analyses for the four paired groups (creative with control by sex and for areas

---

*Dr. Domino (personal communication, 1971) has indicated that of the 9 negatively scored items eliminated from his Cr scale, 3 fall in A-IV--conventional, efficient, and stable--while the majority, 5, are in the low/low corner of A-III: cheerful, contented, organized, kind, and trusting. The remaining item, sociable, is similar in nature to the other items in A-III and is obviously congruent with the general characteristics of the low origent/low intellectent type. Had these negatively scored items been included in the Cr scale, the item overlap for the Governor's School ACL scales expressed algebraically would be: A-I, +2; A-II, +14; A-III, -4; A-IV, +2. The amount of agreement between A-II and Cr would in this case appear even stronger.

of interest) and constructed several different keys. They found
that one key, a 27 item scale, gave better discriminations between the criterion groups than the other scales and have recommended its use.

Ten of these items appear on the Governor's School origence/
intellectence scales with item overlap as follows:

A-I	A-II	
clever	complicated	original
	cynical	reflective
	imaginative	unconventional
A-III	A-IV	
----	assertive	
	intelligent	
	resourceful	

The largest overlap, 6 items, is with the 25 item high origence/
high intellectence scale, A-II, and no items at all appear for
the low-low corner. Setting up a fourfold table for the total
87 items on the Governor's School ACL scales, as was done above
for Domino's overlap, gives a chi-square value of 5.02 which is
significant at the .02 level.

Although these two studies are not strictly cross-validation of the origence/intellectence ACL scales *per se*, the findings
are important for the hypotheses of the present research. It can
be seen that the scales of Domino and of Smith and Schaefer, developed in high school and college settings with subjects identified by overt manifestations of creative behavior, show remarkable congruence with the psychometrically generated A-II scale of
the Governor's School.

If creativity is considered to be a single dimension defined operationally by either of their ACL scales, the concept
can still be explicated by the two dimensions postulated in the
Governor's School study. That is, the results of both Domino and
of Smith and Schaefer are consistent with the origence/intellec-
tence framework and may be interpreted as further support for the
conceptual model proposed.

CONSTRUCT VALIDATION OF
ORIGENCE AND INTELLECTENCE

The term *construct validity* was introduced earlier during
the discussion of the art scale and it is appropriate to refer
to the concept again at this point. In outlining the logic of
construct validation, Cronbach and Meehl indicate that it "takes
place when an investigator believes that his instrument reflects
a particular construct, to which are attached certain meanings"
(1955:290).

In the present study two constructs, origence and intellectence, have been set forth in some detail and particular claim
has been made that they are related to a broader concept--creati-
vity. This relationship may be seen as a link in what Cronbach
and Meehl call a "nomological network." As enunciated by the
authors, "the laws in a nomological network may relate (a) observable properties or quantities to each other; or (b) theoretical constructs to observables; or (c) different theoretical constructs to one another.... A necessary condition for a construct
to be scientifically admissable is that it occur in a nomological
net, at least *some* of whose laws involve observables" (p. 290).

A related term, "validity generalization," has also been
employed in connection with cross-validation (Cronbach, 1960) and
some connotations of that phrase may be pointed out. That is,
origence and intellectence may be considered to be constructs
that have implications for the study of creativity and intelligence that extend beyond the specific results of the Governor's
School and, as will be discussed in the Afterword, may be generalized to other areas of personality study.

The cross-validational results presented in this chapter
are offered as additional evidence in the spirit of the Cronbach
and Meehl exegesis for the viability of origence and intellectence.
Measures of these constructs have been shown to be related to
different kinds of performance in school and in the outside world
including creative behavior observed in subjects much older than
the Governor's School students, as well as by subjects similar in
age and status.

Chapter IX

SEX, MASCULINITY-FEMININITY, AND CREATIVITY

From time to time in the present report, sex differences have been noted on some of the measures studied. These differences appear often on masculinity-feminity (M-F) scales as has been discussed briefly in Chapter VII. The basic problem to be explicated is the relationship of sex, masculinity-femininity, and the differential achievement of males and females--particularly in creative accomplishments.

Although differences between the sexes have long been recognized and have been amply documented,* it is often difficult to infer the nature of these differences by studying them through standard psychological tests. Sex differences in intelligence, for example, have been *minimized* in most tests by the psychometric practice of eliminating items that do show sex differences or by counterbalancing items that favor one sex over the other.

In studying masculinity-femininity, on the other hand, sex differences have been *maximized* by discarding items that fail to discriminate males from females. This technique was employed in the pioneering work of Terman and Miles (1936) and has been followed for the most part in the subsequent development of M-F scales. Despite certain conceptual and psychometric ambiguities because of these procedures, most workers seem to agree with Anastasi's conclusion that "available masculinity-femininity tests provide an index of the degree to which the individual's personality resembles the personality of men or of women in our culture" (1958:497).

Although males clearly exceed females in outstanding achievement in the arts as well as in the sciences (Scheinfeld, 1943), within the male sex there is evidence that femininity is positively related to creativity (MacKinnon, 1962; 1965). It has been suggested that there may be a reverse sex-identification such that more creative women have more masculine characteristics (Littlejohn, 1967). However, the findings of Ravenna Helson based on college women as well as IPAR subjects indicates that a simple unidirectional relationship of biological sex,

---

*An extensive review of sex differences by Joseph E. Garai an Amram Scheinfeld (1968) lists 474 references.

sexual identification, and creativity is unlikely (Helson, 1961; 1968b).

Since origence and intellectence have been found to be related to creativity, an explication of the association between masculinity-femininity and the personality dimensions would be of interest in exploring the M-F/creativity problem.

CORRELATION OF M-F SCALES

In the present research five scales were studied as measures of masculinity-femininity: the Minnesota Multiphasic Personality Inventory Mf scale, which has been discussed above (p.124); the Strong Vocational Interest Blank Masculinity scale, Masc (p.116); two Adjective Check List scales, the MA and FE (p.120); and the Welsh Figure Preference Test FM scale, developed from items differentially preferred by males and females (Littlejohn, 1967; Welsh, 1969a).

Although the dimension of masculinity-femininity is admittedly complex and its psychometric assessment difficult, the intercorrelational matrix given in Table IX-1 for Governor's School boys and girls shows that all 20 correlations are in the expected direction, although two coefficients for the boys and three for the girls fail to achieve statistical significance. That is, scales scored in the feminine direction are positively intercorrelated with each other and negatively correlated with scales scored in the masculine direction. The latter scales are likewise consistent in their correlational pattern.

The table indicates clear-cut sex differences in association with origence and intellectence. For boys there is a marked tendency for femininity to correlate positively and masculinity to correlate negatively with ORIG scores. Only one of the five correlations falls short of the .05 significance level. Although the girls show a similar pattern, three of the correlations are nonsignificant. There is, then, a tendency for high origent subjects to be more feminine and the tendency seems to be stronger for boys than for girls.

The relationship to intellectence, on the other hand, does not show such a consistent pattern. For both sexes the MMPI Mf scale and the SVIB Masc scale are positively correlated with INT scores, but the WFPT FM scale and the ACL FE scale are negatively correlated with this dimension. For girls the ACL MA scale is uncorrelated with intellectence. It may be noted that the pattern of correlations is generally similar for boys and girls but

TABLE IX-1.   MATRIX OF INTERCORRELATIONS FOR MASCU-
              LINITY-FEMININITY SCALES AND DIMENSIONAL
              SCORES ON ORIGENCE AND INTELLECTENCE FOR
              GOVERNOR'S SCHOOL SUBJECTS

| TEST | FEMININE | | | MASCULINE | | COMPOSITE DI-MENSIONAL SCORE | |
	MMPI Mf	WFPT FM	ACL FE	ACL MA	SVIB Masc	ORIG	INT
MMPI Mf	--	.17	.17	-.12	-.60	.39	.14
WFPT FM	(.04)	--	(.06)	-.12	-.24	.30	-.13
ACL FE	.19	(.02)	--	-.46	-.15	(.04)	-.29
ACL MA	-.14	(-.02)	-.34	--	(.07)	-.11	(-.04)
SVIB Masc	-.44	-.09	-.28	.08	--	-.41	(.04)
ORIG	(.02)	.22	(.07)	(-.06)	-.08		
INT	(.04)	(-.07)	-.24	(.00)	.27		

NOTE: Boys above diagonal, N = 522 to 529; Girls below
diagonal, N = 616 to 632. (r) signifies correlations not significant at .05 level or beyond. ACL intratest correlations are
partial r's.

that there are differences in the level of significance. Thus,
femininity as measured by the five scales employed in the present
study is not consistently related to intellectence except for
the ACL FE scale which gives a significant negative correlation
for both sexes.

     For girls there is a significant positive correlation on
the SVIB Masc scale as well as a negative one on the ACL FE;
this implies that masculine girls are higher on intellectence.
For boys the correlational evidence is mixed; the negative correlations for WFPT FM and ACL FE imply that masculinity and intellectence are related, but the positive value for MMPI Mf
scale indicates that femininity is associated with high intellectence.

     These correlational inconsistencies invited further explora-
tion of the relationship between masculinity-femininity and the
dimensions of origence and intellectence. The method employed
in this analysis involves placing the Governor's School subjects
in groups determined by their conjoint scores on origence and
intellectence.

A NINEFOLD ANALYSIS

It will be recalled that the two composite dimensional scores, ORIG and INT, were found to be essentially uncorrelated for both sexes and thus statistically independent (p. 83). It was appropriate, then, to make scatterplots using orthogonal axes to represent the two dimensions; these were made separately for each sex. The location of each student was made in terms of his or her set of scores as a point plotted against the two axes. These points were quite evenly distributed over the bivariate surface indicating once more the statistical independence of the two dimensions.

Cutting scores were then established to divide each dimension into three equal parts--high, medium, and low. Since dimensional scores were considered conjointly, the scatterplot was partitioned perforce into nine sections, or "novants,"* of equal size. Had the scores been perfectly evenly distributed, each novant would have contained exactly one-ninth of the cases (11.11%) and the marginal totals would have been one-third (33.33%) for each segment. Although this ideal distribution was not obtained precisely, Table IX-2 shows that it was closely approximated and was considered satisfactory for the analyses to be reported.

It may be noted that this analytic model also makes possible a consideration of subjects in terms of the kind of fourfold typlogy discussed earlier (p. 76) when cases falling at the extremes of the RA and CMT scores were selected to develop the special scales described in Chapter VI.

For consistency of nomenclature, similar numerical designations have been employed for the present analysis although, in order to differentiate the two applications of this method of identifying extreme groups, arabic numerals have replaced the roman numerals used previously.**

---

*The term "novant" is being used here in a general descriptive sense, not in the special meaning indicated when it was first employed (Welsh, 1965).

**

I	High orig/ low int	II High orig/ high int
III	Low orig/ low int	IV Low orig/ high int

TABLE IX-2. DISTRIBUTIONS OF CASES ON ORIGENCE AND INTELLECTENCE SCORES, ORIG AND INT, IN TERMS OF FREQUENCIES AND PERCENTAGES WITH NOVANT DESIGNATION

BOYS

	Low INT	Medium INT	High INT	Totals
High ORIG	(1) 61 11.64%	(1-2) 37 7.06%	(2) 57 10.88%	155 29.58%
Medium ORIG	(1-3) 58 11.07%	(0) 75 14.31%	(2-4) 59 11.26%	192 36.64%
Low ORIG	(3) 59 11.26%	(3-4) 68 12.98%	(4) 50 9.54%	177 33.78%
Totals	178 33.97%	180 34.35%	166 31.68%	524 100.00%

GIRLS

	Low INT	Medium INT	High INT	Totals
High ORIG	(1) 68 11.02%	(1-2) 63 10.21%	(2) 67 10.86%	198 32.09%
Medium ORIG	(1-3) 69 11.19%	(0) 73 11.83%	(2-4) 65 10.53%	207 33.55%
Low ORIG	(3) 74 11.99%	(3-4) 85 13.78%	(4) 53 8.59%	212 34.36%
Totals	211 34.20%	221 35.82%	185 29.98%	617 100.0%

Thus, in the present analysis, (1) refers to the group high on ORIG/low on INT, (2) high ORIG/high INT, (3) low ORIG/low INT, and (4) low ORIG/high INT. The medium groups have been given composite numbers to indicate their locations between the extreme corner groups: Novant (1-2) refers to the group high on ORIG and medium on INT; Novant (1-3) to medium on ORIG and low on INT; Novant (2-4), medium on ORIG, high on INT; and Novant (3-4), low on ORIG, medium on INT. For the novant in the center, medium on both scores, a (0) designation has been employed to suggest the mathematical origin at the intersection of the axes. Reference to Table IX-2 should make clear the logic of the present nomenclature.

An analysis of variance for each of the masculinity-femininity scales was then carried out in terms of the novant classification.

Analysis of Variance Results

Table IX-3 shows the novant summary of analysis of variance for boys on the MMPI Mf scale and Table IX-4 gives that for girls. Consistent with the nonsignificant correlations noted for the girls on ORIG and INT, Mf is not related to either dimension in the analysis of variance. The boys, however, demonstrate a clear-cut and consistent increase in mean scores along both origence and intellectence. Thus, the lowest group mean, 58.19, appears in Novant (3), while the highest value, 72.11, is obtained for the opposite high/high corner of Novant (2).

The total mean on the MMPI Mf for all of the Governor's School boys at 65.19 is much higher than the norm group value of 50 for the original Minnesota males. This is consistent with the general finding of positive association of the Mf scale to general intelligence and academic achievement in males. It may be noted in this connection that the Governor's School boys fall near the level of most groups of college students (Welsh and Dahlstrom, 1956). Even the most masculine of the present subjects, Novant (3), is feminine on the Mf scale as compared to the norm group.

The girls' total mean, 44.70, is somewhat lower than the original Minnesota females ($M = 50$), although it is not nearly as deviant as the boys' mean. Again, this is typical of its association with scholastic performance (Hathaway and Monachesi, 1963). Both boys and girls are more feminine than the norm groups on the MMPI Mf scale, but only for the boys is there a systematic relationship to the dimensional scores.

The SVIB Masculinity scale shows different patterns for the sexes. For boys, Table IX-5 indicates that the SVIB Masc scale is negatively related to origence but shows no difference along the intellectence dimension. Although the low origent boys are significantly less feminine than the high origent groups, it must be pointed out that all of the novant means for the Governor's School subjects fall below the original group norm. This indicates that the boys are somewhat less typically masculine in interests which is consistent with the MMPI findings.

The Governor's School girls show a borderline and inconsistent relationship to origence on the SVIB Masc scale, but Table IX-6 indicates a significant increase in the masculine direction along intellectence. At the lower end of the dimension the mean is only 19.70, but it rises to 25.16 for the group high on intellectence.

The ACL MA scale, as shown in Table IX-7, is unrelated to either of the dimensions for girls but shows a borderline decrease in means for origence for boys in Table IX-8. Thus, on this scale too, the high origent boys are somewhat less masculine.

By contrast, the ACL FE scale shows highly significant differences in means for both sexes. Table IX-9 indicates that the relationship is significant along both dimensions for the girls with the direction reversed along intellectence from that previously noted. That is, the less intellectent girls are more feminine on the FE scale. For the first time, an increase is noted along origence and the high origent girls are, as has been typical of the boys on other scales, more feminine. Novant (1) emerges as the most feminine corner with Novant (4) the least feminine location for girls on this ACL scale.

It may be noted, however, as seen in Table IX-10, that for the boys the ACL FE scale scores are unrelated to origence although there is a nonsignificant trend in the usual feminine direction. At the same time, there is a highly significant decrease in FE scores along intellectence so that the boys are like the girls on this scale, and the corner Novants (1) and (4) are the most and the least feminine, respectively. Although there is a significant interaction term, it does not seem to be of any great practical importance and does not alter the overall pattern of relationships.

The WFPT FM scale shows a significant negative relationship to intellectence for the boys, Table IX-11, with an even more striking positive relationship to origence. Thus, once

MEAN T SCORE ON MMPI Mf SCALE BY NOVANT CLASSIFICATION ON COMPOSITE SCORES FOR ORIGENCE AND INTELLECTENCE AND SUMMARY OF ANALYSIS OF VARIANCE

TABLE IX-3: BOYS

	Low INT	Medium INT	High INT	Totals
	(1)	(1-2)	(2)	
High ORIG	68.61	71.05	72.11	70.48
	(1-3)	(0)	(2-4)	
Medium ORIG	64.53	64.41	66.41	65.06
	(3)	(3-4)	(4)	
Low ORIG	58.19	63.09	60.38	60.69
Totals	63.83	65.28	66.55	65.19

Summary of Analysis of Variance

Source	df	MS	F	p
Intellectence	2	342.14	3.96	<.025
Origence	2	4257.76	49.32	<.0001
Interaction	4	124.00	1.44	ns
Error	515	86.32		

TABLE IX-4: GIRLS

	Low INT	Medium INT	High INT	Totals
	(1)	(1-2)	(2)	
High ORIG	46.90	43.65	43.69	44.78
	(1-3)	(0)	(2-4)	
Medium ORIG	43.91	44.67	44.06	44.23
	(3)	(3-4)	(4)	
Low ORIG	44.38	44.85	46.47	45.09
Totals	45.04	44.45	44.62	44.70

Summary of Analysis of Variance

Source	df	MS	F	p
Intellectence	2	22.97	.28	ns
Origence	2	52.44	.63	ns
Interaction	4	152.44	1.84	ns
Error	608	82.64		

MEAN T SCORES ON SVIB Masc SCALE BY NOVANT CLASSIFICATION ON COMPOSITE SCORES FOR ORIGENCE AND INTELLECTENCE AND SUMMARY OF ANALYSIS OF VARIANCE

TABLE IX-5: BOYS

	Low INT	Medium INT	High INT	Totals
High ORIG	(1) 35.11	(1-2) 34.73	(2) 37.26	35.81
Medium ORIG	(1-3) 40.71	(0) 43.53	(2-4) 41.64	42.10
Low ORIG	(3) 46.29	(3-4) 45.60	(4) 48.52	46.66
Totals	40.64	42.51	42.21	41.78

Summary of Analysis of Variance

Source	df	MS	F	p
Intellectence	2	137.51	1.39	ns
Origence	2	5222.54	52.93	<.0001
Interaction	4	107.24	1.09	ns
Error	515	98.67		

TABLE IX-6: GIRLS

	Low INT	Medium INT	High INT	Totals
High ORIG	(1) 20.35	(1-2) 21.44	(2) 23.01	21.60
Medium ORIG	(1-3) 20.14	(0) 23.90	(2-4) 25.77	23.24
Low ORIG	(3) 18.69	(3-4) 23.67	(4) 27.11	22.79
Totals	19.70	23.11	25.16	22.56

Summary of Analysis of Variance

Source	df	MS	F	p
Intellectence	2	1588.33	23.88	<.0001
Origence	2	176.02	2.65	<.10
Interaction	4	149.44	2.25	<.10
Error	608	66.52		

MEAN RAW SCORES ON ACL MA SCALE BY NOVANT CLASSIFICATION ON COMPOSITE SCORES FOR ORIGENCE AND INTELLECTENCE AND SUMMARY OF ANALYSIS OF VARIANCE

TABLE IX-7: GIRLS

	Low INT	Medium INT	High INT	Totals
High ORIG	(1) 13.19	(1-2) 11.35	(2) 13.66	12.76
	(1-3)	(0)	(2-4)	
Medium ORIG	11.90	11.64	12.74	12.07
	(3)	(3-4)	(4)	
Medium ORIG	13.65	13.56	12.38	13.30
Totals	12.93	12.30	12.97	12.71

Summary of Analysis of Variance

Source	df	MS	F	p
Intellectence	2	36.26	.97	ns
Origence	2	62.19	1.66	ns
Interaction	4	60.32	1.61	ns
Error	608	37.35		

TABLE IX-8: BOYS

	Low INT	Medium INT	High INT	Totals
High ORIG	(1) 17.61	(1-2) 15.41	(2) 16.30	16.60
	(1-3)	(0)	(2-4)	
Medium ORIG	17.34	18.65	17.20	17.81
	(3)	(3-4)	(4)	
Low ORIG	17.36	19.09	17.58	18.08
Totals	17.44	18.15	17.01	17.54

Summary of Analysis of Variance

Source	df	MS	F	p
Intellectence	2	20.21	.40	ns
Origence	2	118.77	2.32	<.10
Interaction	4	67.24	1.32	ns
Error	515	51.10		

MEAN RAW SCORES ON ACL FE SCALE BY NOVANT CLASSIFICATION ON COMPOSITE SCORES FOR ORIGENCE AND INTELLECTENCE AND SUMMARY OF ANALYSIS OF VARIANCE

TABLE IX-9: GIRLS

	Low INT	Medium INT	High INT	Totals
High ORIG	(1) 31.26	(1-2) 29.71	(2) 27.31	29.43
Medium ORIG	(1-3) 29.22	(0) 27.59	(2-4) 26.15	27.68
Low ORIG	(3) 29.58	(3-4) 28.29	(4) 24.98	27.92
Totals	30.00	28.47	26.24	28.32

Summary of Analysis of Variance

Source	df	MS	F	p
Intellectence	2	772.95	15.77	<.0001
Origence	2	217.65	4.44	<.025
Interaction	4	16.99	.34	ns
Error	608	49.02		

TABLE IX-10: BOYS

	Low INT	Medium INT	High INT	Totals
High ORIG	(1) 26.57	(1-2) 21.89	(2) 19.58	22.88
Medium ORIG	(1-3) 22.97	(0) 24.20	(2-4) 19.39	22.35
Low ORIG	(3) 22.29	(3-4) 22.93	(4) 18.76	21.54
Totals	23.98	23.24	19.27	22.23

Summary of Analysis of Variance

Source	df	MS	F	p
Intellectence	2	1043.18	19.70	<.0001
Origence	2	79.44	1.50	ns
Interaction	4	152.15	2.87	<.025
Error	515	52.95		

MEAN RAW SCORES ON WFPT FM SCALE BY NOVANT CLASSIFICATION ON COMPOSITE SCORES FOR ORIGENCE AND INTELLECTENCE AND SUMMARY OF ANALYSIS OF VARIANCE

TABLE IX-11: BOYS

	Low INT	Medium INT	High INT	Totals
High ORIG	(1) 42.80	(1-2) 41.95	(2) 36.89	40.41
Medium ORIG	(1-3) 36.31	(0) 36.79	(2-4) 33.78	35.72
Low ORIG	(3) 31.49	(3-4) 31.49	(4) 30.72	31.27
Totals	36.90	35.87	33.93	35.60

Summary of Analysis of Variance

Source	df	MS	f	p
Intellectence	2	507.05	3.22	<.05
Origence	2	3647.83	23.14	<.0001
Interaction	4	110.57	.70	ns
Error	513	157.61		

TABLE IX-12: GIRLS

	Low INT	Medium INT	High INT	Totals
High ORIG	(1) 47.40	(1-2) 46.78	(2) 48.60	47.61
Medium ORIG	(1-3) 48.45	(0) 46.44	(2-4) 44.85	46.61
Low ORIG	(3) 42.34	(3-4) 41.01	(4) 41.19	41.52
Totals	45.97	44.44	45.16	45.18

Summary of Analysis of Variance

Source	df	MS	F	p
Intellectence	2	106.36	.73	ns
Origence	2	2146.45	14.71	<.0001
Interaction	4	103.09	.71	ns
Error	607	145.94		

again, Novant (1) has the most feminine mean and Novant (4) the
lowest value on this scale. For girls, Table IX-12 indicates
a significant increase along one dimension only--the high origent
girls get higher scores on the FM scale.

Because different methods of expressing scores were used
for the five scales (raw scores in some cases, T scores in others), it is difficult to collate the results. The expedient
adopted was to convert the nine novant means to standard scores
(z scores) for each of the five scales using the means and standard deviations for each sex separately and reversing the scored
direction for the masculinity scales so that a high z score consistently indicates femininity. The resulting z scores were
then averaged for the origence/intellectence novants and the results are displayed in Table IX-13.

In addition to novant values, the marginal averages have
been calculated as well. The overall average for each sex is,
of course, zero. It should be noted that for any particular distribution of z scores the mean is .00 and the standard deviation
is 1.00.

For both sexes the highest positive average occurs for
Novant (1), and the most negative average appears in the opposite corner, Novant (4). Thus, in terms of masculinity-femininity scales employed, the boys and the girls in the high origence/
low intellectence novant were the most feminine while the low
origence/high intellectence groups were the most masculine. The
sexes are very similar in the order of the average z scores as
indicated by a Spearman rank order correlation of .80 for the
novant values.

There are some sex differences worth noting. The boys
showed a greater range of z scores than the girls; this is consistent with the fact that they also had larger standard deviations on the original scores of all five masculinity-femininity
scales. From the marginal totals it can be seen that for boys
the discrepancy between high origence and low origence is .625
z-score units (from +.337 to -.288), while for girls the difference is only .181 (+.084 to -.097). On the other hand, the discrepancy is greater for girls along intellectence, .275 (+.130
to -.145), as compared to the boys, .142 (+.060 to -.082).

ANALYSIS OF MASCULINE AND FEMININE SUBGROUPS

In addition to the novant analysis on all of the Governor's
School students, special subgroups were studied by identifying

TABLE IX-13.   AVERAGE OF z SCORE MEANS ON ALL M-F
SCALES BY NOVANTS

BOYS

	Low INT	Medium INT	High INT	Totals
High ORIG	(1) +.413	(1-2) +.394	(2) +.205	+.337
Medium ORIG	(1-3) +.043	(0) +.005	(2-4) -.066	-.006
Low ORIG	(3) -.277	(3-4) -.199	(4) -.386	-.288
Totals	+.060	+.067	-.082	.000

GIRLS

	Low INT	Medium INT	High INT	Totals
High ORIG	(1) +.203	(1-2) +.112	(2) -.064	+.084
Medium ORIG	(1-3) +.144	(0) +.003	(2-4) -.157	-.003
Low ORIG	(3) +.043	(3-4) -.119	(4) -.215	-.097
Totals	+.130	-.001	-.145	.000

individual subjects who fell consistently in either the masculine
or the feminine direction on all of the test masculinity-femininity scales. The median of the distribution was used for MMPI Mf,
SVIB Masc, and WFPT FM scales, while the ACL FE and MA scales
were compared to each other.

The actual cutting scores for feminine boys are Mf $\geq$ 65,
Masc $\leq$ 42, FM $\geq$ 51, and FE $\geq$ MA. Boys were assigned to a mascu-
line subgroup if they fell consistently in the opposite direction.
Girls were assigned to subgroups in an analogous manner with cut-
ting scores for femininity of Mf $\leq$ 44, Masc $\leq$ 21, FM $\geq$ 51, and
FE > MA.

By requiring consistency in scoring direction we hoped
to elucidate what was common across all of the scales by ex-
cluding any subject who might be extremely deviant on merely one
scale. This is often a problem when weighted scores are assigned
on the basis of a regression analysis or other statistical procedure where a series of low scores for a subject might be coun-
terbalanced by a single very high score on one scale. The present method of using cutting scores on all scales seems justified
on the basis of the consistent correlational pattern shown in
Table IX-1 (p. 154) which implies some degree of common variance
for all of the masculinity-femininity scales.

Out of the total of 531 boys there were 78 (14.7%) falling consistently in the feminine direction and 73 (13.8%) in the
masculine direction. Of the 632 girls there were 62 (9.8%) each
in the feminine and masculine subgroups. It is of interest to
find that there are relatively more boys in the subgroups than
girls. This is consistent with the more extreme differences
shown in z scores and with the greater variability in standard
deviations noted above.

Table IX-14 gives for each of the four subgroups the number of cases in the origence/intellectence novants. These results tend to confirm the group data analysis of z-score averages and lend further support to the interpretation offered
there.

For masculine boys there is a consistent increase in frequency of cases along intellectence and a decrease along origence
so that 17 subjects fall in the low origent/high intellectent novant, while none fall opposite in the high origent/low intellectent corner. Conversely, 17 of the feminine boys fall in the
latter novant, while only one is low origent/high intellectent
type.

TABLE IX-14.   NOVANT FREQUENCIES FOR MASCULINE AND
FEMININE SUBGROUPS

	Low INT	Medium INT	High INT
High ORIG	(1)	(1-2)	(2)
Medium ORIG	(1-3)	(0)	(2-4)
Low ORIG	(3)	(3-4)	(4)

Masculine Boys

			Totals
0	2	5	7
3	9	7	19
14	16	17	47
Totals 17	27	29	73

Masculine Girls

			Totals
2	5	5	12
3	8	9	20
6	10	14	30
Totals 11	23	28	62

Feminine Boys

			Totals
17	14	7	38
11	9	8	28
5	6	1	12
Totals 33	29	16	78

Feminine Girls

			Totals
9	9	5	23
14	12	4	30
6	3	0	9
Totals 29	24	9	62

A similar pattern of distribution is seen for the masculine girls with 14 cases of low origence/high intellectence and only two falling opposite. Less consistency is shown by the feminine girls. Although none of them fall in the low origent/high

intellectent corner, the greatest frequencies occur for the novants of medium origence/low intellectence and medium on both
dimensions rather than in the opposite corner so clearly displayed by the feminine boys' subgroup.

This discordant result may be mere sampling fluctuation,
but it is possible that it reflects real psychological differences in psychometric identification of femininity in female
subjects. It may be noted that the correlational analysis of
the specific masculinity-femininity scales reported in Table
IX-1 was somewhat less consistent for girls. Likewise, in the
average z-score analysis, intellectence and masculinity were
found to be more strongly related for the girls.

The colligated psychometric evidence in terms of correlation, analysis of variance, and a frequency count of individual
subjects is both consistent and meaningful. It may be interpreted to indicate a positive relationship of femininity to origence and of masculinity to intellectence with the former being
more salient in the case of boys and the latter more so for girls.

CREATIVITY AND MASCULINITY-FEMININITY

The Governor's School results are generally consistent
with previous reports of feminine interest patterns in creative
subjects, particularly males (Myden, 1959; Rees and Goldman,
1961). In the IPAR study of male architects described above,
the MMPI Mf scale showed that although all three groups scored
above the mean of Minnesota normals, these groups were differentiated among themselves. The most creative group, Architects I,
averaged 72; Architects II had a mean of 71; the least creative
group, III, fell lowest at 65.

Helson reported that female mathematicians differed on the
Femininity (Fe) scale of the CPI (Gough, 1964); her creative
group had a mean of 53 while the comparison group fell slightly
below the norm at 49 (Helson, 1961: IV-2). Creative male mathematicians were somewhat higher than their comparison group on
the CPI Fe scale, and both groups fell above the norm (Helson,
1967a). Among college women, more creative subjects were not
more masculine nor did they report more "tomboy" activities in
childhood (Helson, 1966:20).

It must be stressed that the association of femininity with
creativity does not necessarily imply any sexual pathology. In
fact, some studies (*e.g.*, Ellis, 1959) have indicated that homosexuality may be negatively related to creative potential.

Rather, the association seems to be that the creative person is able to recognize and accept characteristics in himself that are conventionally attributed to the opposite sex; this seeming contrasexuality is more often apparent in males than in females.

This kind of an interpretation is similar to that offered by MacKinnon who finds support for the theoretical position of C.G. Jung in this regard. (Jung's views will be discussed in some detail in Chapter X.)

> The more creative a person is the more he reveals an openness to his own feelings and emotions, a sensitive intellect and understanding self-awareness, and wide-ranging interests including many which in the American culture are thought of as feminine. In the realm of sexual identification and interests, our creative subjects appear to give more expression to the feminine side of their nature than do less creative persons. In the language of the Swiss psychiatrist, Carl G. Jung (1956), creative persons are not so completely identified with their masculine *persona* roles as to blind themselves to or deny expression to the more feminine traits of the *anima*. (MacKinnon, 1962:488)

Both the Governor's School results and the findings of the IPAR studies suggest that creative males and creative females alike will show certain feminine characteristics, particularly those tapped by conventional masculinity-femininity scales. This would seem to argue against the hypothesis of reverse-sex identification in creativity--that creative men should be more feminine, but that creative women should be more masculine. A resolution of the seeming contradiction is possible through certain implications of the present results.

First, it is clear that different kinds of M-F scales measure different aspects of masculinity-femininity, and that it is indeed a complex and a multidimensional construct as many workers have pointed out (Engel, 1966; Vroegh, 1968; McCarthy, Anthony, and Domino, 1970).

Masculinity-femininity is often construed as a bipolar dimension; in many studies it is assumed, often implicitly, that a subject scoring at the opposite end of an M-F scale will have personality characteristics directly opposite those of the dimension itself. That is, it is implied that a subject scoring low

on a scale scored in the feminine direction is masculine and that
a subject scoring low on a masculine scale is feminine. If such
a scale is interpreted as a bipolar and unidimensional measure,
it may seem to follow that the opposite ends are opposite in the
characteristics that the scale ostensibly measures. But it may
just as well be argued that the opposite of masculinity is non-
masculinity and not necessarily femininity, and likewise, that
the opposite of femininity is non-femininity and not necessarily
masculinity. This interpretation is, of course, consistent with
the complex and multidimensional nature of masculinity-femininity
both as a theoretical construct and as measured by conventional
M-F scales.

Thus, the hypothetical femininity of creative males and
masculinity of creative females alleged in some studies may be
accounted for by acknowledging the difference in personality
characteristics associated with different kinds of masculinity-
femininity scales and, more importantly, by recognizing the implicit assumption of contrasex traits attributed to low-scoring
subjects on these scales.

An alternate explanation, then, and a hypothesis stemming
from implications of IPAR and Governor's School results, is that
creativity requires a blending of *both* masculine and feminine
characteristics and cannot be accounted for by assumptions of
reverse-sex features on a single bipolar dimension. It may be
noted in this regard that the creative corner of Novant (2),
high origence/high intellectence, is not the most feminine-scoring group of boys nor the most masculine-scoring group of Governor's School girls. Instead, it is an intermediate position
for both sexes. It ranks third in femininity for boys and fourth
in masculinity for girls.

As was pointed out above, the most feminine-scoring group
for both sexes is Novant (1), high on origence and low on intellectence, while the most masculine group is the diagonally opposite novant, (4), low origence/high intellectence.

If, as adumbrated in the discussion above, origence is construed as relatively more feminine in nature and intellectence
as relatively more masculine, then both our empirical results
and theoretical formulations can be accommodated. Creativity will
be associated with sex-related characteristics of both of these
dimensions and creative persons will manifest features of both
masculinity and femininity--even though the latter may be more
conspicuous for males.

SEX ROLE, SEXUAL IDENTIFICATION,
AND FAMILY DYNAMICS

If intellectence is construed as a masculine dimension and origence as a feminine dimension following the interpretation presented here, then it should be possible to examine the consequences of their conjoint relationship and the implications for sex role behavior, sexual identification, and family dynamics. If, in addition, the lower end of each dimension is construed as the lack of the upper end characteristics, then the restrictions imposed by a single bipolar masculinity-femininity conceptualization may be overcome. Thus, low origence may be considered as "non-feminine" and low intellectence as "non-masculine." Since the two personality dimensions are independent, four possible configurations result which have different psychological implications.

For the quadrant high on origence and low on intellectence, the feminine end of origence is congruent with the non-masculine end of intellectence, and would lead to saliency of femininity in sex role behaviors. In the family constellation there would be an identification with the mother. The opposite quadrant, low on origence but high on intellectence, also shows congruence. In this case masculinity would be salient and identification would be with the father.

The two diagonally opposite quadrants have more complicated outcomes. In the quadrant high on both dimensions, the feminine pole of origence is in contrast to the masculine pole of intellectence. This results in incompatibility leading to rejection of conventional social norms for sex role and to manifestation of mixed masculinity and femininity. Ambivalence and confusion is resolved by identification with the self rather than a parent figure.

In the quadrant low on both dimensions there is compatibility of the non-masculine pole of intellectence and the non-feminine pole of origence. The result is an acceptance of conventional social norms for sex role and overt expression of compatible behaviors. That is, the female manifests culturally acceptable femininity and represses masculinity; a converse pattern characterizes the male.

Table IX-15 summarizes the hypothetical interpretation of origence and intellectence and the implications for sexual identification. Clear-cut predictions can be made from this framework and further empirical study is suggested.

TABLE IX-15. HYPOTHETICAL INTERPRETATION OF SEXUAL IDENTIFICATION
AS A FUNCTION OF ORIGENCE AND INTELLECTENCE

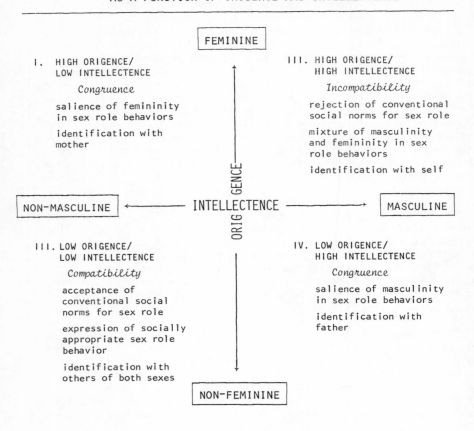

Some reports from the IPAR studies are consistent with the present hypothetical interpretation. In discussing the architects, MacKinnon writes that

> there was often a lack of intense closeness
> with one or both of the parents. Most often
> this appeared in relation to the father than
> to the mother, but often it characterized the
> relationship with both parents. There were
> not strong emotional ties of either a positive
> or a negative sort between parent and child....

> Closely related to this factor of some dis-
> tance between parent and child were ambigui-
> ties in identification with the parents. In
> place of the more usual clear identification
> with one parent, there was a tendency for
> the architects to have identified with both
> parents or with neither. (MacKinnon, 1962:
> 491-92).

It would follow that the most creative architects who fell
high on both origence and intellectence would not have identified with either parent while the less creative architects who
were lower on both dimensions would have identified with both
parents.

Women mathematicians were studied by Ravenna Helson in the
IPAR research program. Although scores on origence and intellectence are not available, their location in the two-dimensional personality model can be inferred from the high scores on the Concept
Mastery Test reported in Chapter II and the relatively low scores
on the art scale as given in Appendix A. Thus, compared with
other IPAR groups they would be expected to fall low on origence
and high on intellectence, which would place them in quadrant
four of Table IX-15 and their identification in the family should
be with the father. Data from a personal history and responses to
open-ended questions in an in-depth interview were evaluated independently by two psychologists. "The interviewers judged more
creative women than comparison women to have identified primarily
with the father ($p < .05$)" (Helson, 1971:216).

In other research Helson studied creative college women
and contrasted them with the other students in a senior class.
One item in her study was a question, "As a child were you closer
to your mother or your father?" She reports that

> most comparison subjects had felt closer to
> their mothers in childhood, a few to their
> fathers.... The creatives found the question
> hard to answer; most of them...said either
> that they had not been close to either parent
> or, more commonly, that they had felt closer
> to the father in some ways and to the mother
> in others." (Helson, 1967a:224)

Again inferring from scores on the art scale and the CMT,
it seems likely that many of the creatives were of the high orig-
ent/high intellectent type and would not have been close to either
parent. The statement that they felt closer to the father in

some ways and to the mother in others may reflect some ambivalence in attitude or an inability to resolve conflicting identification by a rejection of both parents.

The interpretation of the results offered here seems consistent with the proposed model for family identification and
the relationship to masculinity and femininity. It suggests
that the dimensions of origence and intellectence may be of value
in testing hypotheses related to sexual identification.

Chapter X

THEORETICAL INTERPRETATION

The use of Cronbach and Meehl's concept of a "nomological network" in connection with construct validity has been discussed previously where it was pointed out that the strands of retiary relationships may concern theoretical constructs as well as observable properties in all three possible combinations. That is, a theoretician or researcher may seek relationships between observables, between constructs and observables, or between theoretical constructs. Most of the material presented thus far has been concerned with observable relationships, particularly those based on test scores and ratings of observable behavior. These data have been presented as an argument for the viability of the constructs of origence and intellectence supported by demonstrated relationships to behavioral observations and psychometric results.

In this chapter an attempt will be made to collate other theoretical constructs with the two proposed in the present work. In terms of the conceptual and definitional model suggested earlier(Figure II-2, p. 28), we are now operating at a "level of inference" rather than at a "level of observation" where empirical evidence can be adduced in favor of certain interpretations. Theoretical constructs can be related only on logical or rational grounds and for many persons may seem to be less compelling than demonstrable relationships of an empirical nature. It will be of interest, nonetheless, to see whether intellectence and origence can, at this level, be related in some systematic way to a selected number of personality theories and to some of the various concepts that have been put forth to explain creativity.

It has been pointed out that relationships are not always symmetric between theories so that conceptual terms in one theory may not always have counterparts in another framework. For example, it is possible to express modern learning theory in the language of Freud but psychoanalysis cannot always be formulated in the context of learning theory (Rychlak, 1968:16). A similar type of asymmetry seems to hold in the present study.

175

The views about personality held by Sigmund Freud are so well-known that most of the basic terms in his psychoanalytic theory are widely used by laymen and professionals alike. These usages are reflected in the present work, particularly in discussing the MMPI item analysis (Chap. VI) where Freud's terms seem quite natural in such a descriptive task. In this sense it is possible to translate some basic features of the origence/intellectence typology into the language of psychoanalysis, but this would be an exercise in semantics rather than a statement about formal and conceptual relationships. That is, there is no compelling logical reason in the hypothetical psychodynamics of Freud's theory to imply the fourfold typology that emerged from the Governor's School analysis. The similarities are purely descriptive and must be understood in this way.

On the other hand, one of the dissidents from Freud's early circle, Carl Gustav Jung (1875-1961), developed a theory with conceptual elements that can be related logically to the origence/intellectence typology and to certain empirical findings of the present study. Thus, his theory is of value in comprehending hypotheses of this study and, perhaps, the proposed typology may help elucidate some of the Jungian concepts. The first formal theoretical comparison, then, will be with some of the elements in Jung's position.

Following this analysis a comparison will be made with the views of a contemporary theorist, Salvatore R. Maddi, who has developed a comprehensive theory of personality related to "level of activation." Maddi's theory comprises conceptual principles and a typology that may be related both logically and empirically to the Governor's School model.

The position of another contemporary theorist will be examined next. John L. Holland has developed what is basically a personality theory stemming from his work in the area of vocational preference. This comparison rests more on rational analysis than on formal relationships between the elements of Holland's theory and those of the present study.

Finally, a theory specifically related to creativity will be discussed; in the context of scientific research, William D. Hitt has generated a two-dimensional model that shows certain similarities to the results of the Governor's School study.

JUNG'S ANALYTICAL PSYCHOLOGY

It must be acknowledged that Jung's views are not as popular as those of Freud, nor are they well understood. Even the one concept that is widely known, that of the contrast between introversion and extroversion, is frequently misinterpreted. "Freud himself," Jung complains, "interpreted the introverted type as an individual morbidly concerned with himself. But introspection and self-knowledge can just as well be of the greatest value and importance" (1964:60). All too often the extrovert is depicted as well-adjusted, in addition to being outgoing and go-getting, while the introvert is caricatured as a maladjusted and moody misfit. H.J. Eysenck, a contemporary theorist, has demonstrated, however, that the concept of neurosis and the concept of introversion-extroversion can be clearly separated and has found empirical support for their independence (1953). In Eysenck's work all four combinations of neurotic/normal and extroversion/introversion have been identified and many differences in personality characteristics have been described.

Of crucial importance in Jung's concept is the difference between the subjective orientation of the introvert and the objective orientation of the extrovert (Jung, 1921).

The Governor's School typology, as summarized in Chapter VI, clearly suggests that the two types high on intellectence are introversive in temperament while the two low intellectent types are contrastingly extroversive. In Chapter VII, however, the dimensional analysis seems to indicate that the relationship may be more complicated. For example, the MMPI Social Introversion scale, Si, is positively correlated with both dimensions. For boys and girls respectively, the correlational values with INT are .21 and .17; for ORIG they are slightly lower, .15 and .13.

These findings imply that the high origent/high intellectent person of Type II would be the most introverted while the most extroverted would fall in the opposite low/low corner of Type III. The correlational pattern of the four special MMPI scales for the types is consistent with this implication; correlations with Si are as follows:

	Boys			*Girls*	
M-I	M-II		M-I	M-IV	
.18	.40		.26	.33	
M-III	M-IV		M-III	M-IV	
-.22	-.12		-.22	-.15	

For both sexes the highest positive values of correlation for Si are with M-II and the highest negative values are with M-III. Less extreme correlations are shown for M-I (positive) and for M-IV (negative). This implies that Type I is somewhat introversive and Type IV is slightly extroversive. But material from the other tests--the ACL and the SVIB--has been interpreted to imply a reverse situation; that is, on these tests Type I seems to be more extroversive and Type IV more introversive.

Regardless of inconsistencies for the latter two types, the general characteristics of Type II and Type III are relatively clear. The subjective orientation of Jung's introvert seems to be reflected primarily in a combination of high origence and high intellectence with the objectivity of the extrovert falling at low origence and low intellectence. Thus, if introversion-extroversion is considered as a dimension of personality, it would lie diagonally across the axes of origence and intellectence rather than coinciding with the former. Considering the typology of the present work, a high origent/low intellectent person and one in the opposite low origent/high intellectent corner would both have to be classified as mixed types or "ambiverts," although it can be argued that one attitude may tend to predominate.

To the extent that the high origent/high intellectent person is potentially more creative and that this type is more likely to be introversive, it would follow that there should be a positive relationship between introversion and creativity. Findings from the IPAR group confirm this tendency, but its implications have not been elaborated. "Approximately two-thirds of all our creative groups score as introverts, though there is no evidence that introverts as such are more creative than extraverts" (MacKinnon, 1962:490). It will be recalled that introversion is one of the personality characteristics found in Dellas and Gaier's review (1970) which has been referred to above. Although the precise relationship between introversion and creativity may not be clear, the Governor's School study suggests a positive association between the two concepts and is congruent with previous findings in this regard.

Because of the meaningfulness and the familiarity of the introversion-extroversion features of his theory, most psychologists as well as laymen have concentrated their interest on these concepts. Relatively little attention has been paid to the aspects of his theory designated by Jung as "psychological functions."

The total result of my work in this field
...is the presentation of two general types
covering the attitudes which I call extraver-
sion and introversion. Besides these, I have
worked out a fourfold classification corresponding to the functions of thinking, feeling,
sensation, and intuition. Each of these functions varies according to the general attitude,
and thus eight variants are produced. I have
been asked almost reproachfully why I speak of
four functions and not more or fewer. That
there are exactly four is a matter of empirical fact. But...a certain completeness is attained by these four. Sensation establishes
what is actually given, thinking enables us to
recognize its meaning, feeling tells us its
value, and finally intuition points to the pos-
sibilities of the whence and whither that lie
within the immediate facts. In this way we
can orient outselves with respect to the immediate world as completely as when we locate
a place geographically by latitude and longi-
tude. The four functions are somewhat like
the four points of the compass; they are just
as arbitrary and just as indispensable. Nothing prevents our shifting the cardinal points
as many degrees as we like in one direction or
the other, nor are we precluded from giving
them different names. It is merely a question
of convention and comprehensibility. (Jung,
1933:93-94)

Although Jung has stressed the arbitrary designation of
this typology, his theory implicates certain fixed relationships
between the four functional elements. Thinking and feeling are
at opposite poles on a dimension of "rational" or ordering principles in which an evaluation or judgment is made either on cognitive or noncognitive grounds. That is, the individual concludes that some particular experience is true or false on the
one hand, or pleasant or unpleasant on the other. Since thinking and feeling are at contrary poles and follow Jung's principle of "opposition" in the flow of psychic energy, to the extent that a person stresses his thinking function at the conscious level he will relegate feeling to an "inferior" function
in his unconscious. For the person whose preferred or "superi-
or" function in consciousness is feeling, thinking will fall at
the opposite pole.

Sensing and intuiting are located opposite one another on a dimension of "irrational" or nonevaluative principles based on perception. "Sensing" involves the uncritical acceptance of evidence from the five senses in a more or less objective way. Intuition is related more to imagination and an "inner perception" of the potentiality of things without any deliberate interpretation.

When a person is correctly classified into one of the four functional types, the opposite inferior function is determined by this placement and the remaining two must be "auxiliary" functions which can only partially be called into play. A thinking type, for example, must have feeling as an inferior function with sensation and intuition as auxiliaries. A sensing type would have intuiting as inferior with feeling and thinking as auxiliary functions.

Hybrid types are probably more common. "In actual life the function types almost never appear in pure form, but in a variety of mixed types.... Kant, for example, was a pure thinking type, while Schopenhauer must be regarded as an intuitive thinking type. We often find mixtures, but only of 'adjacent' functions...[since] mixture is impossible between the opposites on the two axes: thinking-feeling and sensation-intuition" (Jacobi, 1962:17-18).

Although Jung's expositors complain (*e.g.*, Marshall, 1968: 1) that clear and exact definitions of each of the four functional types have not been enunciated, they believe that the psychological nature of his dimensions has been well established. Thus, it does seem feasible to attempt a collation of Jung's types with the fourfold typology of the present work. Probably the most obvious similarity may be seen in the rationality and objectivity of the low orient/high intellectent type. These characteristics seem to be congruent with thinking, "the function which seeks to apprehend the world and adjust to it by way of thought or cognition, *i.e.* logical inferences" (Jacobi, 1962:12).

Many features of the high orient/high intellectent type, on the other hand, particularly as related to the use of imagination, fantasy, and nonlogical means of arriving at insights would seem compatible with Jung's intuitive type. In both models these types lie adjacent, so there is consistency on that basis as well as in the descriptive features.

If these pairs of types are equated, then the Jungian model requires that his feeling type be aligned with high origence/low intellectence and his sensing type with low origence/low intellectence. The summary description of this low/low type in Chapter VI emphasizes literal acceptance of the world as it is, in addition to conforming to it in conventional ways.

It is more difficult to grasp an essential congruence between feeling and the remaining high origent/low intellectent type. Jung has made it clear that the term "feeling," as he uses it, does not refer to affect or emotion: "'Feeling' here means the faculty of weighing and evaluating experience--in the way one might say "I *feel* that it is a good thing to do' without needing to analyze or rationalize the 'why' of the action" (1964:60). Governor's School Type I has been described as being disinclined to use rational or logical argument in attempting to influence other persons but to be likely to respond without studied or calculated analyses of situations. To this extent, there may be some similarity between these types, but it seems less compelling than that for the other three pairs.*

Since the two dimensions of the present work generate only four distinct types as compared to the eight hypothetical types comprised by Jung's theoretical model, it is logically impossible to find complete accord between them. Hence, the double placement of the high origent/high intellectent type into both intuition and introversion and the low/low type into both sensation and extroversion does not disprove Jung's thesis. At the same time it must be noted that other studies directly aimed at Jungian typology have not been able to find all eight possible types. Only five types emerged from a very carefully conducted study using a Q-sort methodology (Gorlow, Simonson, and Krauss, 1966). Another construct validational study based on an extensive test battery given to large numbers of subjects found many inconsistencies in the Jungian model as assessed by the Myers-Briggs Type Indicator. "The findings suggest that Sensation-Intuition and Thinking-Feeling scales may reflect restricted aspects of the dimensions they are intended to represent, and Judging-

---

*One bit of collateral evidence for the justifiability of equating the intuitive type with high origence and high intellectence comes from the IPAR use of a test based on Jung's theory, the Myers-Briggs Type Indicator (Myers, 1958). "In contrast to an estimated 25% of the general population who are intuitive, 90% of the creative writers, 92% of the mathematicians, 93% of the research scientists, and 100% of the architects are intuitive as measured by this test" (MacKinnon, 1962:489). It will be recalled that the creative architects fell very clearly into the high origent/high intellectent corner. Thus a conceptual colligation of creativity, intuition, and origence/intellectence may be assumed logically.

Perceiving scales may reflect something quite different from their postulated dimensions" (Striker and Ross, 1964:642).

There are two other concepts that are of specific interest because their role in Jung's theory is compatible with findings of the present study and may explain certain characteristics of creative persons. These terms, the *persona* and the *animus/anima*, were mentioned briefly in discussing results of masculinity-femininity scales in Chapter IX. Both concepts are related to his distinction between psychic functions dealing with the "outer world" and those at the deepest level facing the "inner world." It may be noted that not only does Jung recognize differences between conscious and unconscious as do other theorists, but he also distinguishes between the individual's "personal unconscious" and a "transpersonal," or "collective unconscious," common to all human beings.

A series of elements or "arbitrary segments of the psyche" have been enunciated and may be arrayed on a continuum from the level of consciousness to the depth of the collective unconscious. The most important of these "archetypes" or "primordial images" are the persona, ego, self, shadow, and animus/anima (see Jacobi, 1962: Diagram 6).

The term "persona" was derived from this word's original reference to the mask worn by an actor to signify the role he played. As such it indicates only "a mask that *feigns individuality* and tries to make others and oneself believe that one is individual, whereas one is simply playing a part in which the collective psyche speaks.... Fundamentally the persona is nothing real: it is a compromise between individual and society as to what a man should appear to be" (Jung, 1956:167). To the extent that an individual identifies with his persona, he will be overly concerned with superficial appearance and will respond too readily to the world around him. The persona "has two purposes: first, to make a specific impression on other people; second, to conceal the individual's inner self from their prying eyes" (Jacobi, 1964:287).

The concept of animus/anima is related to the inherent bisexuality of all human beings and also to the relationship of contrasexual traits in both males and females. That is, society generally considers certain traits to be typically masculine and appropriate for males while expecting traditional feminine characteristics to appear only in females. Although recognizing certain biological differences and the pertinence of some sex-role distinctions, Jung feels that psychological elements associated with the opposite sex cannot be completely ignored by an individual.

No man is so entirely masculine that he has
nothing feminine in him. The fact is, rather,
that very masculine men have--carefully guarded
and hidden--a very soft emotional life, often
incorrectly described as 'feminine.' A man
counts it a virtue to repress his feminine
traits as much as possible, just as a woman,
at least until recently, considered it unbe-
coming to be 'mannish.' The repression of
feminine traits and inclinations naturally
causes these contrasexual demands to accumulate
in the unconscious. (Jung, 1956:199)

Woman is compensated by a masculine element
and therefore her unconscious has, so to speak,
a masculine imprint. This results in a considerable psychological difference between men
and women, and accordingly I have called the
projection-making factor in women the animus,
which means reason or spirit. The animus corresponds to the paternal Logos just as the
anima corresponds to the maternal Eros.... I
use Eros and Logos merely as conceptual aids
to describe the fact that woman's unconscious
is characterized more by the connective quality
of Eros than by the discrimination and cognition
associated with Logos. (Jung in de Laszlo, 1958:
13)

A man who identifies exclusively with his persona and is
hyper-masculine may be in psychological difficulty just as much
as a man whose identification with his anima has led to homosexuality. A counterpart relationship would hold for women. Jung
argues that a proper balance must be achieved even if it means
flouting some of society's standards and codes of conduct. Creative individuals, because of their independence, autonomy, and
asociality may be better able to recognize and accept their contrasexual tendencies and to express them in overt ways. Society
will then view the creative male as somewhat feminine and the
creative female as somewhat masculine.

These views of Jung are consistent with the findings summarized by Dellas and Gaier (1970:64) and with the results of the
IPAR group; MacKinnon's comments in this regard have been cited
previously. That is, the noncreative individual who is overly
concerned about the face he presents to society and who subordi-
nates his own views to those of his social group may be said to
have identified with the persona. The creative individual who
manifests traits typically assigned by society to the opposite

sex may be expressing the other side of the animus/anima relationship.

In the Governor's School typology it is the low origent/low
intellectent group that seems to exemplify identification with
the persona as shown by this type's conventionality and conformity
and by a ready accession to other people in many matters.

To the extent that high origence/high intellectence is the
creative quadrant, the Jungian position would imply that this
type should be neither the most masculine nor the most feminine
within either sex, but should show instead some characteristics
of the opposite sex. Such a relationship has indeed been shown
in the analyses summarized in Table IX-13 (p.165) where mean z
scores for masculinity-femininity scales are reported. The most
feminine boys are the high origent/low intellectent group of
Novant (1); the most masculine girls are the low origent/high intellectent group of Novant (4). Both boys and girls of Novant (2)
fall between these extremes and may be considered to show a mixture of masculinity and femininity. These results are congruent
with the animus/anima balance specified by Jung's theory although
they are complicated to some extent by the relationship of the
two dimensions themselves to the specific measures of masculinity-
femininity employed in the Governor's School study that have been
discussed previously.

MADDI'S ACTIVATION THEORY

Salvatore R. Maddi (1968) has outlined a theory of personality based on concepts derived from activation theory (Fiske and
Maddi, 1961; Maddi and Propst, 1971). His position assumes that
all persons exhibit a "core tendency" to maintain a customary
level of activation. "Activation is a neuropsychological concept,
referring on the psychological side to the common core of meaning
in such terms as alertness, attentiveness, tension, and subjective excitement, and on the neural side to the state of excitement in a postulated center of the brain" (Maddi, 1968:135). Determinants of activation are subsumed by the concept of "impact"
which includes three dimensions of stimulation--intensity, meaningfulness, and variety--and three sources for this stimulation--
exteroceptive, interoceptive, and cortical. "Impact-modifying"
behavior is instituted whenever the actual level of activation de-
parts from the customary or characteristic level that has emerged
from experience. "When actual activation level is above that
which is customary, *impact-decreasing behavior* occurs, and when
actual activation level is below that which is customary, *impact-
increasing* behavior occurs" (pp. 137-38).

These assumed "core characteristics" are related to "concrete peripheral characteristics" which have been classified under an elaborate typology of 24 independent types. The first major principle of classification is related to customary level of activation and differentiates "high-activation people" from "low-activation people." The second major principle collapses the "favored source of stimulation" from three into two--an "external trait" which regulates impact by sources of stimulation "essentially outside the body (anything from thunderclaps or wind to music or pictures)," and an "internal trait." The internal trait will cause an individual to "turn within the organism (focusing on anything from thoughts or daydreams to pains or dizziness)" (Maddi: 1968:319). The third major principle is

> The distinction between the *active* and the *passive* trait.... The person with the active trait has the habit of initiative, such that he influences his external and even internal stimulus environment, whereas the person with the passive trait is habitually indolent, permitting himself to be influenced by internal and external stimuli over which he has no subjective sense of control. (p. 319)

These three distinctions form a 2x2x2 model which generates eight basic types, each of which may be subdivided on the basis of the salience of the three dimensions of stimulation; that is, a person may have an approach or avoidance *motive* (need or fear) for either intensity, meaningfulness, or variety. Adding these three subdivisions would result in a total of 24 different theoretical types (3x8).

Maddi has concentrated on the eight basic types of his theory and has given a fairly detailed description of each (pp. 320-24). Brief summaries are given in his appendix (pp. 501-02) for only the four active forms with the implication that they are relatively more important for understanding the content of his typology. "All these passive personality types will seem similar to those with the active trait in stated aims, values, and interests. But on finer analysis, those with the passive trait emerge as somewhat unable to practice what they preach" (p. 502).

Since the Governor's School students were selected because of demonstrated ability and achievement, it seems plausible to consider them as exemplifying active rather than passive traits. For this reason, as well as Maddi's own emphasis on the active trait form of his typology, a comparison will be made between these four types and those developed in the present work.

The basic nature of Maddi's principle types is given in the following brief summaries:

The *High-Activation Person* with *active* and *external* traits will be a 'go-getter,' seeking out challenges to meet in the physical and social environment. He will be energetic and voracious in his appetites. If he also has a high *need for meaningfulness*, he will be a pursuer of causes and problems. But if he has a high *need for intensity*, he may pursue action and tumult per se. And if he has a high *need for variety*, he will show curiosity, adventurousness, and impulsiveness.

The *High-Activation Person* with *active* and *internal* traits will pursue impact through thinking, daydreaming, responding to challenges posed by limitations of mind and body, without much regard for the tangible affairs of the external world. He will be subtle and complex. With a high *need for meaningfulness*, he will lead the life of the mind. With a high *need for intensity*, he will pursue sensations and emotions. With a high *need for variety*, he will strive for originality in some creative endeavor.

The *Low-Activation Person* with *active* and *external traits* will be the eternal conversationalist, bent on heading off social and physical disorganization and conflict through negotiation and control. He will tend to be a conformist, and show simplicity in his tastes. If he also has a high *fear of meaningfulness*, he will try to oversimplify problems and avoid ambiguity. With a high *fear of intensity*, he will exert a dampening effect on vigorous, disorganized external events. If he has a high *fear of variety*, he will seek to force routine on the environment, preferring the familiar to the new.

The *Low-Activation Person* with *active* and *internal* traits will be conservative with his own organism by advocating the golden mean, being careful to avoid excesses and indulgences of any kind. He will be simple, uncomplex, devoid of inconsistencies. With a high *fear of meaningfulness*, he will show absence of detailed or diverse thoughts

> and daydreams. With a high *fear of intensity*,
> he will have an especially ascetic emphasis
> about him. With a high *fear of variety*, he
> will force himself to function consistently
> and stably, in a manner devoid of flamboyance.
> (Maddi, 1968:501-02)

Many of the characteristics that he imputes to his types
seem to parallel those found in the Governor's School study and
suggest that some psychological similarity may be found.

1. Maddi's high-activation/external type shares with high
origence/low intellectence features of impulsivity, adventuresome-
ness, and a preference for tangible events and things.

2. Common characteristics for high-activation/internal and
high origence/high intellectence include: subtleness, complexity,
lack of sociability, preference for a few intimate friends, lack
of interest in the obvious, and striving for originality in a creative or imaginative endeavor.

3. Low-activation/external and low origence/low intellectence both show preferences for familiar and conventional activities. They avoid ambiguity and seek routine simplification and
conformity. Problems seem to be resolved by direct social interaction.

4. Consistency and stability appear to be salient for both
low-activation/internal and low origence/high intellectence. The
types also stress personal dependability and they avoid flamboyant
excesses of any kind.

HOLLAND'S VOCATIONAL THEORY

John L. Holland has presented a theory of vocational behavior
in his book, *The Psychology of Vocational Choice* (1966), but the
subtitle of this volume, *A Theory of Personality Types and Model
Environments*, suggests the breadth of his approach and the possible relevance of his position to the results of the Governor's
School study. "For many years," he points out, "it was popular
to interpret a person's scores on vocational interest inventories
and his choice of vocation as a function of his 'vocational interests,' as if these interests were different from or independent of
personality" (p. 2). At the same time, studies of the relationship of vocational test scores to other kinds of human activity
that are not narrowly vocational indicated that a more comprehensive approach was needed. "If vocational preference is

construed as an expression of personality, then 'vocational interests' represent the expression of personality in work, hob-
bies, recreational activities, and preferences. In short, what
we have called 'vocational interests' are simply another aspect
of personality" (p. 3). It will be recalled that the Strong Vocational Interest Blank was treated as a personality test in the
present work.

After extensive collation of results from various areas of
investigation, Holland concluded that most persons in our culture
can be categorized into six theoretical types to which he assigns
the terms, Realistic, Intellectual,* Social, Conventional, Enterprising, and Artistic.

> The types are assumed to represent common
> outcomes of growing up in our culture. Each
> type is described in terms of a theoretical
> model called the *model orientation*. The model
> orientation is a cluster of characteristic
> adaptive behaviors (coping mechanisms), psycho-
> logical needs and motives, self-concepts, life
> history, vocational and educational goals, pre-
> ferred occupations, aptitudes, and intelligence.
> A person's resemblance to *each* of the six model
> orientations is called his *personality pattern*.
> The single model that the person most clearly
> resembles is his personality type. (Holland,
> 1966:16).

Perusal of Holland's descriptions suggested that there were
similarities between certain of his personality types and those
that emerged from the Governor's School study. The general flavor of these descriptions may be seen in the following brief introductory statements extracted from his book:

> *Realistic*. The model type is masculine, physi-
> cally strong, unsociable, aggressive; has good
> motor coordination and skill; lacks verbal and

---

*Holland now prefers the term "Investigative" in referring
to occupations related to this type since "the literal meanings of
'investigative' are to track down, trace out, or to search. These
denotations appear sensible for describing the core activities of
scientists...[and]...appear more useful in combination with other
categories. For example, machinists are classified as Realistic-
Investigative as essentially they track down realistic problems."
He offers as a second reason the fact that the term Intellectual
"offended people in some categories, especially Artistic types"
(Holland, *et al.*, 1970:21).

interpersonal skills; prefers concrete to abstract problems; conceives of himself as being
aggressive and masculine and as having conventional political and economic values....

Intellectual. The model type is task-oriented,
intraceptive, asocial; prefers to think through
rather than act out problems; needs to understand; enjoys ambiguous work tasks; has unconventional values and attitudes; is anal as opposed to oral....

Social. The model type is sociable, responsible,
feminine, humanistic, religious; needs attention;
has verbal and interpersonal skills; avoids intellectual problem solving, physical activity,
and highly ordered activities; prefers to solve
problems through feelings and interpersonal
manipulation of others, is orally dependent....

Conventional. The model type prefers structured verbal and numerical activities and sub-
ordinate roles; is conforming (extraceptive);
avoids ambiguous situations and problems in-
volving interpersonal relationships and physical
skills; is effective at well-structured tasks;
identifies with power; values material posses-
sions and status....

Enterprising. The model type has verbal skills
for selling, dominating, leading; conceives of
himself as a strong masculine leader, avoids
well-defined language or work situations requiring long periods of intellectual effort; is
extraceptive; differs from the Conventional type
in that he prefers ambiguous social tasks and
has greater concern with power, status, and leadership; is orally aggressive....

Artistic. The model type is asocial; avoids
problems that are highly structured or require
gross physical skills; resembles the Intellectual
type in being intraceptive and asocial; but differs from that type in that he has a need for
individualistic expression, has less ego strength,
is more feminine, and suffers more frequently
from emotional disturbances; prefers dealing with
environmental problems through self-expression
in artistic media.... (Holland, 1966:16-17)

There are manifest parallels between the orience/intel-
lectence types and four of Holland's six types, while the remaining two seem to differ on only one of the dimensions that we
have proposed.

1.   Holland's Enterprising type seems similar in many ways
to the Governor's School high orient/low intellectent type.
Some of the common features are impulsiveness, exhibitionistic
tendencies, persuasiveness, interest in selling and dramatics,
dislike of manual and nonsocial activities, avoidance of tasks
requiring persistence and extended concentration, disinclination
for intellectual activities, and an exploitative tendency.

2.   An equation of the high orient/high intellectent type
with Holland's Artistic type is suggested by interest in aesthetic and literary occupations, complexity of outlook, independence
of judgment, intuition, imagination, introversion, femininity,
introspection, lack of sociability, preference for indirect methods of relating to people, rejection of conventional values,
originality, and potential for creative achievement.

3.   The third Governor's School type, low orient/low intellectent, shares many common features with the Conventional
type.   They show the least potential for creative performance
and prefer to function in a well structured context.   Other characteristics include conservatism, practical-mindedness, cheerful attitude, suppression of sex and aggression, sociability,
conformance to custom and tradition, interest in banking and
business occupations, stable attitudes, self-acceptance, simplicity rather than complexity in outlook, self-control, and concern with making a good impression on others.

4.   The Intellectual type is basically similar to the low
orient/high intellectent Type IV.   Both tend to solve problems
through the manipulation of ideas rather than through physical
or social skills and prefer scientific and highly skilled technical occupations.   They tend to be rational, analytic, cognitive, achieving, unsociable, to avoid dependence on others, and
to exert indirect control over others.

The remaining two types in Holland's theory, Social and
Realistic, do not seem to differ much in terms of intellectence
and their characteristics probably would place them somewhere in
the middle of this dimension.   On orience, however, the Social
type would seem to fall relatively high while the Realistic type
would, in all likelihood, be quite low.

The Social person differs from the Enterprising person in being more feminine, introverted, helpful, intellectual, insightful, co-
operative, friendly, responsible (having religious and social values), and less energetic,
aggressive, dominant, sociable, cynical, and
enthusiastic. The Social person differs from
the Conventional person in that the latter is
more self-controlled, hard-headed, masculine,
and submissive. The Social person is more
sociable, dependent and conventional than the
Artistic person. (Holland, 1966:27)

The Realistic person differs from the Intellectual person in that the Realistic person
is more practical (concerned with facts), emotionally stable, masculine, and conventional
(more concerned about success, status, and
leadership) than the Intellectual person. The
Realistic person is less scholarly (less apt
to seek a Ph.D. or daydream about achievement
and learning), original, sociable, insightful
about interpersonal relations, independent, and
self-confident than the Intellectual person.
The Realistic person differs from the Social
and the Enterprising primarily in social skills
and interests. The Realistic person is more
masculine and less original than the Artistic
person. The Realistic person differs from the
Conventional person primarily in that the Realistic person is less responsible and sociable
and more impulsive, stable, submissive, and
self-deprecatory. (Holland, 1966:21-22)

This rational comparison of the Holland and the Governor's
School typologies can be construed only as suggestive of the inferred relationships discussed. No direct empirical comparison
is possible with the present data and it will be necessary to
classify another sample of subjects by both typologies to learn
the actual degree of similarity.*

---

*Mean scores on the modified Strong Vocational Interest
Blank scales for origence and intellectence on more than 200 occupational groups have been made available to the present writer
through the courtesy of Dr. Charles B. Johansson, Director of
Test Development for Interpretive Scoring Systems, National Computer Systems, Minneapolis. There is striking agreement between
the locations predicted by Holland's typology as presently interpreted and the origence/intellectence model.

HITT'S THEORY OF CREATIVITY IN RESEARCH

A two-factor theory of research creativity has been developed by William D. Hitt (1965) based on "the premise...that original thinking and logical reasoning are complementary aspects of
creative thinking. These facets of behavior are mutually dependent forces which, when acting together, can produce creative
ideas that are new and have some value" (p. 127).

An empirical test of his hypothesis was made by studying
a random sample of 200 male subjects from a research laboratory
in the physical sciences and engineering. Research performance
was assessed by a specially constructed supervisory rating scale.
The items on the scale were intercorrelated and the matrix sub-
jected to factor analysis which "produced two correlated but
distinct dimensions of research performance, which were labeled
'originality' and 'logical reasoning' "* (p. 128).

Scores on these two factors were then used in a second
phase of the study (Hitt and Stock, 1965). A sample of 96 subjects from the same research laboratory was drawn so that 24 subjects fell in each of the four quadrants generated by ratings
either above or below average on the two dimensions conjointly,
that is, (1) high originality/low logical reasoning, (2) high on
both, (3) low on both, and (4) low on originality but high on
logical reasoning.

A conventional analysis of variance technique was used to
test the overall significance for these groups on scores from an
extensive battery of tests comprising general mental ability
(the Wonderlic Personnel Test), ten specific intellectual aptitudes from Guilford's Structure-of-Intellect model (see above
pp. 41-45), and eight personality characteristics from the Gordon
Personal Inventory and the Gordon Personal Profile.

Highest mean scores were obtained by the two groups above
average on rated originality for six of seven measures on Guilford's *divergent*-thinking tests: Alternate Uses, Associational
Fluency, Consequences, Expressional Fluency, Ideational Fluency,
and Plot Titles. These groups were also highest on personality
measures for Original Thinking and Ascendancy. In contrast, the
two groups below average on rated originality had the highest
means on Cautiousness and Emotional Stability.

*The groups above average on logical reasoning excelled on
one *divergent* test, Match Problems, but it was noted that

---

*The reference axes were correlated to the extent of .61
(John D. Stock, personal communication, 1969).

"Although the test involves *divergent* production, the solutions can be obtained by application of logical reasoning" (Hitt and Stock, 1965:139). These groups were also highest on a Guilford *evaluation* test (Seeing Problems), on general intelligence, and on personality scales for Vigor and Responsibility. The groups below average on logical reasoning had highest mean scores on Guilford's *cognition* test, Social Institutions, and on the personality scale for Personal Relations.

It is of interest to note that on the only Guilford *convergent*-thinking test included, Gestalt Transformation, the highest mean was achieved by the group below average on both ratings. Hitt and Stock point out that this test is in a multiple-choice format and comment, "In pure and simple terms, it appears that many of the brightest researchers who took the tests are in disagreement with the scoring key. This test obviously should be used with caution" (p. 139).

The results of this study are important for the present work both from a theoretical viewpoint and also in terms of the substantive findings. The fact that a two-dimensional model was required to account for variation in rated research performance supports the general argument advanced earlier that creativity is not adequately conceptualized by a single factor. Although a greater number of dimensions may be identified ultimately, the need for at least two distinct dimensions has been demonstrated for research creativity in Hitt's convincing study.

The subjects studied are obviously different from the Governor's School students--as were the IPAR scientists discussed above (Chap. VIII)--but the dimensions that emerged from the analysis show certain congruences with the two dimensions of the present work, origence and intellectence.

In particular, the contrast of personality measures for Ascendancy and Original Thinking with those for Cautiousness and Emotional Stability on Hitt's dimension of originality suggests that it might be related to origence. For the Governor's School subjects, positive correlations with origence were found for two ACL scales, Aggression and Autonomy, with negative correlations for Self Control and Personal Adjustment (p. 119) above. The high positive correlation for all of the MMPI clinical scales with origence and the negative correlation for K and L (p. 123) is likewise consistent with the implications of Hitt's results.

On his dimension of logical reasoning, the association of general mental ability is paralleled in the present work by

positive correlation for both the CMT and the D-48 with intellectence. Both of the Governor's School low intellectent types
(I's and III's) showed more interest in personal and social interaction than the other types; this seems to parallel Hitt's
findings for Social Institutions and Personal Relations.

Finally, it may be pointed out that the Governor's School
boys falling in Novant (2)--high origence/high intellectence--
were rated highest on originality by their teachers.

ORIGENCE AND INTELLECTENCE AS GENERAL DIMENSIONS OF PERSONALITY

The comparison given above of origence and intellectence
with some basic concepts from three different personality theories may be interpreted as evidence at the level of inference
for the generalizability of the proposed dimensions. The views
of a traditional theorist, Jung, and those of a contemporary
personologist, Maddi, were both found to be compatible with the
two-dimensional model of the present work. Likewise, a personality theory derived from vocational preference, that of Holland,
was shown to be congruent with the concepts of origence and intellectence. Their specific relation to creativity was found
consistent with Hitt's theory of research creativeness and, at
the level of observation, with empirical findings of the IPAR
group as we have noted previously.

It seems fair to conclude that origence and intellectence
may be considered relevant to the study of personality in general as well as to the specific area of creativity. To be sure,
although two dimensions appear to be a minimal number to use in
personality study, it is possible to get by with only one. Carl
Rogers, for example, utilizes a single dimension, "self-actualization," which embraces only two basic types, the ideal "fully
functioning person" at one end with the "maladjusted person" opposite (Rogers, 1959). By contrast, R.B. Cattell may be found
at the other extreme; he has identified more than three dozen
separate dimensions of personality although he is sometimes content to work with merely 16 of them (Cattell, 1965).

Personality is obviously too broad an area and too complicated a construct to be comprehended in any detailed manner by
one dimension or even by two. At the same time, such a seemingly self-evident assertion raises two quite separate questions:
How many dimensions of personality *are* there? How many dimensions are *needed* in the study of personality?

There is no ultimate answer to the first question--it is a theoretical matter that cannot be resolved either rationally or logically although it can be discussed and debated in both frameworks. That is, there are an infinite number of dimensions which can be postulated and individual theorists will differ widely both in the nature and the number of the dimensions that they propose. The problem is similar to that posed by Warren Weaver in discussing what he calls "imperfections of science."

> It is widely recognized that any natural event has a number of possible explanations. It has been demonstrated that if a certain body of experience can be usefully interpreted through one particular theory, there is always, in fact, an infinite number of other theories each of which will equally well accommodate the same body of experience. There may be very important aesthetic reasons for preferring certain of the theories. (Weaver, 1961:110)

To the extent that "aesthetic reasons" are subjective judgments or predilections stemming from personal preferences of the theorist, it may be that an answer can be sought in this realm. That is, the kind of theory a person sets forth, including both the number and nature of dimensions postulated, may be a reflection more of the theorist himself than of any objective reality inherent in the phenomena encompassed by his theory. Freud, Jung, Adler, Sullivan, and many other personality theorists all worked with emotionally disturbed individuals, yet their theories treat psychopathology as well as normal mental functions in quite different ways.

It would be an interesting study in itself to compare different theorists on the very dimensions or concepts that they themselves propose.* For example, the present writer has found

---

*The comments of a Jungian are of interest in this regard. "We can also discern a dominant archetype underlying the doctrine of various thinkers, particularly the psychologists. When Freud sees the beginning and principle of everything that happens in sexuality, Adler in the striving for power, these too are ideas expressing an archetype.... Jung's teaching is also based on an archetype which finds its expression particularly in 'tetrasomy,' four-bodiedness (*cf*. the theory of the four functions, the pictorial arrangement of the four, orientation by the four cardinal points, etc.).... and probably the universal distribution and magical significance of the cross or the four-part circle may be explained by the archetypal character of the quaternity" (Jacobi, 1962:46).

many marked personality differences between Freud and Jung when they are compared by a composite Adjective Check List describing the men completed by graduate students in a seminar on personality theory. At the same time these theorists were highly similar on the special ACL scales for orgence and intellectence-- falling high on both dimensions as expected of creative persons (Welsh, 1975). Although the task of relating great men to their work has been left mostly to conventional biographical procedures, there is no reason to exclude psychological measurement from the task.

A plausible hypothesis, then, would be that personality characteristics may account for some of the differences found in the postulates and positions of personality theorists. This implies that an attempt to answer the first question raised must take the theorist himself into account.

The second question, however, may be answered in somewhat more objective terms. At least Leon H. Levy makes a forthright statement that bears on the problem of the number of dimensions needed in personality study.

> The value of a dimension in the study of
> personality depends on the precision with
> which it can be defined, the extent to which
> it is tied to empirical operations, and the
> range and kinds of phenomena it explains and
> predicts. And the more precisely it may be
> measured, the better. Thus, although Cat-
> tell has postulated a wider array of dimen-
> sions--for which he has constructed a bewilder-
> ing array of neologisms--than any other re-
> searcher, Holt's (1962) criticism that they
> lack intuitive meaning seems irrelevant. The
> only criteria against which the dimensions
> can be legitimately evaluated are those for
> any scientific construct: Do they pay their
> way empirically? (Levy, 1970:200-01)

The number, as well as the kind, of personality dimensions needed, then, can be answered only in an empirical context de- termined partly by the purpose and aim of the theorist. A com- plex multi-dimensional theory of intellectual functioning cannot be faulted *per se* if it fails to identify creative persons or does not differentiate their products. On the other hand, a theory of, say, remote association that does clearly claim to be related to creativity and yet demonstrates a systematic relationship only to measures of intellectual performance must be appraised and ex- amined in that light.

Thus, it seems proper to evaluate the two dimensions of personality proposed in the present research in the framework of Levy's statement: origence and intellectence have been defined extensively; they are closely tied to empirical operations; they can be measured with reasonable accuracy by a number of different objective instruments; they explain, and perhaps predict, not only results specific to the area of creativity, but also some other phenomena of interest in personality study.

"There are some enterprises in which a careful disorderliness is the true method."

Herman Melville, *Moby Dick*, Chap. 82

One of the difficulties in approaching the issue of creativity stems from the tendency to consider creativity in absolute terms and to conceptualize it in a quantitative framework. This is one of the consequences of the cognitive approach favored by many researchers as discussed in Chapter III. Creativity is construed by them to be an ability like intelligence and, just as a high IQ score is considered to be indicative of intelligence, so a person must give the correct answer on some "creative thinking" test to be seen as creative. A clear implication is that a person scoring low in this kind of cognitive performance lacks creativity.

However, if creativity is conceptualized as a combination of personality and ability traits in the context of societal requirements, then a qualitative and relative judgment can be employed in place of the quantitative and absolute evaluation of the cognitive approach. Departure from this latter position has been urged by Carl Rogers, for example, in a discussion of the creative process. "The action of the child inventing a new game with his playmates; Einstein formulating a theory of relativity; the housewife devising a new sauce for the meat; a young author writing his first novel--all of these are...creative, and there is no attempt to set them in order of more or less creative" (Rogers, 1954).

In the framework of origence and intellectence the following hypothesis is proposed to account for differential evaluation of creativity: A person is likely to be judged as creative if he falls high on origence and high on intellectence *relative* to the central tendency of his own peer status group.

A general predictive summary may be set forth now in the form of hypotheses to be tested in future research. Discussion of the proposed dimensions in the framework of other theoretical positions just concluded as well as the empirical results previously presented seem to converge on a few basic points that have predictive implications.

It is hypothesized that there will be *psychological simi-larity* related to position along each dimension and that there will be *categorical congruity* for the types generated by the two dimensions. Thus, all persons falling at the same position on origence and on intellectence will be of the same general personality type and will show typical and characteristic behavior both covertly and overtly; they will be found more often in contexts or environments compatible with their personality features, and they will respond to similar aspects of their "life space" (Lewin, 1936).

Using the present study's fourfold classification, it is possible to summarize a number of characteristics that would be predicted from the two-dimensional model; these are displayed in Table A-1. For example, two individuals equally high on origence and equally low on intellectence will be similarly interactive and sociable, they will respond to other persons in a direct manner, and will be found in occupations that involve working with others. They will be more at home in tasks that do not require close supervision or close adherence to stringent rules and they will be particularly responsive to immediate reward and recognition of an accomplishment. Counterpart predictions can be made for other configurations of position along the two dimensions.

It follows that the closer any two individuals (or groups) are in the framework of origence/intellectence space, the more alike they will be in the characteristic features associated with the position. Conversely, the more distant two persons are in terms of the dimensions, the less alike they will be in these characteristics.

There is a *consistency corollary*, then, of categorical congruity. It is predicted that of two persons in the same origence/intellectence position, the one who is more consistent in all of the characteristics of that particular location will be more effective in his performance and better satisfied with himself.

For example, suppose that two students are equally low on both dimensions but that they have been enrolled in two different sections of a beginning psychology course. One section is taught by a disciplined and well-organized lecturer following a standard textbook in which clear-cut assignments are made in advance. Examination is by objective quizzes previously announced

TABLE A-1. SUMMARY OF CHARACTERISTICS ASSOCIATED WITH
ORIGENCE-INTELLECTENCE DIMENSIONAL TYPES*

INTRAPERSONAL ORIENTATION

I. *Extroversive* exhibitionistic acting out	II. *Introverted* withdrawing ruminative
II. *Extroverted* outward directed responsive	IV. *Introversive* inward directed speculative

INTERPERSONAL CONDUCT

I. *Sociable* outgoing many acquaintances amicable	II. *Asocial* isolative few friends impersonal
II. *Social* friendly indiscriminate sociality benevolent	IV. *Unsocial* shy guarded sociality humanitarian

DIRECTION OF ACTIVITY

I. *Interactive* interdependent responder	II. *Proactive* autonomous detached viewer
III. *Reactive* dependent follower	IV. *Active* independent leader

*

I High orig/low int	II High orig/high int
III Low orig/low int	IV Low orig/high int

TABLE A-1 (continued)

NATURE OF SELF CONCEPT

I. Self-seeking egocentric	*II. Self-centered* egotistic
III. Self-effacing allocentric	*IV. Self-confident* egoistic

ATTITUDES AND BELIEFS

I. Irregular uncommon "don't conform"	*II. Unorthodox* unconventional "take risks"
III. Orthodox common "play safe"	*IV. Regular* conventional "follow rules"

COGNITIVE STYLE

I. Imaginative fantasy improvisation simile	*II. Intuitive* insight meditation metaphor
III. Customary industry persistence allegory	*IV. Rational* logic deliberation analogy

TABLE A-1.   (continued)

COGNITIVE DEVELOPMENT

I. *Proto-integration without differ-entiation*	II. *Integration with differentiation*
diffuse global imprecise	synthesis organization composition
III. *Proto-differentia-tion without integration*	IV. *Differentiation with integration*
fragmented detailed unrelated	analysis specification resolution

VOCATIONAL PREFERENCE

I. *Histrionic*	II. *Intellectual*

action
performing and
  dramatic arts
sales occupations
	ideas
	arts and humanities
	related occupations
	  (*e.g.*, journalist)

III. *Pragmatic*	IV. *Scientific*
practical problems commerce and business service occupations	concepts sciences and mathe-matics related occupations (*e.g.* statistician)

---

with an explicit grading system. The second student, however, is in an experimental section with no regularly scheduled class hours but with frequent and unstructured group meetings during which the student may suddenly be called upon to discuss some new and unassigned topic. Grades are based on an independent

project or paper that the student must work out on his own.
There is consistency in the case of the first student, and he
should perform relatively better in the course and express more
positive feelings about his experience. The inconsistency for
the second student would result in poorer performance and in addition, might lead to other behavior such as dropping the course,
transferring to the first section, or seeking help from a friend
who is an advanced psychology major. The student will express
negative feelings about his experience and it is possible that
he might be more dissatisfied with himself as well as with psychology.*

Psychiatric patients and other maladjusted groups as compared to matched control subjects should manifest less consistency in characteristics, particularly intrapersonal and interpersonal traits of behavior. A paranoid schizophrenic, for example, may simultaneously show features of impulsivity and ego-
centricity associated with high orience/low intellectence as
well as the detached rationality and intellectualized objectivity
characteristic of the opposite low orience/high intellectence
corner. It might be noted also that patients should respond better to a type of therapy that is appropriate to their dimensional
location, just as students should react to instructional consistency.

This corollary may be used to explain other phenomena. For
example, the location of the Strong Vocational Interest Blank
scale for Army Officers (Figure VII-1, p. 111) is relatively
low on orience for males and in the middle on intellectence;
this would correspond to Holland's Realistic occupational type
(pp. 188-89 above). During peacetime with a volunteer army it
would be expected that most of the individuals choosing a military career would have personality characteristics appropriate
for that location in the dimensional space. Persons who had
different traits of personality would either not sign-up to begin with, or, finding themselves in an inconsistent context,
would drop out as soon as possible. During a war or circumstances
when individuals are drafted, many different personality types
will find themselves, often against their will, in situations
that are not consistent with their own characteristics. This
would be expected to result in more breaches of military discipline, lower morale, poorer performance, and other evidence of
inefficiency as a consequence of the inconsistency.

---

*A study by Domino (1968) found evidence for this viewpoint
and the author argues that "it might be extremely worthwhile to
fit the curriculum to the student by providing...[a] setting
which most effectively utilizes his potential" (p. 259).

Thus, it is our contention that many other phenomena of interest in human behavior as well as personality characteristics related to creativity and intelligence--the original focus of our study--may be susceptive to investigation in terms of the concept of origence and intellectence and the fourfold typology generated by this two-dimensional personality model. If the model proves feasible, then we should expect formulations to generate specific predictions within the framework of the general hypotheses of psychological similarity, categorical congruity, and the consistency corollary.

APPENDIX A

IPAR RESULTS

Architects. One of the groups of subjects studied in the living-in assessment was a sample of 40 American architects who had been nominated as the most outstandingly creative practitioners in the United States. For convenience, this sample was referred to as Architects I (MacKinnon, 1961). Two additional samples were studied somewhat less intensively, since they could not all be assessed at the Institute itself but were evaluated mostly by mailout of questionnaires and test instruments. Architects II comprised a sample of 43 subjects matched for age and geographic location of practice and who had had at least two years' working experience with one of the originally nominated creative architects. A third group, Architects III, without any experience with the creative architects, was selected to be representative of architects-in-general. No females were included in any of the groups.

Average scores on the BW Art Scale for the three groups were: I, 37.1; II, 29.5; and III, 26.1 (p. V-16). Not only does the creative group score higher than the other two groups, as expected, but also all three average much above the mean score for people-in-general. To the extent that the profession of architecture can be expected to attract persons who are more creative than the ordinary citizen, these results make sense. In a like manner, the significantly higher mean score for Architects I is certainly support for the scale's construct validity as a measure related to creativity.

Mathematicians. A group of 44 women mathematicians was studied by the assessment procedures at IPAR. "The sample includes virtually all creatively productive women mathematicians under the age of 65 in the United States and Canada at the time of the study" (Helson, 1961:IV-1). The sample was divided into two subgroups that were not as sharply differentiated in terms of the criterion of creativity as the architects had been. There were 16 Women Mathematicians I "rated as more creative than the average mathematician engaged in research" and 28 in Group II "rated as average or somewhat less creative than average." But Helson stresses that even the average mathematician engaged in research may be considered creative "so that we really have to do here, not with creative and uncreative persons, but with creative and very creative persons" (p. IV-2).

Differences in the means are in the expected direction of the BW Art Scale with the I's averaging 28.1 and II's, 26.9.

Men mathematicians were studied mostly by mailout procedures and were not assessed at the Institute. There were 26 creatives in Group I and 22 less

205

creative mathematicians in Group II. Again the means fell in the expected di-
rection--I, 26.9 and II, 19.4.*

There are two points of interest here; first, creative women were less
sharply differentiated from comparison women on the art scale, and second, both
groups of women had higher averages than their male counterpart groups. The
latter difference is consistent with other results. In the original group of
people-in-general, 75 males showed an average of 15.1 on BW while 75 females
averaged 18.1. Similar differences between sexes in favor of females have
been reported for grade school children (Watson, 1964) and for high school
students (Littlejohn, 1967). The Governor's School subjects of the present
study show the same kind of trend (Welsh, 1969a).

The implications of these sex differences and their relationship to
creativity and masculinity-femininity are discussed in Chapter IX.

Research Scientists. A sample of 45 research scientists was studied by
assessment procedures at IPAR. These men were all working in industrial research settings and had varied education and training; most were physicists,
mathematicians, and electronics engineers. They were selected to be typical
of scientists of that level of creativity rather than representing renowned or
outstandingly creative scientists in different settings (Gough, 1961:III-6).

Like the groups of mathematicians, subgroups were formed within a fairly
homogeneous sample. For the research scientists, three groups of 15 each were
selected on the basis of an index derived from a statistical analysis of super-
visor and peer ratings (p. III-7).

A very nice progression from most creative to least creative subgroups
appeared for BW: I, 30.7; II, 22.1; and III, 19.2. Like Men Mathematicians
II, even Scientists III fell above the mean for men-in-general.

A correlation was run for all of the 45 subjects for the art scale
against criterion ratings of creativity "and the coefficient of .41 is in fact
the highest observed for any of the tests or questionnaires tried in the assessment" (p. III-16).

Writers. A mixed group of 56 professional writers and 10 student writers
was studied before the IPAR psychologists had completely worked out their assessment procedures. Thus, not all of the nominated writers were studied completely and the division into more or less creative subgroups was less clearly
specified (Barron, 1961:II-3).

The mean BW score for 20 Writers I is reported as 31.5 (p. V-16), but in a
later publication the mean for 19 Writers I is given as a slightly higher value

---

*In a later report with a total sample of 60 men, the art scale means
were reported to be 27.5 for creatives and 18.5 for comparison mathematicians
(Helson and Crutchfield, 1970:253).

of 32.9 (Barron, 1965:22). Since an average score for the less creative writers was not reported, there is no way of knowing whether they were differentiated by the art scale. At any rate, it can be seen that Writers I did score far above the mean for people-in-general as expected.

Summary for all Groups

For each of the groups discussed above, means on the BW Art Scale were higher on the average than the mean for people-in-general. If one assumes a 50-50 statistical probability for each difference falling in this direction, then the combined probability for all eleven groups having means higher than people-in-general is 1/2 raised to the eleventh power; this comes out to only one chance in 2048--surely an unlikely occurrence on this basis.

Using the same statistical argument for the direction of differentiation within groups also gives a significant probability value: Architects I and Scientists I have only one chance in three of being highest, and women and men Mathematicians I each have one chance in two of being higher. The combined probability that the most creative subgroups would by chance all exceed the less creative is only one chance out of 36.

It seems fair to conclude that the art scale has some claim as an index positively associated with creativity.

STUDENT GROUPS

Artists. A study of art students enrolled in the Newcomb Art School of Tulane University was reported by John C. Rosen (1955). He administered the BW Art Scale to 44 students, 22 in the first year and 22 in advanced classes. Eight members of the art faculty were tested and a matched group of non-artist faculty was also given the scale.

The mean scores in order of magnitude were: art faculty, 41.1; advanced students, 40.7; beginning students, 39.0; and non-artists, 22.1. Although the first three groups did not differ significantly from each other, the order was in the expected direction. The non-artist faculty group was, however, significantly lower than all three art groups.

Faculty ratings of the originality of the students' work showed a significant correlation of .40 with the art scale. Grade point average (approximately half of the courses were not studio art classes) correlated slightly lower with the BW although the correlation of .34 was still statistically significant.

Writers. Students in a creative writing course at the University of North Carolina, Chapel Hill, were tested with the Revised Art Scale (Welsh, 1959). There were 16 subjects each in one advanced section and two regular sections. The advanced section averaged higher on the RA with 46.4 while the regular sections had means of 40.9 and 39.1.

For the two regular sections the instructors ranked the students for their originality and creativity as judged by stories written during the term. Rank order correlations of .40 and .35 were obtained which fail to reach statistical significance because of the small number, but which are at least consistent in direction with other findings.

It is interesting to note that not only were these student writers far above the level of people-in-general, but also that they scored much higher than the creative writers studied by Barron (see pp. 206-07 above). Some light may be shed on this difference by comments that Barron offered in a discussion of this group of subjects.

> Although all these writers were actively engaged in creative work, they did differ widely among themselves in the goals of their work and in the audiences they reached. Thirty of them were writers of wide renown who are generally considered important artists in the field of writing; their names were obtained by asking three faculty members in the English Department and one in the Drama Department at the University of California to nominate writers of a conspicuously high degree of originality and creativeness. Twenty-six others are successful and productive writers who were not nominated as outstandingly creative, but who have clearly made their mark in the field of writing.... I wish to make it quite clear that I am not suggesting that one group is creative and the other is not.... I must say quite honestly that some of the writers nominated as outstandingly creative appeared to me to be less creative than many of those who were not so nominated, and among the writers who were not mentioned by the nominators (and hence by this exclusion defined simply as representative of their craft) were persons of a high order of creative ability. (1968:237)

Perhaps, if Barron is right about the level of creativity, had the BW scores been reported for Writers II, their mean might have exceeded that for Writers I and might be closer to the North Carolina groups. At any rate, it is encouraging to find that persons whose stock in trade is verbal facility may score as high as those in graphic and pictorial arts.

Undergraduate Women. In addition to her work with mathematicians, Ravenna Helson has studied two senior classes at Mills College in Oakland, California, a private liberal arts college for women. Various subgroups from the total of 135 subjects were chosen in different ways for special analyses. Of particular interest is a group of 23 women who scored high on an index of imaginative and artistic interests. Within this group were 12 subjects who had also been among the 36 women nominated by the faculty "as having shown outstanding potential for creative work in the arts, sciences, or humanities"

(Helson, 1966b:4). The creative subgroup had a mean art scale score of 37.1 while the other subgroup averaged 29.8; the difference was significant at the .05 level using a one-tailed t test. It should be noted that not only was the mean score for the more creative subgroup higher than the less creative, but also that both scored far above the mean of people-in-general as would be consistent with their high scores on the index of imaginative and artistic interest.

For both senior classes of the Mills College women, correlations of the art scale scores with the creativity criterion were .38 and .15. It is noted, however, that these correlations may be attenuated by the distributions of scores since "the mean scores of both creatives and comparison subjects--36 and 31 respectively--are quite high" (1967b:219).

A follow-up study after five years, with retesting on some of the same instruments originally used, showed that creatives still scored higher on the art scale, 35.9 to 29.2 (p. 233). An evaluation was made of creativity manifested since graduation from college by these subjects. One finding of special significance is a comparison of a subgroup of 13 subjects who had not been rated as creative while in college but who were high on manifest creativity since that time, with a subgroup of 14 who had been nominated by the faculty as creative and had also been high on creativity since. This latter, "nominated" group scored higher on a number of measures including the art scale. Therefore, it seems that a "group that might be considered to have been overlooked appears less highly qualified than the group identified by the faculty" (p. 234).

Siblings of the Mills College Women were also studied. A subgroup of 22 creatives having brothers and sisters showd an art scale mean of 35.9 compared to 77 other subjects with a mean of 29.2. Six brothers of creatives averaged 24.3 while brothers of the others scored 21.2.

Sex differences are shown here as in other studies noted above, since the sisters in both groups scored higher than brothers; for the creatives the mean was 33.4 contrasted with 27.3. "The most conspicuous finding shown...is the consistent superiority of the creatives and their brothers and sisters on intuition, complexity of outlook, and the other cognitive traits relevant to creativity" (1968a:595). There is thus a tendency for an intrafamilial association of art scale scores.

High School. Charles E. Schaefer (1968) studied 400 male and 400 female students selected from 10 high schools in the New York metropolitan area. Each of eight groups ($N = 100$) was matched for sex, school attended, class in which enrolled, grade level, and grade point average. Four groups were used as controls for groups selected as creative on the basis of teacher nomination and cut-off scores on Guilford's Alternate Uses and Consequences tests. Boys were either "artistic," which included art and writing, or scientific, but girls were placed in either art or writing since so few produced a scientific work or product that could be evaluated by teachers.

The Revised Art Scale was used and mean scores for the groups are: artistic boys--creative 37.5, control 30.6; scientific boys--creative and control, 31.5 and 30.0, respectively; art girls--creative and control, 37.7 and 35.8; writing girls--creative and control, 38.7 and 36.6. All of the differences are in the expected direction but only the first is statistically significant. There was also a significant difference for sex with girls averaging higher as is typically found.

Schaefer pointed out that both scientific groups of boys are relatively low and quite similar in value on RA. It is suggested that this "may be attributed to a field-related preference by scientists for a number of designs that are simple, balanced, and orderly in nature. In this connection, both the creative and the control boys in the science field shows remarkably similar scores on the Order Scale of the Adjective Check List (ACL), while the creative groups in the other specialties scored markedly lower than their controls" (1968:1101). This is an interesting observation and is discussed in Chapter VII, p. 118.

The failure of RA to achieve statistical significance between creatives and controls for the girls is attributed to the possibility "that academically talented adolescent girls in these fields generally possess a relatively high level of artistic appreciation" (p. 1102). (See Chapter IX for a discussion of the relationship of sex to creativity.)

It may be noted that all eight groups averaged higher on the RA than most high school groups previously reported and this raises two questions; first, whether there may be some regional differences, particularly in school situations, and second, whether there may be some trend over time for higher scores on the art scale. Most high school groups tested at an earlier time fell into the 20-25 range of means; more recent studies seem to have risen to the 25-30 level while all of Schaefer's groups, control and creative alike, scored in the 30's. Whether this is a meaningful trend or merely a statistical drift related to test instrument familiarity or sophistication cannot be easily determined.

Primary Grades. An extensive analysis of data from the Figure Preference Test was carried out by Stuart E. Golann in his doctoral dissertation, "The Creativity Motive" (1961), based on large groups of subjects at the grade school level. Of special interest are two subgroups of pupils.

Children in the third and fifth grades selected works of art from those of their peers to be shown at a county art exhibit. Scores on the Revised Art Scale for 12 subjects whose art work was chosen had a mean of 31.8 while the mean for the entire group of 139 pupils was only 22.7.

In his eighth grade group, 11 children whose work was awarded a prize in a nationally sponsored art competition averaged 36.5 on RA compared to 26.5 for the total group of 200 pupils.

Although these subgroups had not been selected by any formal criterion specified as creativity, the results are clearly in the expected direction.

It is singularly striking that whether the children were honored by peers or by competent adult judges, the selected subgroups scored significantly higher on the art scale.

Another extensive study which did not use a formal creativity criterion but which is also of interest because of results on the art scale was conducted by W. Gene Watson (1964). He studied three matched groups of 132 subjects each from all of the grades from third through ninth. The three groups were differentiated on the basis of scores on standard intellectual measures into a mentally retarded group and normal pupils who were either in regular classes or in special classes for the gifted.

The retardates averaged 22.5 on RA while those in regular classes had a mean of 30.8 and the gifted pupils were slightly higher at 31.5. Thus, although the mental retardates who might be considered noncreative on *a priori* grounds scored significantly lower on the art scale, the two normal groups did not differ. This latter finding is important since it indicates that children designated as "gifted" merely because of intellectual superiority, in this case, an IQ score over 125 on the Wechsler Intelligence Scale for Children, were not different on the art scale from children in the middle range of intelligence who fell between 90 and 110 on the California Short-Form Test of Mental Maturity. Other findings related to art scale scores and intelligence are summarized in Chapter V (pp. 73-75).

ORIGINALITY

Graduate Students. Originality is an important element in creativity and is often used as a synonym for creativity itself. In some of the early assessment procedures at IPAR, several groups of graduate students and medical students were studied. The faculties of the various departments from which the students were selected had rated the students on three variables: Personal Soundness, Originality, and Scholarly Promise. Results from the first rated variable, Personal Soundness, have been reported by Frank Barron (1968: Chap. 5), but material on the other variables must be gotten from unpublished IPAR papers.

Scores on the BW Art Scale were correlated with rated Originality for three different groups of graduate students and one group of medical students. The size of the groups and the coefficients of correlation are as follows for the four groups respectively: 30, .30; 40, .45; 32, .19; and 40, .29. (H.G. Gough, personal communication). All of the correlations are in the expected direction and the largest value reaches a respectable level of significance.

Military Officers. The psychologists at IPAR studied a group of 100 captains in the U.S. Air Force who "are not themselves especially selected for originality in relation to the population in general. Nevertheless...some of the 100 captains are regularly original in comparison with the remainder, while others are regularly unoriginal in relation to the entire group" (Barron, 1968: 202).

A special index of originality was developed from a battery of eight measures including the Rorschach inkblots, Thematic Apperception Test, Unusual Uses, and other Guilford tests (see Chapter III, pp. 41-45). The 15 subjects scoring highest on the Originality index were compared with the 15 lowest scoring subjects on a number of tests. The more original subgroup was significantly higher on the art scale with a mean of 19.4 compared to 12.7 for the less original. Although both subgroups fall near the mean for people-in-general, consistent with Barron's observations as noted above, there seems to be some relationship even within this limited range of scores between the art scale and originality.

ARTISTIC AND AESTHETIC INTERESTS

Aesthetic Judgment. The art scale was included in a study of aesthetic sensitivity by Irvin L. Child (1962). Subjects were asked to indicate their preferences for paintings shown in postcard-size reproductions. Scores on the BW were positively correlated with "aesthetic value" as determined by judges for two groups of 22 undergraduates each; the correlation coefficient for Yale subjects was .32 while a significant correlation of .45 was obtained for Stanford students. For these subjects, the art scale was negatively related to "group preference" as discussed below.

In a later study using 138 Yale students, a statistically significant correlation of .18 was obtained between BW and "aesthetic judgment" although Child comments that "this correlation may well be connected entirely with a common relation to variables of art background; for when these are controlled, it drops to +.09. The relationship seems remarkably low in view of the way the Art Scale was developed" (1965:502). Yet, as pointed out above in Chapter IV, WFPT items were not themselves meant in any way to be aesthetic objects and were deliberately drawn *not* to have any obvious artistic merit. It is a tenable hypothesis that the crucial variable in the relationship is a temperamental or personality characteristic that leads certain people to have an interest in art, to have better taste or aesthetic judgment, and to obtain higher scores on the art scale. If any one of the variables is controlled, the remaining relationships are bound to be attenuated.

Preference for Paintings. In the IPAR assessment of graduate students, one of the tasks used was the sorting of a set of 105 postcard-size reproductions of paintings. For a group of 40 male graduate students the distribution of scores on the art scale was such that eliminating the four middle cases resulted in two distinct subgroups separated by 20 points on BW.

The high art scale subgroup and the low subgroup showed opposite tendencies for many of the paintings. Liked *best of all* by the highs and *least of all* by the lows were works by Picasso, Modigliani, Gris, Toulouse-Lautrec, and Vuillard. Liked best by the lows and least by the highs were paintings by Veneziano, Botticelli, Corot, Lippi, Leonardo, Gainsborough, Raeburn, and Clouet. An interpretation was made of these disparate sets of preferences and rejections.

The high art scale subgroup "approves the modern, the radically experimental, the primitive, and the sensual, while disliking what is religious, aristocratic, traditional, and emotionally controlled" (Barron, 1952:392).

The low art scale subgroup on the other hand "approves good breeding, religion, and authority, and rejects the daring, the esoteric, the 'unnatural,' and the frankly sensual" (p. 390).

CONFORMITY AND INDEPENDENCE

These two concepts seem to be negatively related although they are not necessarily the opposite sides of the same coin. Traditionally it has been held that creative persons are basically nonconformists and are relatively more independent than most people.

Although a measure of independence *per se* has not been developed for the WFPT, a measure of "conformance" is afforded by the CF scale. This scale was developed by finding a set of items on which there was the greatest agreement in preferences by 150 people-in-general and approximately 50 artists. There are 38 items on the CF scale, 13 "Like" and 25 "Don't Like" (Welsh, 1959), and it is scored in the direction of agreement with the consensus. A high score, then, indicates conforming to group preferences.

Because of the manner in which items were selected, the scale tends toward a skew distribution of scores with most groups showing a mean near 27 or 28 and very few individual scores falling below 20. The original subjects showed the following means and standard deviations: men, 27.9 and 5.4; women, 28.3 and 5.0. A group of 100 male neuropsychiatric patients fell only slightly lower with a mean of 27.1 while 53 Chamber of Commerce office managers were somewhat higher at 28.7. Younger age groups typically fall lower on CF than adults, and the Governor's School adolescents show this trend; the mean for boys is 26.3 with the girls slightly below at 25.6.

It might be expected that the art scale and CF would be negatively related despite the fact that a group of artists was used in developing the conformance scale. Negative correlations were found for the Governor's School subjects. For the boys, correlations with CF are -.56 for the BW and -.55 for RA; for girls, the values are -.50 and -.47. A similar level of correlation has been reported for 177 female college students with a correlation between BW and CF of -.48 (Wrightsman and Cook, 1965).

Campus Conformity. Although the CF scale has not been widely used in studies to the extent that the art scale has been, there is one case in which both scales were scored. These data were given in an unpublished undergraduate term paper in Social Psychology at the University of North Carolina by Lou Johnson and Jenny Whitehurst (personal communication, 1960). Twenty-three undergraduate women living in the same sorority house were given the WFPT and were rated on a five-point scale for "conformity" in dress, speech patterns, campus attitude, dating behavior, and sorority attitude.

Despite the small size of the sample, statistics for the two scales
are typical; the mean and standard deviation for CF was 27.0 and 4.00, for
RA, 30.1 and 15.9. Correlation between the two scales was -.39. Neither
the use of slang in speech or enthusiasm in sorority attitude were related
to either scale. However, girls high on CF were most conforming in dress (r =
.47), defined as "Ivy League" at that time; least conforming in dress was a
subgroup low on CF and high on RA. The opposite subgroup, high on CF and low on
RA, showed the least participation in campus activities. The high RA girls
had more social life with the subgroup low on CF and low on RA having fewest
dates.

It is possible that the pattern of the two scales may lead to better understanding of conforming behavior than either by itself. At any rate, the
art scale seems to show some negative relationship to conformance in a college
setting.

Independence of Judgment. An experimental approach based on the work
of Solomon Asch has frequently been followed in which subjects are placed in
the position of being a member of a group ostensibly formed to give judgments about such matters as the relative lengths of different lines (see Baughman and Welsh, 1962:234-39). Individual members give their reports aloud and
it is arranged that the actual subject gives his judgment toward the last. On
certain trials the rest of the group, who are actually confederates of the experimenter, give contrived reports that are contrary to the evidence of actual
stimulus material.

The question to be determined is whether the real subject will yield to
the false group reports or will remain independent. In one study (Barron,
1968: Chap. 14) it was reported that about 25% of college students remained independent while about 25% yielded on eight to twelve of the experimental trials.

These two groups were differentiated by the BW scale with 43 independent
subjects obtaining a higher mean at 20.4, while 42 yielders had an average of
16.8.

In the study of aesthetic judgment discussed above, Child reported negative correlations between art scale scores and degree of individual agreement
with group preference; although with the small numbers, neither value was significant, the correlations for Stanford subjects was -.19, for Yale, -.37 (1962:
505). Thus, while high BW subjects tended to agree with the aesthetic value
of the paintings, they tended to disagree with group preferences. This may be
interpreted as greater independence, or less conformance, in aesthetic judgment.

PERSONAL COMPLEXITY

In an early attempt to formulate a general concept of the BW Art Scale,
Barron focused on one of the most obvious characteristics of the items in the
measure, namely that many were either relatively simple or rather complex in

general appearance. Of course, the nature of the items in the scale is in
fact more complex than this simple dichotomy implies; this was true of the
original factor analysis that suggested the development of the art scale discussed above (Chap. IV, p. 61).

Moving from these stimulus characteristics of the scale, Barron decided
that "the designations *Complex person* and *Simple person* will be employed to
indicate a modal high scorer and a modal low scorer, respectively" (1953:165).
He then reviewed the IPAR findings from the study of the 40 graduate students
cited above plus some data from other graduate students, medical students, and
undergraduates.

In a summary, the following pattern of relationships to the art scale
and the personality variable of complexity was given:

1. It is related positively to personal tempo, verbal fluency, impulsive-
    ness, and expansiveness.

2. It is related negatively in one sample to naturalness, likeability,
    lack of deceitfulness, adjustment, and abundance values, but in
    other samples a revised form of the measure shows no significant
    relationship to these variables....

3. It is related positively to originality, good taste, and artistic
    expression, and its revised form in two other samples shows signi-
    ficant positive correlations with intellect, sense of humor, breadth
    of interest, and cathexis of intellectual activity (none of which
    were significantly related to it in the first sample).

4. It is related positively to sensuality, sentience, esthetic inter-
    est, effeminacy, and femininity in men.

5. It is related negatively to rigidity and constriction.

6. It is related negatively to control of impulse by repression, and
    positively to expression of impulse and to breakdown of repression.

7. It is related negatively to political-economic conservatism, to
    subservience to authority, to ethnocentrism, and to social conformity.

8. It is related positively to independence of judgment.

(Barron, 1953:171-72)

An objection to the designation of the stimulus dimension as simplicity/
complexity (S/C) was raised by E.W. Moyles, Read D. Tuddenham, and Jack Block
(1965) on the basis that an important aspect, symmetry/asymmetry (S/A) had been
ignored. They commented in a footnote: "One may speculate that Barron focused
upon S/C rather than S/A...inasmuch as S/A applied to *persons* is more an anatomi-
cal than a psychological variable. However, his usage could easily lead to the

indiscriminate use of the Barron-Welsh Art Scale for the invidious categoriza-
tion of 'simple' *vs* 'complex' people" (Moyles *et al.*, 1953:686).

The results of their study, that the two dimensions* can be disentangled
in the WFPT and that they are not important general influences in individual
preferences, is tangential to the present summary. There is no doubt, however, that the term "simple" tends to have negative connotations as contrasted
with "complex" despite Barron's disclaimer: "It was emphasized that these
types have both their effective and their ineffective aspects, so far as human
functioning is concerned. At times there is considerable merit in the simple
view, while on other occasions some ease may profitably be sacrificed for
greater phenomenal richness" (p. 171).

CROSS-CULTURAL STUDIES

Since the WFPT was developed and validated in the United States, it is
important to learn whether or not the findings reported from American groups
can be generalized to other cultures. The test was intended to be useful in
other cultures and would, it was hoped, make comparison possible on the various scales of the test.

An important series of studies has been conducted in India by Manas
Raychaudhuri, Rabindra Bharati University, Calcutta, and his associates in
the area of creativity and related psychological dimensions.

Artists. An essential cross-validation of the art scale was accomplished
using a group of 60 artists and a matched group of 75 university graduate students. The artists comprised two subgroups, 35 students in fine arts and 25
commercial art students who were "picked up randomly from a list of 'promising
and creative' students of the Institution supplied by the faculty members"
(Raychaudhuri, 1963:14). The mean RA score for the fine artists was 41.7 and
for the commercial artists, 39.6, while the non-artists fell at 24.6 The fine
artists thus scored higher on the art scale, although their mean was not statistically different from the commercial artists.

Both artist groups, however, were significantly higher than the non-
artist graduate student group. These findings on RA parallel very closely the
report of Rosen using BW (as reported in Chapter IV and in this Appendix,
p. 207), and constitute an additional replication of the art scale's ability
to differentiate artists from non-artists. It may be noted that the latter
group had an average that is higher than that for people-in-general; for the
most part, student groups tend to average in the 20 to 30 range so that Raychaudhuri's results are typical in every regard.

---

*Other studies have also questioned the equation of symmetry with sim-
plicity and asymmetry with complexity (Grove and Eisenman, 1970).

Musicians. Since musicians do not express themselves in visual and pictorial ways as painters and other graphic artists do, it would be reassuring to find that the art scale might be useful with this "non-visual" group. Raychaudhuri compared a group of 30 professional musicians who had been "nominated as 'creative' by a panel of 'experts' in music" to a matched group of 50 subjects "engaged in the non-artistic professions *viz.*, Office-Work, Sales, Business, etc." (Raychaudhuri, 1966:68).

The musicians obtained a mean RA of 29.0 which, although lower than the artists cited above, was significantly above the non-artist professional's mean of 19.9. Again, it may be noted that the non-student control group is closer to the mean of people-in-general than university students.

Delinquents and Criminals. An interesting study was carried out by Maitra, Mukerji, and Raychaudhuri (1967) to determine whether or not scales from the WFPT would distinguish "the perceptual preference style of the delinquents and the criminals who, despite their ineptness, show considerable artistic creativity" (p. 7).

There were four groups of 20 subjects each, two experimental and two control. One experimental group was "composed of 20 juveniles of 14-18 age group showing considerable artistic creativity who are now detained at the State Borstal for their delinquent behavior" while the other was "composed of adult offenders of 29-34 age group who are serving sentences in a Calcutta jail and showed creativity in music and painting" (p. 8). Control groups which showed normal social behavior but gave no evidence of artistic creativity were selected to match the experimental groups in age.

A median test was used to demonstrate that scores on RA were significantly higher for the experimental groups; for the adolescents, values were 28.5 and 24.5, for the adults, 30.5 and 20.0. Artistic adults were somewhat more clearly distinguished from their non-artistic controls than the adolescent groups.

Conformance as measured by the CF scale was also reported and the groups were significantly separated in the expected direction by this scale also. The medians for the juveniles were 17.5 *versus* 22.5, while the adults had medians of 21.5 *versus* 28.5. The latter value for control adults is very close to that for ordinary adult American men and women and suggests that preferences for figures of the kind in the WFPT are relatively independent of culture.

Rural and Urban Groups. In India, at least, there seems to be no difference between urban and rural adults on the RA scale. Raychaudhuri (1965) tested three matched groups of subjects: 50 adults of West Bengal who lived in rural areas and had not been exposed to cosmopolitan city life, 50 adults who lived in Calcutta, and 60 adults having both rural and urban background who were nominated by a panel of experts as having artistic ability in painting, music, or literature. A subgroup was formed by selecting randomly 25 subjects from the second group of urban dwellers who were given two lectures on modern art and abstract painting after the initial testing.

All groups were given the art scale, the Rorschach scored for number of good form responses, and an inventory scale of intolerance of ambiguity. Contrary to the hypotheses of the study, the urban and rural groups did not differ significantly on any of the measures; RA means were 24.5 and 23.2. The artistic group, however, had significantly higher scores on the art scale (*M* = 40.8), a greater number of Rorschach responses, and more tolerance for ambiguity It is of interest that exposure to lectures raised the tolerance of ambiguity scores for that subgroup but did not change the number of Rorschach responses or the scores on the art scale.

Raychaudhuri comments that the latter "two tests are, in a sense, disguised--permitting little conscious comprehension of the underlying testing principles and the state of assessment devices. But the inventory used here requires the subject to evaluate on cognitive-ideational level certain ambiguous issues and to indicate his conscious acceptance or rejection for them. While the perceptual style and preferences explored by the other two tests stem from more stable and deeper substratum of personality-organization, the inventory elicits data from relatively surface, conscious and intellectual areas of personality" (p. 191). It can be pointed out, once again, that the artistic group which included subjects from painting, music, and literature showed a mean score typical of American artists.

Egyptian Groups. The WFPT has been given to a number of groups in Egypt and seems to differentiate artists, architects, and sculptors from non-artist student groups (Michel Wahba, personal communication) and has been employed successfully as a test with illiterate subjects.

A comparison of average proportion of "Like" responses to individual items for the Egyptian groups and a number of American groups show them to be very similar (Welsh, 1969b). This finding strengthens the implications of Raychaudhuri's work in India and suggests that the test and the art scale may be successfully employed with different cultures.

American Indians. A modified version of the WFPT containing only 144 items was given to 25 subjects from the Attawapiskatt Indian group in Canada by John and Irma Honigmann, University of North Carolina, Chapel Hill. It was possible to score the art scale, and the mean and standard deviation are 30.4 and 8.2, respectively; unlike most groups, men were slightly higher at 32.2 on RA while women averaged 28.5. Since the sex groups comprised only 13 and 12 cases each, perhaps not too much emphasis should be placed on the difference. At the same time, the relatively high RA men for the entire group needs to be explained in view of the Honigmanns' report (personal communication) that the Attawapiskatt do not seem to be at all creative or artistic.

Richard Preston, University of North Carolina, tested a small group of Cree and Objibwa children. All but one of the subjects scored above 20 on RA and the median value was 34; the highest score was 49 and the lowest only 7.

American Chinese. Some work has been carried out with another modified version of the WFPT by Don Lim who indicated in a preliminary report that there seemed to be no differences between Chinese and non-Chinese adolescents in their preferences (see Welsh, 1959:18-19).

Other Studies. Although the art scale is not included in the modified form of the WFPT developed by Robert Van de Castle, he has reported the use of the test to study perceptual maturity with various groups including Cuna Indians of Central America (1962, 1965; see Also Aiken, 1967:15-19).

MISCELLANEOUS GROUPS

Golann (1961) has assembled mean scores on the art scale for various groups of subjects from a number of unpublished studies. In descending magnitude of BW, the numbers of subjects and the means are: 80 Ph.D. candidates, 24; 44 upper division college students, 22; 80 medical seniors, 21; 92 college students, 19; 50 Vassar College alumnae, 14; 26 medical inpatients, 14; 149 neuropsychiatric patients, 13.

MacKinnon (1961b) interpreted a BW mean of 21.5 for student engineers as indicating the need for stimulation of aesthetic interests in this group if they are to become creative.

A selected group of 37 "leaders and innovators" in Irish management was studied by some members of IPAR under the direction of Frank Barron. The mean BW score was only 18.4, close to that for ordinary American groups. "This finding may have real implications for further education and personal development of these managers. It is becoming increasingly recognized in the technologically advanced countries that uglification of both cities and countryside will occur if those in charge of matters are not alert to questions of esthetic value. The proper design of environment requires an artist's eye" (Barron and Egan, 1968).

A group of 125 male neuropsychiatric patients with various diagnoses in the Veterans Administration Hospital, Palo Alto, California, had a mean RA score of 20.7 with *SD* 11.9 (Lim and Ullman, 1961). It is interesting that this group fell somewhat higher than the patients cited above by Golann and also the Minneapolis VA patients noted in Chapter IV (see also Welsh, 1959). The Palo Alto group was also somewhat lower than the midwest patients on conformance with a mean CF score of 25.7 and a somewhat greater standard deviation of 6.0. Whether these differences represent sampling fluctuations, diagnostic vagaries, or regional differences cannot be determined.

The present writer has calculated a mean score on RA of 13.7 for managers in Chamber of Commerce offices from various sections of the United
States; their relatively high CF score was previously cited.

Higher than any of these miscellaneous groups is the reported mean BW
score of 31.5 for 15 team members of the first American expedition to attempt
climbing Mount Everest (Barron, 1965:22). That mountain climbers tend to
score higher than most noncreative groups is particularly interesting in light
of some of the items that appeared on scales developed in the present research
(see Table VI-2, "Activities").

OTHER STUDIES

Social Attitudes. An extensive investigation of social attitudes and
other variables was conducted by Lawrence S. Wrightsman and Stuart W. Cook
(1964) using 177 paid volunteer subjects. They were female, white college
students under the age of 25 and most of them were from southern or border
states. A factor analysis of 73 personality, attitude, and aptitude variables
was carried out which resulted in a nine factor solution.

The art scale had a loading of -.59 on factor I, "rigidity," and -.25
on III, "anti-Negro attitudes," thus indicating that high BW scores tend to
be associated with less rigid and less prejudiced attitudes. The conformance
scale was also used and had a positive loading of .35 on rigidity which is consistent with the negative relation between CF and the art scale previously
noted. CF also had a loading of .34 on VII, "tolerance for unpleasantness,"
which, judging from other variables loaded on this factor, seems also to imply
a need for social approval. Neither of the WFPT scales were loaded on the
aptitude factor, IV; this is consistent with the argument advanced earlier that
the test seems to be relatively free from intellectual requirements as measured by standard intelligence tests.

Social Intelligence. The art scale was found to be unrelated to academic
intelligence in a study by Lee Sechrest and Douglas N. Jackson (1961). A
forced-choice form of BW was used with 60 female subjects who were in the first
year of nurses training and were almost all 18 years of age. Although an r of
only -.07 was obtained with academic intelligence, a significant correlation
of .35 with "social intelligence" was found. It was noted in Chapter II that
the relationship of social intelligence and ordinary intelligence test scores
may be complex.

Curiosity. Hy Day has pursued the relationship between creativity and
curiosity (1968a) and in one study found a significant correlation, .22, between BW and a Test of Specific Curiosity in a group of 247 seventh and eighth
grade pupils in a Canadian junior high school (1968b). A larger group ($N =$
429) of 7th, 8th, and 9th graders from the same school showed a somewhat lower
correlation, .14, but even this value is significant beyond the .01 level.

Perceptual Speed. James Bieri, Wendy M. Bradburn, and M. David Galinsky studied sex differences in perceptual behavior (1958). Their subjects were 62 female and 50 male undergraduates, of whom 41 were from Radcliffe and 35 from Harvard College. The BW mean and standard deviation for women were 30.89 and 12.52, with a range of scores from 6 to 52; for men the values were 28.00, 12.46, and 2 to 54. Once again the sex differences in favor of female groups are evident.

One of the measures used in the study was Witkin's Embedded Figures Test which was correlated significantly with the art scale for men, -.36, but not for women (r = -.08). A comparison was made of means on BW for the ten most extreme scorers on Embedded Figures. For females, the ten high scorers averaged 26.80 and, while the low scorers fell higher at 32.10, the difference was not significant. Males showed a difference significant at the .03 level, 20.90 to 34.90. Apparently males higher on the art scale show greater perceptual speed in this kind of task.

Motion Picture Preference. Robert E. Roy utilized the art scale in a study (1970) based on the theory of creativity proposed by Stark (1965), which suggests that there are two distinct types of creativity. One type, "experiential," is related to meaning, experience, and expansion of consciousness; it is measured by Rorschach movement responses. The second, "novelty," is related to novelty *per se*, action, and problem-solving; it can be measured by many of Guilford's originality tests such as Plot Titles, Consequences, and Unusual Uses.

College students who had consistently expressed preferences for motion pictures designated as examples of the two types of creativity were used as subjects. Although the Rorschach and the Guilford tests failed to distinguish the two groups, the Myers-Briggs Type Indicator and the art scale showed significant differences. The RA mean for 14 experiential subjects was 43.07 while 12 novelty subjects averaged 32.50.

Drug Users. A study of undergraduate students who are admitted users of hallucinogenic drugs has been conducted at the University of Vermont. Howard Savin (personal communication, 1969) has reported that 26 experimental subjects who voluntarily participated in the study averaged 41.3 on RA while 29 controls fell significantly lower at 25.9.

Undergraduate Achievement. Gale H. Roid (1967) studied 872 undergraduate students at the University of Oregon electively enrolled in one of two psychology courses, "Personality" or "Individual Differences and Development." Students were randomly assigned to sections with four different instructional formats: traditional lecture with frequent quizzes, lectures and frequent papers, self-study instruction and quizzes, or self-study and papers. In addition to course grades, a measure of satisfaction with the course and the type of instruction was obtained by a method likely to insure maximum candor from the students.

A test battery including the WFPT had been given to the students and in Roid's study a number of scales were systematically examined by analysis of variance for the conditions and the combinations of conditions in the experimental design. The art scale showed several significant differences between groups.

Students higher on RA expressed more satisfaction in writing papers than in taking objective quizzes in discussion sections of the course; students lower on RA showed a reversed pattern and preferred the quizzes. Irrespective of the type of teaching format, students with higher RA scores obtained higher final course grades. They also tended to have higher overall grade point averages.

In this study, scores on RA were significantly related to college achievement and to satisfaction with type of instruction. It is of particular interest that the high RA student preferred the more independent and personalized activity of writing papers to the more structured and impersonal objective quizzes.

Originality and Complexity. Of specific importance in the present context is a study employing the BW scale carried out by Russell Eisenman (1969) with a large group (N = 302) of undergraduate students at Temple University. Two other tests were given, Unusual Uses (list all of the uses you can think of for a brick, a paper clip, and a pencil) and Complexity (preferences for polygons with different numbers of sides). In addition, when subjects had completed the tests, they were asked to rate the degree to which they liked being in the study and also to indicate what they considered the purpose of the study to be. Responses to the last request such as "creativity," "originality," or "test of thinking" were counted as being aware of the purpose. Unusual Uses results were scored for Fluency (total number of responses) and Originality (number of responses that occurred only once per hundred); also an Originality/Fluency ratio was calculated.

Correlations with the art scale were as follows: Fluency, .27; Originality, .38; Originality/Fluency, .39; Complexity, .55; Liking, .02; and Awareness, .03. The latter two correlations are statistically insignificant while the first four are beyond the .001 level of probability. Complexity showed a similar pattern although the coefficients are slightly lower.

BW and Complexity can both be considered to be more subtle measures in this study than Unusual Uses since Originality and Originality/Fluency scores were significantly correlated with both Awareness and Liking while Fluency showed a significant correlation with Liking. It will be recalled that Raychaudhuri commented on the relatively disguised nature of the art scale (p.218).

A factor analysis of the intercorrelational matrix of the seven variables employed by Eisenman has been carried out by the present writer. Four clear-cut factors emerged in the rotated solution. The first factor shows significant loadings on all three Unusual Uses variables with the loading on Fluency particularly high, plus a significant loading on Liking. The second

factor has high loadings on Complexity and BW with moderate loadings on
Originality and the Originality/Fluency ratio. The third factor has high
loadings on Awareness and Liking with a moderate loading on the ratio. The
last factor has a high loading on the ratio and a moderate loading on Originality. It is important to note that the art scale and Complexity had
loadings on the second factor only while the Unusual Uses variables loaded
across all four factors.

These results imply that the art scale and Complexity share an independent dimension quite different from Unusual Uses. While Originality and
the ratio are loaded on this dimension, Fluency is not. Thus, if creativity
is defined operationally by scores on the art scale, only the Originality
scores on the Unusual Uses test will be related to this dimension.

HEREDITY AND ENVIRONMENT

Although the crux of the problem is often implied by the phrase heredity
"versus" environment, most persons are becoming somewhat more sophisticated
about this matter and recognize that it is not an either/or problem but rather
one of the relative proportions of the total variance in a set of measures
from various sources of influence.

This problem was studied by Frank Barron in Italy using 59 pairs of
like-sex twins, 30 identical (monozygotic) and 29 fraternal (dizygotic).
One of the test measures employed was the Barron-Welsh Art Scale on which the
following results were obtained:

> The correlation in the monozygotic group is .58; in
> the dizygotic group, .07. The MZ correlation is signi-
> ficantly different from zero, but the DZ is not; they are
> significantly different from one aother (t of 3.05, p less
> than .01), and a high heritability component is indicated
> by the Holzinger heritability coefficient of .55. Whether
> what is inherited is a preference for complexity or a greater
> ability to discriminate in the esthetic realm is not alto-
> gether clear.... (1969:123)

It will be recalled that in Ravenna Helson's Mills College Study, siblings
of creative subjects tended also to get higher scores and it was suggested that
there may be some intrafamilial trend on the art scale. In view of Barron's
finding, this suggestion seems strengthened. But, to pursue the argument developed earlier, it seems likely that what is inherited (if in fact it actually
is genetically determined) is a personality or temperamental trait rather than
some specific kind of aesthetic preference or discrimination. Barron comments
further:

> For the entire sample of 118 subjects, the mean score
> on the Art Scale is 28, as compared with a mean of 14 for
> American high school groups, a highly significant difference.
> In view of the historical contribution of Italy to the arts,

> it seems possible that a higher than average level of
> esthetic discrimination may be carried in the Italian
> gene pool. (Barron, 1969:123)

This genetic hypothesis is merely absurd, but the invidious comparison
with American children is factually incorrect. All of the group means reported by Golann, Watson, Harris, Littlejohn, and the present writer fall into
the 20-30 range on the art scale and Schaeffer's means are even higher.

EXPERIMENTAL MANIPULATION OF SCORES

Among the procedures employed during IPAR assessment was a contrived
situation in which subjects were tested to see whether or not they would yield
to group pressure and change their responses (see p. 214 above). Barron has
commented in this connection that "it is interesting as a sidelight on the
centrality of esthetic choice that figures of the Art Scale are more impervious
to pressure from a fabricated consensus in the Crutchfield procedure than are
any other stimulus materials; although about 75% of all subjects will yield to
group pressure in other matters, less than 10% will yield when the judgment involves simple-symmetrical figures versus complex-assymmetrical ones" (1965:25).

It is, however, possible to alter scores on the art scale by systematic
experimental procedures. Richard N. Carrera (1968) administered 100 figures
from the WFPT including the 60 RA items to a group of 23 delinquents 10 to 15
years of age. After the initial presentation in which the subjects responded
in the usual way, an experimental subgroup was systematically reinforced on the
RA item responses by the experimenter's comments of "Good" or "Fine" to a response in the creative (high score) direction and "No" or "Uh-uh" to noncreative
responses. A significant upward shift occurred for the experimental group but
repeated administration for the control group showed little change in scores.

In an extension of this study (Carrera, Moore, and Levy, 1969) 60 undergraduate students served as subjects. They were divided into two subgroups,
high and low, on the basis of their initial RA score using a cutting score of
30. The experimenters were successful in altering their relative positions
by reinforcing noncreative responses of the highs and creative responses of
the lows.

On follow-up testing, both subgroups tended to return to their original
base line but the low group remained relatively high. That is, low RA subjects having been taught to respond like highs shifted in that direction.
"A possible implication is that it might be possible to instill creative modes
of response in low creatives with relatively long lasting results" (p. 3).
Since the highs quickly returned to their original level, "this finding suggests that aesthetic preferences associated with high creativity are much more
resistant to change than those associated with low creativity." These results seem to be congruent with those reported for aesthetic judgment as well
as for the personal independence of high scoring subjects on the art scale.

Teaching Creativity. A series of studies by George I. Brown (1964, 1965, 1966) on the teaching of creativity have also shown meaningful shifts in scores on the art scale. Subjects were students in sections of a unversity junior level course in elementary school teaching. An experimental section was taught to develop a "creative self" and methods for "triggering" it. One experimental group of 18 subjects tested in February and May showed BW means of 29.67 and 30.94, but the May-triggered mean was 38.72; counterpart means for 24 subjects in a control group were 32.71, 35.04, and 30.58 (1964:445).

In another study which used triggered noncreativity in addition to the triggered creativity, the following sequence of means for 25 subjects appeared: 25.56, 28.12, 44.36 for triggered creativity and 10.44 for triggered noncreativity (1965:47).

Role Playing. R.O. Kroger, University of Toronto, has studied the effect of the classroom setting (1967) and specific role assumption (1968) on test scores. He used selected items from the WFPT, including many from the art scale and items from the Strong Vocational Interest Blank. Appropriate differences in responses by undergraduate subjects were found in contrasting results obtained under a "military" or an "artistic" type of setting and also when the subjects were instructed to take the role of a military officer or a creative artist.

PERSONALITY CHARACTERISTICS

Graduate Students. In the IPAR study of graduate students described above in the discussion of painting preferences, an analysis was made of their self-description on an early version of Gough's Adjective Check List (see Chap. VI, p.95). In Barron's report (1952:393) he gave the following lists of adjectives with the level of discrimination between the two groups.

High art scale: (.05)--gloomy, loud, unstable, bitter, cool, dissatisfied, pessimistic, emotional, irritable, pleasure-seeking; (.10)--aloof, sarcastic, spendthrift, distractible, demanding, indifferent; (.15)--anxious, opinionated, temperamental, quick.

Low art scale: (.05)--contented, gentle, conservative, unaffected, patient, peaceable; (.10)--serious, individualistic, stable, worrying, timid, thrifty; (.15)--dreamy, deliberate, moderate, modest, responsible, foresighted; (.20)--conscientious.

Undergraduates. The Adjective Check List (ACL) and RA were given to a group of 74 undergraduate students and a comparison made of the self-descriptions of the ten highest subjects on RA with the ten lowest scorers (Welsh, 1959:15). Adjectives most consistently checked by the two groups are:

High art scale: adventurous, aggressive, argumentative, artistic, charming, cold, complicated, cynical, demanding, dominant, egotistical, flirtatious, impatient, impulsive, individualistic, lazy, mischievous, outspoken, realistic, rebellious, self-seeking, selfish, sharp-witted, shrewd, sly, snobbish, stubborn, touchy, unconventional, and wise.

Low art scale: conservative, contented, conventional, easy-going, industrious, persevering, pleasant, sentimental, and thorough.

Psychiatric Patients. A similar analysis was made on the ACL for 40 psychiatric patients who had also been given the WFPT (Welsh, 1959:15). Adjectives showing the greatest differences are listed below.

High art scale: sarcastic, despondent, hurried, inhibited, suggestible, absent-minded, affected, humorless, moody, rebellious, reserved, self-centered, snobbish, touchy, unstable, and versatile.

Low art scale: fussy, civilized, dependable, mannerly, natural, pleasure-seeking, cheerful, easygoing, industrious, mature, obliging, pleasant, and soft-hearted.

Hospital Patients. Karl V. Schultz and W.E. Knapp worked with 367 male non-psychiatric patients in the Oakland Veterans Administration Hospital, California. They compared self-descriptions on a specially constructed 100 item list of terms with scores on the 62 item card form of the Barron-Welsh Art Scale. After an informal cluster analysis they described the high and low scorers as follows:

> The self-descriptions of the low [low BW] group suggest that individuals in this group see themselves as having a low level of self-esteem and lacking in self-confidence bordering on depressive helplessness ('Always look on the dark side,' 'Tired,' 'Worn out'). These self-descriptions also seem to include a quality of anxious restlessness ('Always on the go,' 'Impatient,' 'On edge,' 'Push myself'). The inclination to seek security through conformity might conceivably be inferred from 'Play it safe,' and 'Self-conscious.'
>
> A review of the items checked significantly more often by the [high BW] group suggests rather different qualities. Persons in this group seem to see themselves as having a higher level of self-esteem, being more independent, and having a somewhat more autonomous approach to life ('Pretty clear about what I believe,' 'Thinker,' 'Rugged,' 'Like to figure things out,' and 'Different than others'). These qualities, when related to additional items such as 'Broke,' 'Nervous,' and 'Never had the breaks' might be thought of as suggesting an inner readiness to engage in problem solving in the face of odds. (Schultz and Knapp, 1959:581-84)

Although it is not possible to compare directly the results from the four analyses given above because of lack of comparability of the lists used for self-description, some general trends are apparent. It may be noted that relatively more terms appear for high scorers on the art scale. Perhaps the low scorers find fewer appropriate terms in the list for them to use. It may also mean that the lows are somewhat more guarded or are less candid in describing themselves and do not check many of the seemingly negative terms that the highs use. It may, on the other hand, imply a greater similarity in self-concept and in self-description among the lows with the highs being more diffuse and idiosyncratic.

The highs appear to be more self-oriented, independent, and willing to act autonomously while the lows are more group-oriented, accepting, and willing to seek security by conformity. The highs are rebellious but the lows accept things as they are. The lows may also be somewhat more inclined to accept themselves as they are and to be more self-consistent in the way that they describe themselves. They seem also to be more dependable, deliberate, and better organized. High scorers regard themselves as unstable and impulsive.

Despite the tentative nature of this summary, it does seem fair to say that there are marked differences in the self-concepts of the groups at the upper and lower ends of the art scale.

APPENDIX B

Name: STRONG VOCATIONAL INTEREST BLANK (SVIB)

Publisher: STANFORD UNIVERSITY PRESS
            STANFORD, CALIFORNIA 94305

Description: The SVIB (Men's form, T399) is a 399-item revision of the 400-item form previously used. The Governor's School testing was carried out with the 400-item booklet and the Men's form was employed with the girls as well as the boys. The revised manual (see ref. [2] below) indicates the comparability of the forms despite certain changes in the items and in the scales. The subject indicates his agreement with the test items by marking a special answer sheet in the appropriate direction--"Like," "Indifferent," "Dislike," "Like Most," "like Least," etc.

Purpose: This test was developed to assess a subject's similarity of interests to those of men in various occupational groups. It has been shown that people are more likely to find satisfaction in occupations for which their interests are similar than in those where they are dissimilar.

Scoring: These procedures are so complicated that it is practically impossible to use hand-scoring with the SVIB. A number of different scoring services are available and are listed in the revised manual.

Norms: Raw scores on each of the occupational scales are converted to T scores based on the distributions of scores obtained by persons actually in that particular occupation. Both manuals describe the procedures followed.

References

(1) Strong, E.K., Jr. *Manual for Strong Vocational Interest Blanks for Men and Women.* Palo Alto: Consulting Psychologists Press, 1959.

     This manual describes in detail the familiar form of the SVIB that was used in testing the Governor's School subjects.

(2) Campbell, D.P. *Manual for Strong Vocational Interest Blanks, revised.* Stanford: Stanford University Press, 1966.

Details of the current form of the SVIB are given in the revised manual which replaces the previous edition (1959) by E.K. Strong, Jr. It contains technical data about scale development and other psychometric characteristics of the test, but also devotes a section to interpretation of results. A list of more than a hundred references includes the important publications of Strong himself.

(3) Welsh, G.S. "Verbal interests and intelligence: comparison of Strong VIB, Terman CMT, and D-48 scores of gifted adolescents." *Educational and Psychological Measurement,* 1967, *27,* 349-52.

Three SVIB scales (Advertising Man, Lawyer, and Author-Journalist) were used as measures of verbal interest. Governor's School students with high verbal interests tended to score higher on a verbal test of intelligence (CMT) than a nonverbal test (D-48).

Name: GOUGH'S ADJECTIVE CHECK LIST (ACL)

Publisher: CONSULTING PSYCHOLOGISTS PRESS
577 COLLEGE AVENUE
PALO ALTO, CALIFORNIA 94306

Description: The ACL is a brief, easily administered personality test comprising a list of 300 commonly used adjectives which the subject is asked to check, thus indicating those that are "self-descriptive." As the test manual indicates, "it may be completed in 10 or 15 minutes, even by unsophisticated subjects, arouses little resistance or anxiety, and yields a wealth of potentially useful information."

Purpose: This test was especially developed for personality assessment of subjects in the normal range and has also been used widely with superior and gifted persons. It is a flexible instrument and a subject may use it to describe another person, or "it may be used by raters, judges, or observers in research or other situations as a convenient method of recording and tabulating personality attributes of persons being evaluated."

Scoring: Because of the large number of scales now available, handscoring is not feasible and it is recommended that machine or computer programmed scoring be utilized. Information is available from the publisher.

Norms: Raw scores on the 24 scales and indices currently used are converted to T scores based on statistics derived from more than 1300 men and 600 women. The norm group comprises a wide range of persons but better educated subjects are more heavily represented.

References

(1) Gough, H.G., and Heilbrun, A.B. *The Adjective Check List Manual*. Palo
     Alto: Consulting Psychologists Press, 1965.

         The manual is the major source of information about the test. It de-
     scribes the rationale and development of the ACL and furnishes scale de-
     scriptions and scoring procedures for them. An extensive bibliography is
     included.

(2) MacKinnon, D.W. "Creativity and images of the self." In White, R.W.
     (ed.), *The Study of Lives*. New York: Atherton Press, 1963.

         This study of creativity in architects has important implications for
     the assessment of adolescents as well as adults. MacKinnon describes
     various types of analyses that were carried out on the ACL and testifies
     to its utility by commenting that "it is remarkable that so simple a
     device as a list of three hundred adjectives can reveal so much about a
     person."

(3) Cashdan, S., and Welsh, G.S. "Personality correlates of creative potential
     in talented high schools students." *Journal of Personality*, 1966, *34*,
     445-55.

         Some of the findings with the ACL from Governor's School subjects are
     reported in this article and tend to parallel many observations made by
     MacKinnon.

Name: MINNESOTA MULTIPHASIC PERSONALITY INVENTORY (MMPI)

Publishers: THE PSYCHOLOGICAL CORPORATION
                304 EAST 45TH STREET
                NEW YORK, NEW YORK 10017

Description: The MMPI is an objective personality test consisting of 550 items
in the form of verbal statements to which the subject responds "True" or "False"
by marking a special answer sheet.

Purpose: Although the MMPI was originally developed to assess personality
characteristics associated with neuropsychiatric disorders and with problems of
adjustment, it has been found to be very useful in the normal range for assessment and for personality research.

Scoring: Individual records may be scored by hand but it is worthwhile to utilize
machine scoring methods when more than a few dozen subjects have been tested.
Information on scoring services is available from the publisher and the test
manual (see ref. [1]) may be consulted in this regard.

Norms: Raw scores on the MMPI are converted to T scores based on statistics derived from "Minnesota Normals." The norm group was developed from visitors to the University of Minnesota Hospitals who were not themselves under the care of a physician. The average age of this group was about 34 years and about ten grades of school had been completed.

References

(1) Hathaway, S.R., and McKinley, J.C. *Minnesota Multiphasic Personality Inventory Manual*, revised 1967. New York: The Psychological Corp., 1967.

    The revised manual should be consulted since it contains information about the different formats in which the MMPI appears and describes various scoring procedures that are now available.

(2) Dahlstrom, W.G., and Welsh, G.S. *An MMPI Handbook: A Guide to Use in Clinical Practice and Research*. Minneapolis: University of Minnesota Press, 1960.

    This handbook is the basic reference for information on the development and use of the MMPI and contains an extensive bibliography. The test manual states that "all users of the MMPI are urged to read the Handbook carefully."

(3) Hathaway, S.R., and Monachesi, E.D. *Adolescent Personality and Behavior*. Minneapolis: University of Minnesota Press, 1963.

    This volume will be invaluable in understanding the meaning of the MMPI in the adolescent age range both from the practical and the research points of view.

Name: D-48 NON-VERBAL INTELLIGENCE TEST (D-48)

Publisher: CONSULTING PSYCHOLOGISTS PRESS
               577 COLLEGE AVENUE
               PALO ALTO, CALIFORNIA   94306

Description: The D-48 is a non-language intelligence test comprising 44 actual items and four practice items. These are in the form of sets of dominoes in which the subject must discern the relationship in each series and fill in the appropriate numbers on an answer sheet for the last domino which is blank in the test booklet. This test is timed--25 minutes are allotted and subjects are informed at the end of 15 minutes that 10 minutes remain. Almost 20% of the Governor's School subjects completed all of the items but none got them all correct.

Purpose: No verbal ability, except for reading the instructions, is required for the D-48 and the test manual describes it as "essentially a non-verbal analogies test measuring primarily the 'g' or general factor in intelligence."

Scoring: A template is placed over the answer sheet and handscoring is easily accomplished. There is no "correction for guessing" since the chances of getting both halves on this basis are only one in 49 (1/7 times 1/7).

Norms: The manual gives abbreviated percentile tables for French adults (the test was adapted from the form developed by the Centre de Psychologie Appliquée) with different years of schooling. Means and standard deviations for children in French secondary schools and for a few groups of American students are also given. Since these norms were not suitable, *T* scores on the Governor's School subjects were developed and are given in Table 13 (Welsh, 1969a).

References

(1) Black, J.D. *Preliminary Manual, The D-48 Test.* Palo Alto: Consulting Psychologists Press, 1963.

     The manual is a revision and adaptation of that for the French edition and describes the background and development of the test; 11 references, mostly foreign, are included.

(2) Gough, H.G., and Domino, G. "The D-48 Test as a measure of general ability among grade school children. *Journal of Consulting Psychology,* 1963, *27,* 344-49.

     This paper describes the use of the test with fifth and sixth graders and gives correlations with school achievement.

(3) Domino, G. "Comparison of the D-48, Cattell Culture Fair, and Army Beta Tests in a sample of college males." *Journal of Consulting Psychology,* 1964, *28,* 468-69.

(4) Cantwell, Zita M. "Relationships between scores on the Standard Progressive Matrices (1938) and on the D-48 test of non-verbal intelligence and three measures of academic achievement." *Journal of Experimental Education,* 1966, *34,* 28-31.

     Subjects in this study were undergraduate females.

(5) Rafi, A.A. "The progressive matrices and the dominoes (D-48) test: a cross-cultural study." *The British Journal of Educational Psychology, 1967, (1), 37,* 117-19.

     Male college students in Lebanon were subjects in this study.

(6) Horn, J.L., and Bramble, W.J. "Second-order ability structure revealed
     in rights and wrongs scores." *Journal of Educational Psychology*, 1967,
     58, 115-22.

     Analysis of an extensive battery of intelligence tests given to prison
     inmates shows the D-48 to have high loadings on "fluid intelligence" as
     contrasted with "crystallized intelligence" measured with conventional in-
     formation tests.

     See also: SVIB ref. (3); CMT ref. (2).

SPECIAL SCALES FOR THE STRONG VOCATIONAL INTEREST BLANK*
DEVELOPED BY GEORGE S. WELSH

S-I (high origence/low intellectence) 27 items			S-II (high origence/high intellectence) 44 items			
10-D	120-D	203-D	5-L	35-D	146-I	292-least
24-D	128-D	205-L	6-L	40-L	163-L	299-most
31-I	144-D	213-L	7-D	57-L	172-L	309-most
63-L	146-D	302-most	9-L	65-D	190-D	319-most
65-L	148-D	317-most	15-D	71-L	195-L	326-gardening
91-D	153-L	339-more	17-I	78-L	223-D	333-enjoyed
107-D	159-L	345-physical	20-L	84-L	225-L	334-chance
108-D	185-D	355-many	21-D	112-L	231-L	353-book
110-L	200-L	382-yes	27-L	119-L	251-I	355-few
			28-L	126-L	271-I	369-yes
			31-L	144-L	272-I	380-no

S-III (low origence/low intellectence) 28 items			S-IV (low origence/high intellectence) 31 items		
7-L	105-L	242-L	5-I	107-L	240-L
49-L	127-L	258-L	12-D	115-L	243-I
56-I	145-D	271-L	17-D	120-L	297-least
66-I	180-L	286-I	33-D	128-L	302-least
67-L	192-L	299-least	52-I	146-L	305-least
70-L	195-D	324-waiter	70-D	148-L	313-most
71-D	244-L	333-produces	72-L	196-D	317-least
100-L	227-L	334-safe	83-L	206-I	342-inside
103-L	228-L	369-no	91-L	223-L	383-not sure
		383-yes	101-L	225-I	395-sometimes
					399-rarely

*These scales have been related to a model for personality study that contrasts two independent dimensions, "intellectence" and "origence." See Welsh, G.S. "Vocational Interests and Intelligence in Gifted Adolescents," *Educational and Psychological Measurement*, 1971, 31. 155-64. See also pp. 76-81 and 88-95 in the present work.

GOVERNOR'S SCHOOL COMBINED ITEM ANALYSIS

SVIB

S-I HIGH ORIGENCE - LOW INTELLECTENCE

(27 items in current form)*

		Item No.	Choice	Statement
PART I.	OCCUPATIONS	10	D	Author of technical book
		24	D	Civil Engineer
		31	I	Editor
		63	L	Music Teacher
		64	*I*	*Office Clerk*
		65	L	Office Manager
		91	D	Statistician
PART II.	SCHOOL SUBJECTS	107	D	Calculus
		108	D	Chemistry
		110	L	Dramatics
		120	D	Mathematics
		128	D	Physics
PART III.	AMUSEMENTS	144	D	Chess
		146	D	Bridge
		148	D	Solving mechanical puzzles
		153	L	Amusement parks
		157	*L*	*"Rough house" initiations*
		159	L	Full-dress affairs
		185	D	Making a radio set
PART IV.	ACTIVITIES	200	L	Organizing a play
		203	D	Teaching adults
		205	L	Being called by a nickname
		213	L	Acting as yell-leader
PART V.	PECULIARITIES OF PEOPLE	*253*	*D*	*People who get rattled easily*
PART VI.	PREFERENCES	302	Most	Enrico Caruso, singer
		317	Most	Chairman, Entertainment Committee

*There were 32 items on the original SVIB scale, items dropped in the current form are shown in italics.

GOVERNOR'S SCHOOL COMBINED ITEM ANALYSIS--SVIB *(continued)*

		Item No.	Choice	Statement
PART VII.	COMPARISON BETWEEN TWO ITEMS	339	Prefer	Selling article, quoted 10% above competitor (to) selling article quoted 10% below competitor
		345	Prefer	Physical activity (to) Mental activity
		355	Prefer	Many acquaintances (to) Few intimate friends
		359	*Prefer*	*Jealous people (to) Conceited people*
PART VIII.	RATING YOUR ABILITIES AND PERSONALITY	382	Yes	Put drive into the organization
		385	*Yes*	*Win confidence and loyalty*

SVIB

S-II HIGH ORIGENCE - HIGH INTELLECTENCE

(44 items in current form)*

		Item No.	Choice	Statement
PART I.	OCCUPATIONS	5	L	Artist
		6	L	Astronomer
		7	D	Athletic Director
		9	L	Author of novel
		15	D	Bank Teller
		17	I	Building Contractor
		20	L	Cartoonist
		21	D	Cashier in bank
		27	L	College Professor
		28	L	Consul
		31	L	Editor
		34	*L*	*Explorer*
		35	D	Factory Manager
		40	L	Foreign Correspondent
		57	L	Magazine Writer
		64	*D*	*Officer clerk*
		65	D	Office manager

*There were 56 items on the original SVIB scale, items dropped in the current form are shown in italics.

GOVERNOR'S SCHOOL COMBINED ITEM ANALYSIS--SVIB (continued)

	Item No.	Choice	Statement
Part I. Occupations (cont.)	71	L	Poet
	78	L	Reporter, general
	84	L	Sculptor
	87	*I*	*Ship Officer*
	96	*D*	*Typist*
PART II. SCHOOL SUBJECTS	112	L	English Composition
	119	L	Literature
	126	L	Philosophy
PART III. AMUSEMENTS	144	L	Chess
	146	I	Bridge
	163	L	Art galleries
	172	L	Poetry
	176	*I*	*"New Republic"*
	181	*L*	*"Atlantic Monthly"*
PART IV. ACTIVITIES	190	D	Operating machinery
	195	L	Arguments
	223	D	Methodical work
	225	L	Continually changing activities
	231	L	Climbing along edge of precipice
PART V. PECULIARITIES OF PEOPLE	251	I	Irreligious people
	252	*I*	*People who have done you favors*
	261	*I*	*People with gold teeth*
	264	*I*	*Blind people*
	267	*D*	*People who always agree with you*
	271	I	Fashionably dressed people
	272	I	Carelessy dressed people
PART VI. PREFERENCES	292	Least	Steadiness and performance of work
	299	Most	Freedom in working out one's own methods of doing things
	309	Most	Booth Tarkington, author
	319	Most	Chairman, Program Committee

GOVERNOR'S SCHOOL COMBINED ITEM ANALYSIS--SVIB (continued)

		Item No.	Choice	Statement
PART VII.	COMPARISON BETWEEN TWO ITEMS	326	Prefer	Gardening (to) House to house canvassing
		333	Prefer	Activity which is enjoyed for its own sake (to) Activity which produces tangible returns
		334	Prefer	Taking a chance (to) Playing safe
		353	Prefer	Reading a book (to) Going to movies
		354	*Prefer*	*Belonging to few societies (to) Belonging to many societies*
		355	Prefer	Few intimate friends (to) Many acquaintances
PART VIII.	RATING YOUR ABILITIES AND PERSONALITY	*366*	*No*	*Am quite sure of myself*
		369	Yes	Have more than my share of novel ideas
		380	No	Plan my work in detail

SVIB

S-III LOW ORIGENCE - LOW INTELLECTENCE

(28 items in current form)*

		Item No.	Choice	Statement
PART I.	OCCUPATIONS	7	L	Athletic Director
		16	*L*	*Bookkeeper*
		22	*L*	*Certified Public Accountant*

*There were 35 items on the original SVIB scale; items dropped in the current form are shown in italics.

GOVERNOR'S SCHOOL COMBINED ITEM ANALYSIS--SVIB (continued)

	Item No.	Choice	Statement
Part I. Occupations (cont.)	49	L	Laboratory Technician
	56	I	Machinist
	66	I	Orchestra Conductor
	67	L	Pharmacist
	70	L	Playground Director
	71	D	Poet
	87	*D*	*Ship Officer*
	100	L	Worker in Y.M.C.A., K. of C., etc.
PART II. SCHOOL SUBJECTS	103	L	Arithmetic
	105	L	Bookkeeping
	127	L	Physical Training
PART III. AMUSEMENTS	145	D	Poker
	168	*L*	*Pet canaries*
	180	L	"Popular Mechanics"
PART IV. ACTIVITIES	192	L	Giving "first aid" assistance
	195	D	Arguments
	224	L	Regular hours for work
	227	L	Saving money
	228	L	Contributing to charities
PART V. PECULIARITIES OF PEOPLE	242	L	People who are natural leaders
	258	L	Very old people
	264	*L*	*Blind people*
	265	*L*	*Deaf mutes*
	271	L	Fashionably dressed people
PART VI. PREFERENCES	286	I	Create a new artistic effect, *i.e.*, improve the beauty of the auto
	299	Least	Freedom in working out one's own methods of doing the work
PART VII. COMPARISON BETWEEN TWO ITEMS	*323*	*Prefer*	*Chauffeur (to) Chef*
	324	Prefer	Head waiter (to) Lighthouse tender
	333	Prefer	Activities which produces tangible returns (to) Activity which is enjoyed for its own sake

GOVERNOR'S SCHOOL COMBINED ITEM ANALYSIS--SVIB (continued)

		Item No.	Choice	Statement
Part VII.	*Comparison between Two Items (cont.)*	334	Prefer	Play safe (to) Taking a chance
PART VIII.	RATING YOUR ABILITIES AND PERSONALITY	369	No	Have more than my share of novel ideas
		383	Yes	Stimulate the ambition of my associates

SVIB

S-IV LOW ORIGENCE - HIGH INTELLECTENCE

(31 items on current form)*

		Item No.	Choice	Statement
PART I.	OCCUPATIONS	5	I	Artist
		12	D	Auto Racer
		17	D	Building Contractor
		33	D	Employment Manager
		52	I	Lawyer, Corporation
		70	D	Playground Director
		72	L	Politician
		83	L	Scientific Research Worker
		91	L	Statistician
PART II.	SCHOOL SUBJECTS	101	L	Algebra
		107	L	Calculus
		115	L	Geometry
		120	L	Mathematics
		128	L	Physics
PART III.	AMUSEMENTS	146	L	Bridge
		148	L	Solving mechanical puzzles
PART IV.	ACTIVITIES	196	D	Interviewing men for a job
		206	I	Meeting and directing people
		223	L	Methodical work
		225	I	Continually changing activities

*There were 33 items on the original SVIB scale; items dropped in the current form are shown in italics.

GOVERNOR'S SCHOOL COMBINED ITEM ANALYSIS--SVIB (continued)

		Item No.	Choice	Statement
PART V.	PECULIARITIES OF PEOPLE	240	L	Optimists
		243	I	People who assume leadership
PART VI.	PREFERENCES	297	Least	Opportunity to understand just how one's superior expects work to be done
		302	Least	Enrico Caruso, singer
		305	Least	Charles Dana Gibson, artist
		313	Most	Treasurer of a society or club
		317	Least	Chairman, entertainment committee
PART VII.	COMPARISON BETWEEN TWO ITEMS	342	Prefer	Inside work (to) Outside work
PART VIII.	RATING YOUR ABILITIES AND PERSONALITY	383	Not sure	Stimulate the ambition of my associates
		385	*Not sure*	*Win confidence and loyalty*
		394	*Best*	*Best-liked friends are equal to me in ability*
		395	Best	Become annoyed at times when handling complaints
		399	Best	Never make wagers

SPECIAL SCALES FOR GOUGH'S ADJECTIVE CHECK LIST*
DEVELOPED BY GEORGE S. WELSH

UN (*Uncommon Response*)
*37 items**

22	104	161	223	243	283	294
35	107	187	225	250	284	
52	114	189	227	264	286	
56	126	192	234	274	288	
62	135	208	237	277	289	
72	137	210	238	281	293	

CO (*Consensus, or Common Response*)
35 items

2	26	53	95	132	201
3	31	60	96	134	205
4	32	63	103	140	222
8	33	80	110	145	233
10	45	83	111	181	278
13	49	93	113	196	

MA (*Male Response*)
38 items

7	33	64	136	200	229	296
8	34	79	143	204	247	298
14	41	90	147	213	251	
15	44	95	183	214	267	
23	48	105	186	226	271	
25	58	128	193	228	279	

FE (*Female Response*)
49 items

6	31	71	87	117	157	220	252	295	
13	42	77	88	120	158	221	258		
16	43	80	93	121	167	230	261		
18	45	82	97	129	177	233	266		
29	46	85	99	154	179	240	278		
30	61	86	109	155	219	244	291		

A-I (*high origence/low intellectence*)
21 items[+]

4	42	73	101	200	299
18	48	88	141	224	
30	55	97	180	241	
34	61	98	188	287	

A-II (*high origence/high intellectence*)
25 items

9	66	90	124	191	245	300
39	67	92	142	197	262	
40	71	114	166	199	276	
54	76	118	168	206	282	

A-III (*low origence/low intellectence*)
17 items

13	115	177	278
31	139	178	295
46	140	181	
103	151	270	
108	165	272	

A-IV (*low origence/high intellectence*)
24 items

8	58	132	169	246
17	65	143	174	252
19	75	150	185	265
33	79	153	204	269
47	83	164	230	

*Item numbers are given for the adjectives as they appear in the ACL test booklet and the manual (Gough, H.G. and Heilbrun, A.B., Jr. *The Adjective Check List Manual*, Palo Alto: Consulting Psychologist Press, 1965).

[+]High and low are used in a relative sense and refer to the extremes of score distributions obtained by gifted adolescents on the Revised Art Scale of the Welsh Figure Preference Test (origence) and on the Terman Concept Mastery Test (intellectence). See also pp. 76-81 and 95-97 in the present work.

SPECIAL SCALES FOR THE ADJECTIVE CHECK LIST
DEVELOPED BY GEORGE S. WELSH

A-1 (*high origence/*
  low intellectence)

adventurous	fussy
attractive	gloomy
charming	lazy
clever	polished
confused	quarrelsome
cool	relaxed
daring	sexy
dependent	sophisticated
easy-going	unselfish
flirtatious	worrying
frivolous	

A-II (*high origence/*
  high intellectence)

aloof	leisurely
complicated	original
conceited	outspoken
cynical	quiet
disorderly	rebellious
dissatisfied	reflective
dreamy	restless
egotistical	spunky
forceful	temperamental
forgetful	unconventional
hostile	uninhibited
imaginative	zany
individualistic	

A-III (*low origence/*
  low intellectence)

appreciative	organized
cheerful	pleasant
contented	pleasure-
good-natured	seeking
hasty	practical
humorous	touchy
jolly	trusting
kind	understanding
mild	wholesome

A-IV (*low origence/*
  high intellectence)

alert	methodical
assertive	moderate
autocratic	optimistic
clear-thinking	painstaking
conventional	persistent
deliberate	preoccupied
discreet	resourceful
efficient	shy
enterprising	stable
fair-minded	stubborn
intelligent	thorough
logical	tolerant

SPECIAL SCALES FOR THE MINNESOTA MULTIPHASIC
PERSONALITY INVENTORY (MMPI)*
DEVELOPED BY GEORGE S. WELSH

M-I (high origence/low intellectence) 54 items							M-II (high origence/high intellectence) 53 items						
TRUE						FALSE	TRUE				FALSE		
5	91	224	322	395	459	8	11	176	377	475	6	206	343
24	99	244	327	398	469	55	21	226	412	491	12	229	369
28	106	248	334	404	505	122	39	277	429	506	57	249	391
40	110	250	344	410	507	162	78	292	433	523	67	268	415
41	143	252	345	416	562	221	81	299	441		80	279	443
59	146	256	349	437	565	237	101	305	453		111	297	480
71	147	266	363	444		261	131	307	474		140	329	489
84	165	287	375	456		528	171	317	473		191	332	548
													550

M-III (low origence/low intellectence) 50 items							M-IV (low origence/high intellectence) 42 items						
TRUE				FALSE			TRUE	FALSE					
1	241	394	518	30	170	381	46	27	132	231	389	504	
58	263	413	525	32	233	401	119	33	136	262	406	545	
95	283	457	527	36	235	454	160	62	138	271	418	551	
96	295	476	566	38	236	464	180	82	142	284	439		
98	309	483		52	267	522	201	89	181	296	442		
115	368	488		128	270	539	289	93	189	346	479		
198	373	490		148	324		478	94	203	350	481		
228	379	510		149	336			117	208	383	484		

*These scales were developed in a study of creativity and intelligence in gifted adolescents and have been cross-validated with adults. They have been interpreted in a framework of two independent dimensions of personality, "intelligence," and "origence." See Welsh, G.S. "Color Preference of Gifted Adolescents," *Sciences del'Art--Scientific Aesthetics* 1970, 7, 55-61; "Vocational Interests and Intelligence in Gifted Adolescents," *Educational and Psychological Measurement*, 1971, 31, 155-164; "A Two-Dimensional Model for Research in Social Science," *Research Previews* (Institute for Research in Social Science, Chapel Hill), 1972, 19, 14-23. See also pp. 76-81 and 97-102 in the present work.

MMPI

M-I HIGH ORIGENCE--LOW INTELLECTENCE

(54 items)

A. *(13 items): misanthropic and negative attitudes toward others.*

24. No one seems to understand me. (*true*)

28. When someone does me a wrong I feel I should pay him back if I can, just for the principle of the thing. (*true*)

59. I have often had to take orders from someone who did not know as much as I did. (*true*)

71. I think a great many people exaggerate their misfortunes in order to gain the sympathy and help of others. (*true*)

110. Someone has it in for me. (*true*)

224. My way of doing things is apt to be misunderstood by others. (*true*)

250. I don't blame anyone for trying to grab everything he can get in this world. (*true*)

252. No one cares much what happens to you. (*true*)

344. Often I cross the street in order not to meet someone I see. (*true*)

404. People have often misunderstood my intentions when I was trying to put them right and be helpful. (*true*)

416. It bothers me to have someone watch me at work even though I know I can do it well. (*true*)

469. I have often found people jealous of my good ideas, just because they had not thought of them first. (*true*)

507. I have frequently worked under people who seem to have things arranged so that they get credit for good work but are able to pass off mistakes onto those under them. (*true*)

B. *(4 items): tension and excitement.*

5. I am easily awakened by noise. (*true*)

248. Sometimes without any reason or even when things are going wrong I feel excitedly happy, "on top of the world." (*true*)

M-I (continued)

266. Once a week or oftener I become very excited. (*true*)

505. I have had periods when I felt so full of pep that sleep did not seem necessary for days at a time. (*true*)

C. (*2 items*): *need for stimulation and change.*

99. I like to go to parties and other affairs where there is lots of loud fun. (*true*)

146. I have the wanderlust and am never happy unless I am roaming or traveling about. (*true*)

D. (*2 items*): *lowered energy level.*

40. Most any time I would rather sit and daydream than to do anything else. (*true*)

41. I have had periods of days, weeks, or months when I couldn't take care of things because I couldn't "get going." (*true*)

E. (*2 items*): *indecision, inadequacy.*

122. I seem to be about as capable and smart as most others around me. (*false*)

147. I have often lost out on things because I couldn't make up my mind soon enough. (*true*)

F. (*5 items*): *bizarre symptomatology.*

106. Much of the time I feel as if I have done something wrong or evil. (*true*)

334. Peculiar odors come to me at times. (*true*)

345. I often feel as if things were not real. (*true*)

349. I have strange and peculiar thoughts. (*true*)

363. At times I have enjoyed being hurt by someone I loved. (*true*)

M-I (continued)

G. (2 items): impulsive and compulsive symptoms.

   459. I have one or more bad habits which are so strong that it is no use in fighting against them. (true)

   565. I feel like jumping off when I am on a high place. (true)

H. (2 items): denial of symptoms.

   55. I am almost never bothered by pains over the heart or in my chest. (false)

   528. I blush no more often than others. (false)

I. (5 items): lack of resentment, tolerance of others.

   91. I do not mind being made fun of. (true)

   162. I resent having anyone take me in so cleverly that I have had to admit that it was one on me. (false)

   165. I like to know some important people because it makes me feel important. (true)

   287. I have very few fears compared to my friends. (true)

   444. I do not try to correct people who express an ignorant belief. (true)

J. (3 items): permissive morality.

   410. I would certainly enjoy beating a crook at his own game. (true)

   437. It is all right to get around the law if you don't actually break it. (true)

   456. A person shouldn't be punished for breaking a law that he thinks is unreasonable. (true)

K. (3 items): family.

   224. My parents have often objected to the kind of people I went around with. (true)

   237. My relatives are nearly all in sympathy with me. (false)

   327. My mother or father often made me obey even when I thought that it was unreasonable. (true)

M-I (continued)

L. (3 items): childhood.

143. When I was a child, I belonged to a crowd or gang that tried to stick together through thick and thin. (true)

398. I often think, "I wish I were a child again." (true)

562. The one to whom I was most attached and whom I most admired as a child was a woman. (Mother, sister, aunt, or other woman.) (true)

M. (4 items): worry and pessimism.

84. These days I find it hard not to give up hope of amounting to something. (true)

322. I worry over money and business. (true)

375. When I am feeling very happy and active, someone who is blue or low will spoil it all. (true)

395. The future is too uncertain for a person to make serious plans. (true)

N. (4 items): interests.

8. My daily life is full of things that keep me interested. (false)

221. I like science. (false)

256. The only interesting part of newspapers is the "funnies." (true)

261. If I were an artist, I would like to draw flowers. (false)

MMPI

M-II HIGH ORIGENCE - HIGH INTELLECTENCE

(53 items)

A. (10 items): asociality, lack of social interests.

57. I am a good mixer. (false)

171. It makes me uncomfortable to put on a stunt at a party even when others are doing the same sort of thing. (true)

M-II *(continued)*

229. I should like to belong to several clubs or lodges. *(false)*

292. I am likely not to speak to people until they speak to me. *(true)*

307. I refuse to play some games because I am not good at them. *(true)*

377. At parties I am more likely to sit by myself or with just one other person than to join in with the crowd. *(true)*

391. I love to go to dances. *(false)*

415. If given the chance I would make a good leader of people. *(false)*

453. When I was a child I didn't care to be a member of a crowd or gang. *(true)*

473. Whenever possible I avoid being in a crowd. *(true)*

B. (9 *items*): *introversive withdrawal, emotional subjectivity.*

67. I wish I could be as happy as others seem to be. *(false)*

81. I think I would like the kind of work a forest ranger does. *(true)*

268. Something exciting will almost always pull me out of it when I am feeling low. *(false)*

299. I think that I feel more intensely than most people do. *(true)*

305. Even when I am with people I feel lonely much of the time. *(true)*

317. I am more sensitive than most other people. *(true)*

443. I am apt to pass up something I want to do because others feel that I am not going about it in the right way. *(false)*

489. I feel sympathetic towards people who tend to hang on to their griefs and troubles. *(false)*

506. I am a high strung person. *(true)*

C. (9 *items*): *denial of physical and mental symptoms and fears.*

131. I do not worry about catching diseases. *(true)*

176. I do not have a great fear of snakes. *(true)*

M–II (continued)

191. Sometimes, when embarrassed, I break out in a sweat which annoys me greatly. *(false)*

279. I drink an unusually large amount of water every day. *(false)*

332. Sometimes my voice leaves me or changes even though I have no cold. *(false)*

343. I usually have to stop and think before I act even in trifling matters. *(false)*

412. I do not dread seeing a doctor about a sickness or injury. *(true)*

480. I am often afraid of the dark. *(false)*

523. I practically never blush. *(true)*

D. *(7 items): interests and attitudes.*

6. I like to read newspaper articles on crime. *(false)*

12. I enjoy detective or mystery stories. *(false)*

78. I like poetry. *(true)*

80. I sometimes tease animals. *(false)*

140. I like to cook. *(false)*

429. I like to attend lectures on serious subjects. *(true)*

550. I like repairing a door latch. *(false)*

E. *(6 items): permissive morality, attitudinal frankness.*

101. I believe women ought to have as much sexual freedom as men. *(true)*

277. At times I have been so entertained by the cleverness of a crook that I have hoped he would get by with it. *(true)*

297. I wish I were not bothered by thoughts about sex. *(false)*

441. I like tall women. *(true)*

475. When I am cornered I tell that portion of the truth which is not likely to hurt me. *(true)*

548. I never attend a sexy show if I can avoid it. *(false)*

M-II (*continued*)

F. (*6 items*): *recognition of basic id urges and impulses.*

11. A person should try to understand his dreams and be guided by or take warning from them. (*true*)

39. At times I feel like smashing things. (*true*)

111. I have never done anything dangerous for the thrill of it. (*false*)

329. I almost never dream. (*false*)

433. I used to have imaginary companions. (*true*)

472. I am fascinated with fire. (*true*)

G. (*4 items*): *rejection or denial of conventional religiosity.*

206. I am very religious (more than most people). (*false*)

249. I believe there is a Devil and a Hell in afterlife. (*false*)

369. Religion gives me no worry. (*false*)

491. I have no patience with people who believe there is only one true religion. (*true*)

H. (*2 items*): *family.*

21. At times I have very much wanted to leave home. (*true*)

226. Some of my family have habits that bother and annoy me very much. (*true*)

MMPI

M-III LOW ORIGENCE - LOW INTELLECTENCE

(50 items)

A. (*12 items*): *sociable gregariousness, personal objectivity.*

52. I prefer to pass by school friends, or people I know but have not seen for a long time, unless they speak to me first. (*false*)

M-III (continued)

148. It makes me impatient to have people ask my advice or otherwise interrupt me when I am working on something important. *(false)*

170. What others think of me does not bother me. *(false)*

233. I have at times stood in the way of people who were trying to do something, not because it amounted to much but because of the principle of the thing. *(false)*

267. When in a group of people I have trouble thinking of the right things to talk about. *(false)*

309. I seem to make friends about as quickly as others do. *(true)*

324. I have never been in love with anyone. *(false)*

336. I easily become impatient with people. *(false)*

368. I have sometimes stayed away from another person because I feared doing or saying something that I might regret afterwords. *(true)*

394. I frequently ask people for advice. *(true)*

454. I could be happy living all alone in a cabin in the woods or mountains. *(false)*

518. I have often felt guilty because I have pretended to feel more sorry about something than I really was. *(true)*

B. *(11 items)*: *conventional, orthodox, fundamentalistic religiosity.*

58. Everything is turning out just like the prophets of the Bible said it would. *(true)*

95. I go to church almost every week. *(true)*

98. I believe in the second coming of Christ. *(true)*

115. I believe in a life hereafter. *(true)*

373. I feel sure there is only one true religion. *(true)*

413. I deserve severe punishment for my sins. *(true)*

464. I have never seen a vision. *(false)*

476. I am a special agent of God. *(true)*

M-III *(continued)*

    483. Christ performed miracles such as changing water into wine. *(true)*

    488. I pray several times every week. *(true)*

    490. I read in the Bible several times a week. *(true)*

C. *(9 items)*: *admission of symptoms, fears, and phobias.*

    36. I seldom worry about my health. *(false)*

    128. The sight of blood neither frightens me nor makes me sick. *(false)*

    263. I sweat very easily even on cool days. *(true)*

    270. When I leave home I do not worry about whether the door is locked and the windows closed. *(false)*

    401. I have no fear of water. *(false)*

    510. Dirt frightens or disgusts me. *(true)*

    522. I have no fear of spiders. *(false)*

    525. I am made nervous by certain animals. *(true)*

    539. I am not afraid of mice. *(false)*

D. *(5 items)*: *mental alertness and practicality.*

    32. I find it hard to keep my mind on a task or job. *(false)*

    198. I daydream very litte. *(true)*

    228. At times I feel that I can make up my mind with unusually great ease. *(true)*

    236. I brood a great deal. *(false)*

    379. I very seldom have spells of the blues. *(true)*

E. *(5 items)*: *denial of basic id urges and impulses.*

    30. At times I feel like swearing. *(false)*

    38. During one period when I was a youngster I engaged in petty thievery. *(false)*

M-III (continued)

241. I dream frequently about things that are best kept to myself. (*true*)

381. I am often said to be hotheaded. (*false*)

457. I believe that a person should never taste an alcoholic drink. (*true*)

F. (5 *items*): *interests*

1. I like mechanics magazines. (*true*)

149. I used to keep a diary. (*false*)

283. If I were a reporter I would very much like to report sporting news. (*true*)

295. I liked "Alice in Wonderland" by Lewis Carroll. (*true*)

566. I like movie love scenes. (*true*)

G. (3 *items*): *family.*

96. I have very few quarrels with members of my family. (*true*)

235. I have been quite independent and free from family rule. (*false*)

527. The members of my family and my close relatives get along quite well. (*true*)

MMPI

M-IV LOW ORIGENCE - HIGH INTELLECTENCE

(42 items)

A. (12 *items*): *positive regard for others, philanthropic and altruistic attitudes.*

89. I takes a lot of argument to convince most people of the truth. (*false*)

93. I think most people would lie to get ahead. (*false*)

M-IV *(continued)*

117. Most people are honest chiefly through fear of being caught. *(false)*

136. I commonly wonder what hidden reason another person may have for doing something nice for me. *(false)*

138. Criticism or scolding hurts me terribly. *(false)*

271. I do not blame a person for taking advantage of someone who lays himself open to it. *(false)*

284. I am sure I am being talked about. *(false)*

289. I am always disgusted with the law when a criminal is freed through the arguments of a smart lawyer. *(true)*

383. People often disappoint me. *(false)*

406. I have often met people who were supposed to be experts who were no better than I. *(false)*

504. I do not try to cover up my poor opinion or pity of a person so that he won't know how I feel. *(false)*

551. Sometimes I am sure that other people can tell what I am thinking. *(false)*

B. *(8 items)*: *denial of somatic symptoms, fears, and worries.*

62. Parts of my body often have feelings like burning, tingling, crawling, or like "going to sleep." *(false)*

119. My speech is the same as always (not faster or slower, or slurring; no hoarseness). *(true)*

189. I feel weak all over much of the time. *(false)*

296. I have periods in which I feel unusually cheerful without any special reason. *(false)*

346. I have a habit of counting things that are not important such as bulbs on electric signs, and so forth. *(false)*

439. It makes me nervous to have to wait. *(false)*

442. I have had periods in which I lost sleep over worry. *(false)*

484. I have one or more faults which are so big that it seems better to accept them and try to control them rather than to try to get rid of them. *(false)*

M-IV (continued)

C. (3 *items*): *denial of bizarre symptoms.*

    27. Evil spirits possess me at times. (*false*)

    33. I have had very peculiar and strange experiences. (*false*)

    350. I hear strange things when I am alone. (*false*)

D. (8 *items*): *expression of ability and self-confidence.*

    46. My judgment is better than it ever was. (*true*)

    82. I am easily downed in an argument. (*false*)

    94. I do many things which I regret afterwards (I regret things more or
         more often than other seem to). (*false*)

    142. I certainly feel useless at times. (*false*)

    160. I have never felt better in my life than I do now. (*true*)

    389. My plans have frequently seemed so full of difficulties that I have
         had to give them up. (*false*)

    418. At times I think I am no good at all. (*false*)

    481. I can remember "playing sick" to get out of something. (*false*)

E. (4 *items*): *denial of basic id urges and impulses.*

    181. When I get bored I like to stir up some excitement. (*false*)

    208. I like to flirt. (*false*)

    231. I like to talk about sex. (*false*)

    545. Sometimes I have the same dream over and over again. (*false*)

F. (4 *items*): *social ineptness, lack of social ease.*

    180. I find it hard to make talk when I meet new people. (*true*)

    201. I wish I were not so shy. (*true*)

    262. It does not bother me that I am not better looking. (*false*)

    479. I do not mind meeting strangers. (*false*)

M–IV (continued)

G. *(2 items): interests.*

132. I like collecting flowers or growing house plants. *(false)*

203. If I were a reporter I would very much like to report news of the theater. *(false)*

H. *(1 item): family*

478. I have never been made especially nervous over trouble that any members of my family have gotten into. *(true)*

REFERENCES

Adair, F.L. An analysis of intelligence test scores and WFPT scales for two groups of subjects. Unpublished study, Franklin and Marshall College, 1969.

Aiken, L.R., Jr. *A review of research on the Welsh Figure Preference Test*. Greensboro, N.C.: Creativity Research Institute of the Richardson Foundation, 1967.

Albert, R.S. Genius: Present-day status of the concept and its implications for the study of creativity and giftedness. *American Psychologist*, 1959, *24*, 743-53.

Allport, G.W. *Personality: A psychological interpretation*. New York: Holt, Rinehart & Winston, 1937.

Allport, G.W. *The use of personal documents in psychological science*. New York: Social Science Research Council, 1942.

Allport, G.W. *Pattern and growth in personality*. New York: Holt, Rinehart & Winston, 1961.

Anastasi, A. *Differential psychology: Individual and group differences in behavior*. New York: Macmillan, 1958.

Anastasi, A. (Ed.) *Individual differences*. New York: Wiley, 1965.

Anastasi, A. *Psychological testing*. (3rd ed.) New York: MacMillan, 1968.

Andrews. F.M. Factors affecting the manifestation of creative ability by scientists. *Journal of Personality*, 1965, *23*, 140-52.

Barron, F. Personality style and perceptual choice. *Journal of Personality*, 1952, *20*, 385-401.

Barron. F. Complexity-simplicity as a personality dimension. *Journal of Abnormal & Social Psychology*, 1953, *68*, 163-72.

Barron, F. The disposition toward originality. *Journal of Abnormal and Social Psychology*, 1955, *51*, 478-85.

Barron, F. Creative vision and expression in writing and painting. In D.W. MacKinnon (Ed.) *The creative person*.
Berkeley: University of California Extension, 1961, Chap. 2.

Barron, F. The psychology of creativity. In T.M. Newcomb (Ed.),
New directions in psychology II. New York: Holt, Rinehart
and Winston, 1965, 3-134.

Barron, F. *Creativity and personal freedom*. New York: Van
Nostrand, 1968.

Barron, F. *Creative person and creative process*. New York:
Holt, Rinehart and Winston, 1969.

Barron, F., & Egan, D. Leaders and innovators in Irish management. *Journal of Management Studies*, 1968, *5*, 41-61.

Barron, F., & Welsh, G.S. Artistic perception as a possible
factor in personality style: its measurement by a figure
preference test. *Journal of Psychology*, 1952, *33*, 199-203.

Baughman, E.E., & Welsh, G.S. *Personality: A behavioral science*.
Englewood Cliffs, N.J.: Prentice-Hall, 1962.

Bieri, J., Bradburn, W.M., & Galinsky, M.D. Sex differences in
perceptual behavior. *Journal of Personality*, 1958, *26*,
1-12.

Black, J.D. *Preliminary manual, the D-48 Test*. Palo Alto,
Calif.: Consulting Psychologists Press, 1963.

Bronowski, J. The creative process. *Scientific American*, 1958,
199, 59-65.

Brown, G.I. An experiment in the teaching of creativity. *School
Review*, 1964, *72*, 437-50.

Brown, G.I. A second study in the teaching of creativity.
Harvard Educational Review, 1965, *35*, 39-54.

Brown, G.I. *Operational creativity: a strategy for teacher
change*. Paper presented at the meeting of the American
Educational Research Association, Chicago, February, 1966.

Bryan, J. Who needs computers with mathematical prodigies like
these? *Horizon*, 1970, *12*, 46-47.

Buros, O.K. (Ed.), *The seventh mental measurements yearbook.*
    Highland Park, N.J.: Gryphon, 1965.

Burt, C. The evidence for the concept of intelligence. In
    S. Wiseman (Ed.) *Intelligence and ability.* Baltimore:
    Penguin, 1967.

Butcher, H.J. *Human intelligence: Its nature and assessment.*
    London: Menthuen, 1968. (Republished: New York, Harper &
    Row, 1973).

Calandra, A. Angels on a pin. *Saturday Review,* December 21,
    1968, p. 60.

Campbell, D.P. *Manual for Strong Vocational Interest Blanks,
    revised.* Stanford: Stanford University Press, 1966.

Campbell, D.T., & Fiske, D.W. Convergent and discriminant
    validation by the multitrait-multimethod matrix. *Psycho-
    logical Bulletin,* 1959, *56,* 81-105.

Cantwell, Zita M. Relationships between scores on the Standard
    Progressive Matrices (1938) and on the D-48 Test of non-
    verbal intelligence and three measures of academic achieve-
    ment. *Journal of Experimental Education,* 1966, *34,* 28-31.

The Governor's School. *Carnegie Corporation of New York:
    Quarterly,* 1964, *12,* 1-4.

Carrera, R.N. *Effects of differential reward on stable aesthetic
    preferences.* Paper presented at the meeting of the South-
    eastern Psychological Association, Roanoke, April 1968.

Carrera, R.N., Moore, B., & Levy, T. *Stability and generaliza-
    tion of aesthetic preferences following systematic manipu-
    lation.* Paper presented at the meeting of the Southeastern
    Psychological Association, New Orleans, April 1969.

Cashdan, S., & Welsh, G.S. Personality correlates of creative
    potential in talented high school students. *Journal of
    Personality,* 1966, *34,* 445-55.

Cattell, R.B. *Description and measurement of personality.* New
    York: World Book, 1946.

Cattell, R.B. *The scientific analysis of personality.* Baltimore:
    Penguin, 1965.

Cave, Richard and Charles Boutwell. Personal communication, 1963.

Child, I.L. Personal preferences as an expression of aesthetic sensitivity. *Journal of Personality*, 1962, *30*, 496-512.

Child, I.L. Personality correlates of esthetic judgment in college students. *Journal of Personality*, 1965, *33*, 476-511.

Colman, R.W. Comparison of three creativity measures. Unpublished master's thesis, University of North Carolina, Chapel Hill, 1966.

Cox, C.M. *Genetic studies of genius*. Vol. II. *The early mental traits of three hundred geniuses*. Stanford: Stanford University Press, 1926.

Cronbach, L.J. *Essentials of psychological testing*. (2nd ed.) New York: Harpers, 1960.

Cronbach, L.J., & Meehl, P.E. Construct validity in psychological tests. *Psychological Bulletin*, 1955, *52*, 283-302.

Cropley, A.J. A note on the Wallach-Kogan tests of creativity. *British Journal of Educational Psychology*, 1968, *38*, (2), 197-200.

Crutchfield, R. The creative process. In D.W. MacKinnon (Ed.), *The Creative Person*. Berkeley: University of California Extension, 1961, Chap. 6.

Dahlstrom, W.G., & Welsh, G.S. *An MMPI handbook: A guide to use in clinical practice and research*. Minneapolis: University of Minnesota Press, 1960.

Day, H. A curious approach to creativity. *The Canadian Psychologist*, 1968, *9*, 485-97. (a)

Day, H. Role of specific curiosity in school achievement. *Journal of Educational Psychology*, 1968, *59*, 37-43. (b)

Day, H.I., & Langevin, R. Curiosity and intelligence: two necessary conditions for a high level of curiosity. *Journal of Special Education*, 1969, *3*, 263-68.

de Laszlo, V.S. (Ed.) *Psyche and symbol: a selection from the writings of C.G. Jung*. Garden City, N.Y.: Doubleday, 1958.

Dellas, M., & Gaier, E.L.   Identification of creativity: The individual. *Psychological Bulletin,* 1970, *73,* 55-73.

Domino, G.   Comparison of the D-48, Cattell Culture Fair, and Army Beta Tests in a sample of college males. *Journal of Consulting Psychology,* 1964, *28,* 468-69.

Domino, G.   Differential prediction of academic achievement in conforming and independent settings. *Journal of Educational Psychology,* 1968, *59,* 256-60.

Domino, G.   Identification of potentially creative persons from the Adjective Check List. *Journal of Consulting and Clinical Psychology,* 1970, *35,* 48-51.

Domino, G.   Personal communication, 1971.

Drake, L.E. & Oetting, E.R.   *An MMPI codebook for counselors.* Minneapolis: University of Minnesota Press, 1959.

Edwards, A.J.   *Individual mental testing.* Part I. *History and theories.* Scranton, Pa.: International Textbook, 1971.

Eisenman, R.   Creativity, awareness, and liking. *Journal of Consulting and Clinical Psychology,* 1969, *33,* 157-60.

Eisenman, R., & Robinson, N.   Complexity-simplicity, creativity, intelligence, and other correlates. *Journal of Psychology,* 1967, *67,* 331-34.

Ellis, A.   Homosexuality and creativity. *Journal of Clinical Psychology,* 1959, *15,* 576-79.

Engel, I.M.   A factor-analytic study of items from five masculinity-femininity tests. *Journal of Consulting Psychology,* 1966, *30,* 565.

Eysenck, H.J.   *The structure of human personality.* New York: Wiley, 1953.

Fiske, D.W., & Maddi, S.R. (Eds.) *Functions of varied experience.* Homewood, Ill.: Dorsey, 1961.

Fliegler, L.A. & Bish, C.E.   The gifted and talented. *Review of Educational Research,* 1959, *29,* 408-50.

Friedlander, M.J.   *On art and connoisseurship.* Boston: Beacon Press, 1960.

Garai, J.E., & Scheinfeld, A. Sex differences in mental and
    behavioral traits. *Genetic Psychology Monographs*, 1968,
    77, 169-299.

Gaudreau, J. Interrelations among perception, learning ability
    and intelligence in mentally deficient school children.
    Journal of Learning Disabilities, 1968, *1*, 301-06.

Getzels, J.W., & Csikszentmihalyi, M. The study of creativity
    in future artists: The criterion problem. In O.J. Harvey
    (Ed.), *Experience, structure and adaptability*. New York:
    Springer, 1966.

Getzels, J.W., & Jackson, P.W. *Creativity and intelligence*.
    New York: Wiley, 1962.

Ghiselin, B. *The creative process*. New York: Mentor, 1955.

Gilbert, G.M. *Personality dynamics: A biosocial approach*. New
    York: Harper & Row, 1970.

Ginsberg, G.P., & Whittemore, R.G. Creativity and verbal ability:
    A direct examination of their relationship. *British Journal
    of Educational Psychology*, 1968, *38*, Vol. 2, 133-39.

Golann, S.E. The creativity motive. Unpublished doctoral dis-
    sertation, University of North Carolina, Chapel Hill, 1961.

Golann, S.E. The creativity motive. *Journal of Personality*,
    1962, *30*, 588-600.

Golann, S.E. The psychological study of creativity. *Psycho-
    logical Bulletin*, 1963, *60*, 548-65.

Goodenough, F.L. *Mental testing: its history, principles, and
    applications*. New York: Rinehart, 1949.

Gordon, W.J.J. *Senectics: The development of creative capacity*.
    New York: Harpers, 1961.

Gorlow, L., Simonson, N.R., & Krauss, H. An empirical investi-
    gation of the Jungian typology. *British Journal of Social
    and Clinical Psychology*, 1966, *5*, 108-17.

Gough, H.G. A nonintellectual intelligence test. *Journal of
    Consulting Psychology*, 1953, *17*, 242-46.

Gough, H.G. Techniques for identifying the creative research
     scientist. In D.W. MacKinnon (Ed.), *The creative person.*
     Berkeley: University of California Extension, 1961, Chap. 3.

Gough, H.G. *Manual for the California Psychological Inventory.*
     (Revised ed.) Palo Alto, Calif.: Consulting Psychologists
     Press, 1964.

Gough, H.G. Personal communication, 1970.

Gough, H.G. & Domino, G. The D-48 Test as a measure of general
     ability among grade school children. *Journal of Consulting
     Psychology,* 1963, *27,* 344-49.

Gough, H.G., & Heilbrun, A.B. *The Adjective Check List Manual.*
     Palo Alto, Calif.: Consulting Psychologists Press, 1965.

Gough, H.G., McKee, M.G., & Yandell, R.J. Adjective check list
     analyses of a number of selected psychometric variables.
     Technical Memorandum, May 1955, Officer Education Research
     Laboratory, OERL-TM-55-10.

Grove, M.S., & Eisenman, R. Personality correlates of complexity-
     simplicity. *Perceptual and Motor Skills,* 1970, *31,* 387-91.

Guilford, J.P. *Personality.* New York: McGraw-Hill, 1959. (a)

Guilford, J.P. Three faces of intellect. *American Psychologist,*
     1959, *14,* 469-79. (b)

Guilford, J.P. *The nature of human intelligence.* New York:
     McGraw-Hill, 1967. (a)

Guilford, J.P. Creativity: yesterday, today, and tomorrow.
     Journal of Creative Behavior, 1967, *1,* 3-14. (b).

Hadamard, J. *The psychology of invention in the mathematical
     field.* New York: Dover, 1954.

Harris, R.A. Creativity in marketing. In P. Smith (Ed.),
     Creativity. New York: Hastings House, 1959, 143-66.

Harris, T.L. An analysis of the responses of adolescents to the
     Welsh Figure Preference Test and its implications for
     guidance purposes. Unpublished doctoral dissertation,
     University of North Carolina, Chapel Hill, 1961.

Hathaway, S.R., & McKinley, J.C. A multiphasic personality
schedule (Minnesota): I. Construction of the schedule.
Journal of Psychology, 1940, *10*, 249-54.

Hathaway, S.R. & McKinley, J.C. *Minnesota Multiphasic Personality Inventory, Revised Manual*. New York: The Psychological
Corporation, 1967.

Hathaway, S.R., & Monachesi, E.D. *Adolescent personality and
behavior: MMPI patterns of normal, delinquent, dropout, and
other outcomes*. Minneapolis: University of Minnesota Press,
1963.

Helson, R. Creativity, sex, and mathematics. In D.W. MacKinnon
(Ed.) *The creative person*. Berkeley: University of
California Extension, 1961, Chap. 4.

Helson, R. Personality of women with imaginative and artistic
interests: the role of masculinity, originality, and other
characteristics in their creativity. *Journal of Personality*,
1966, *34*, 1-25.

Helson, R. Personality characteristics and developmental history
of creative college women. *Genetic Psychology Monographs*,
1967, *76*, 205-56. (a)

Helson, R. Sex differences in creative style. *Journal of
Personality*, 1967, *35*, 214-33. (b)

Helson, R. Effect of sibling characteristics and parental values
on creative interest and achievement. *Journal of Personality*, 1968, *36*, 589-607.

Helson, R. Women mathematicians and the creative personality.
Journal of Consulting and Clinical Psychology, 1971, *36*,
210-20.

Helson, R., & Crutchfield, R.S. Mathematicians: the creative
researcher and the average Ph.D. *Journal of Consulting and
Clinical Psychology*, 1970, *34*, 250-57.

Hitt, W.D. Toward a two-factor theory of creativity. *Psychological Record*, 1965, *15*, 127-32.

Hitt, W.D., & Stock, J.R. The relationship between psychological
characteristics and creative behavior. *Psychological Record*,
1965, *15*, 133-40.

Hoepfner, R., & O'Sullivan, M. Social intelligence and IQ. *Educational and Psychological Measurement*, 1968, *28*, 339-44.

Hofstaetter, P.R. The changing composition of intelligence: a study in T-technique. *Journal of Genetic Psychology*, 1954, *85*, 159-64. Also in S. Wiseman (Ed.), *Intelligence and ability*. Baltimore: Penguin, 1967.

Hogben, L. *From cave painting to comic strip: a kaleidoscope of human communication*. New York: Chanticleer Press, 1949.

Holland, J.L. *The psychology of vocational choice: A theory of personality types and model environments*. Waltham, Mass.: Blaisdell, 1966.

Holland, J.L., Viernstein, M.C., Kuo, H.M., Karweit, N.L., & Blum, Z.D. A psychological classification of occupations. Research Report No. 90, Center for Social Organization of Schools, Johns Hopkins University, 1970.

Honigman, John J. and Irma. Personal communication, 1959.

Hook, S. Science and methology in psychoanalysis. In S. Hook (Ed.), *Psychoanalysis, scientific method, and philosophy*. New York: Grove, 1960.

Horn, J.L., & Bramble, W.J. Second-order ability structure revealed in rights and wrongs scores. *Journal of Educational Psychology*, 1967, *58*, 115-22.

Horst, P. *Personality: Measure of dimensions*. San Francisco: Jossey-Bass, 1968.

Hudson, L. *Contrary imaginations: A psychological study of the young student*. New York: Schocken, 1966.

Hudson, L. (Ed.) *The ecology of human intelligence*. Baltimore: Penguin, 1970.

Jacobi, J. *The psychology of C.G. Jung*. (6th ed.) New Haven: Yale University Press, 1962.

Jacobi, J. Symbols in an individual analysis. In C.G. Jung (Ed.), *Man and his symbols*. New York: Doubleday, 1964, 272-303.

Jacobson, L.L., Elenewski, J.J., Lordahl, D.S. & Liroff, J.H. Role of creativity and intelligence in conceptualization. *Journal of Personality and Social Psychology*, 1968, *10*, 431-36.

Johnson, Lou & Jenny Whitehurst. Personal communication, 1960.

Jung, C.G. *Psychologische typen*. Zurich: Rascher, 1921. (English translation, *Psychological types*. In *Collected works*. Vol. 6. Princeton: Princeton University Press, 1971.)

Jung, C.G. *Modern man in search of a soul*. New York: Harcourt, Brace, 1933.

Jung, C.G. *Two essays on analytical psychology*. New York: Meridian, 1956.

Jung, C.G. Approaching the unconscious. In C.G. Jung (Ed.), *Man and his symbols*. New York: Doubleday, 1964, 18-103.

Kassenbaum, G., Couch, A.S., & Slater, P.E. The factorial dimensions of the MMPI. *Journal of Consulting Psychology*, 1959, *23*, 226-36.

King, L.D. Personality and aesthetics: two studies of poetic communication. Unpublished Master's Thesis, University of North Carolina, Chapel Hill, 1969.

Köhler, W. *The mentality of apes*. (Tr. by E. Winter) New York: Harcourt, Brace & World, 1925. (Republished: Baltimore, Penguin, 1957).

Kroger, R.O. Effects of role demands and test-cue properties upon personality test performance. *Journal of Consulting Psychology*, 1967, *31*, 304-12.

Kroger, R.O. Effects of implicit and explicit task cues upon personality test performance. *Journal of Consulting and Clinical Psychology*, 1968, *32*, 498.

Lewin, K. *Dynamic theory of personality*. New York: McGraw-Hill, 1935.

Lewin, K. *Principles of topological psychology*. New York: McGraw-Hill, 1936.

Lewis, H.M. *Open windows onto the future: Theory of the Governor's School of North Carolina*. Winston-Salem: Governor's School (Drawer H, Salem Station), 1969.

Levy, L.H. *Conceptions of personality: Theories and research*. New York: Random, 1970.

Lim, D.T., & Ullmann, L.P. A contribution to Welsh Figure Pref-
    erence Test norms. *Research Reports of Veterans Administra-
    tion Hospital, Palo Alto, Calif.*, No. 14, May 1961.

Littlejohn, Mary T. A comparison of the responses of ninth-
    graders to measures of creativity and masculinity-femininity.
    Unpublished doctoral dissertation, University of North
    Carolina at Chapel Hill, 1966.

Littlejohn, M.T. Creativity and masculinity-femininity in ninth
    graders. *Perceptual and Motor Skills*, 1967, *25*, 737-43.

Loevinger, J. Objective tests as instruments of psychological
    theory. In D.N. Jackson & S. Messick (Eds.), *Problems in
    human assessment*. New York: McGraw-Hill, 1967.

MacKinnon, D.W. (Ed.) *The creative person*. Berkeley: University
    of California Extension, 1961.

MacKinnon, D.W. Creativity in architects. In D.W. MacKinnon
    (Ed.), *The creative person*. Berkeley: University of
    California Extension, 1961, Chap. 5. (a)

MacKinnon, D.W. Fostering creativity in students of engineering.
    Journal of Engineering Education, 1961, *52*, 129-42. (b)

MacKinnon, D.W. The nature and nurture of creative talent.
    American Psychologist, 1962, *17*, 484-95.

MacKinnon, D.W. Creativity and images of the self. In R.W.
    White (Ed.), *The study of lives*. New York: Atherton Press,
    1963.

MacKinnon, D.W. Personality and the realization of creative po-
    tential. *American Psychologist*, 1965, *20*, 273-81.

Madaus, G.F. Divergent thinking and intelligence: Another look
    at a controversial question. *Journal of Educational
    Measurement*, 1967, *4*, 227-35.

Maddi, S.R. Motivational aspects of creativity. *Journal of
    Personality*, 1965, *33*, 330-47.

Maddi, S.R. *Personality theories: A comparative analysis*.
    Homewood, Ill.: Dorsey Press, 1968.

Maddi, S.R., & Propst, B.S. Activation theory and personality.
    In S.R. Maddi (Ed.), *Perspectives on personality: A compara-
    tive approach*. Boston: Little, Brown, 1971.

Maitra, A.K., Mukerji, K., & Raychaudhuri, M.   Artistic creativity among the delinquents and the criminals: Associated perceptual style. *Bulletin, Council of Social and Psychological Research, Calcutta,* 1967, *9,* 7-10.

Marshall, I.N.   The four functions: A conceptual analysis. *Journal of Analytical Psychology,* 1968, *13,* 1-32.

Mattocks, Arthur.   Personal communication, 1960.

McCarthy, D., Anthony, R.J., & Domino, G.   A comparison of the CPI, Franck, MMPI, and WAIS masculinity-femininity indexes. *Journal of Consulting and Clinical Psychology,* 1970, *35,* 414-16.

McClelland, D.C.   The calculated risk: An aspect of scientific performance.   In C.W. Taylor & F. Barron (Eds.), *Scientific creativity: Its recognition and development.*   New York: Wiley, 1963.

McCurdy, H.G.   *The personality of Shakespeare.*   New Haven: Yale University Press, 1953.

McCurdy, H.G.   *The personal world: An introduction to the study of personality.*   New York: Harcourt, Brace & World, 1961.

McCurdy, H.G.   Shakespeare: King of infinite space. *Psychology Today,* 1968, *1,* (11), 38-41, 66-69.

McNemar, Q.   Lost: Our intelligence. Why? *American Psychologist,* 1964, *19,* 871-82.

Mednick, Martha.   Personal communication, 1964.

Mednick, M.T., & Andrews, F.M.   Creative thinking and level of intelligence. *Journal of Creative Behavior,* 1967, *1,* 428-31.

Mednick, S.A.   The associative basis of the creative process. *Psychological Review,* 1962, *69,* 220-32.

Mednick, S.A., & Mednick, M.T.   *Manual, the Remote Associates Test, Form 1.*   Boston, Mass.: Houghton-Mifflin, 1967.

Meehl, P.E.   The dynamics of "structured" personality tests. *Journal of Clinical Psychology,* 1945, *1,* 296-303.   (Also reprinted in Welsh and Dahlstrom, 1956).

Miles, T.R. Contributions to intelligence testing and the theory
    of intelligence. I. On defining intelligence. *British
    Journal of Educational Psychology,* 1957, *27,* 153-65. Also
    in S. Wiseman (Ed.), *Intelligence and ability.* Baltimore:
    Penguin, 1967.

Miller, W.S. *Manual: Miller Analogies Test.* New York: The
    Psychological Corporation, 1960.

Mitchell, M. The Revised Art Scale of the WFPT as a personality
    assessment instrument with educable mentally handicapped
    children. Unpublished doctoral dissertation, University of
    North Carolina, 1968.

Mitchell, Marlys. Personal communication, 1969.

Mosier, C.I. Problems and designs of cross-validation. *Educa-
    tional and Psychological Measurement,* 1951, *11,* 5-11.

Moyles, E.W., Tuddenham, R.D., & Block, J. Simplicity/Complexity
    or Symmetry/Asymmetry? A re-analysis of the Barron-Welsh
    Art Scales. *Perceptual and Motor Skills,* 1965, *20,* 685-90.

Münsterberg, E., & Mussen, P.H. The personality structures of
    art students. *Journal of Personality,* 1953, *21,* 457-66.

Murray, H.A. (and collaborators) *Explorations in personality.*
    New York: Oxford, 1938.

Myden, W. Interpretation and evaluation of certain personality
    characteristics involved in creative production. *Perceptual
    and Motor Skills,* 1959, *9,* 139-58.

Myers, I.B. *Some findings with regard to type and manual for
    Myers-Briggs Type Indicator, Form E.* Swarthmore, Pa.:
    Author, 1958.

Naor, N. Configurational analysis of the Strong Vocational
    Interest Blank (SVIB) and concomitant personality variables.
    Unpublished doctoral dissertation, University of North
    Carolina, Chapel Hill, 1970.

Nicholls, J.G. Creativity in the person who will never produce
    anything original and useful: The concept of creativity as
    a normally distributed trait. *American Psychologist,* 1972,
    27, 717-27.

Osborn, A.F. *Applied imagination.* New York: Scribner's, 1953.

Pankove, E. The relationship between creativity and risk taking in fifth-grade children. Unpublished doctoral dissertation, Rutgers State University, 1967.

Pearson, J.S., Swenson, W.M., and Rome, H.P. Age and sex differences related to MMPI response frequency in 25,000 medical patients. *American Journal of Psychiatry*, 1965, *121*, 988-95.

Piers, E.V. Adolescent creativity. In J.F. Adams (Ed.), *Understanding adolesence*. Boston: Allyn & Bacon, 1968.

Preston, Richard. Personal communication, 1959.

Rafi, A.A. The progressive matrices and the dominoes (D48) tests: A cross-cultural study. *The British Journal of Educational Psychology*, 1967, *37*, (1), 117-19.

Raychaudhuri, M. Some perceptual characteristics of incipient artists. *Indian Journal of Psychology*, 1963, *38*, 13-17.

Raychaudhuri, M. Aesthetic interest, education, milieu differences, and tolerance of ambiguity. *Archivos Panameños de Psicologia*, 1965, *1*, 181-98.

Raychaudhuri, M. *Studies in artistic creativity: Personality structure of the musician*. Calcutta: Rabindra Bharati University, 1966.

Rees, M.E., & Goldman, M. Some relationships between creativity and personality. *Journal of General Psychology*, 1961, *65*, 145-61.

Roe, A. *The making of a scientist*. New York: Dodd-Mead, 1952.

Rogers, C.R. Toward a theory of creativity. *ETC: A Review of General Semantics*, 1954, *11*, 249-60.

Rogers, C.R. A theory of therapy, personality, and interpersonal relationships, as developed in the client-centered framework. In S. Koch (Ed.), *Psychology: A study of a science*. New York: McGraw-Hill, 1959, Vol. 3.

Roid, G.H. Welsh Figure Preference Test scores and student reactions to various college teaching methods. Unpublished master's thesis, University of Oregon, 1967.

Rosen, J.C.   The Barron-Welsh Art Scale as a predictor of origi-
    nality and level of ability among artists.   *Journal of
    Applied Psychology*, 1955, *39*, 366-67.

Roy, R.E.   Motion picture preference as a criterion variable in
    the study of creativity.   Unpublished master's thesis,
    West Virginia University, 1970.

Rychlak, J.F.   *A philosophy of science for personality theory*.
    Boston: Houghton Mifflin, 1968.

Saunders, M.   *A cross-validation of the Welsh origence-intelli-
    gence keys for the Strong Vocational Interest Blank*.
    Greensboro, N.C.: Creativity Research Institute of the
    Richardson Foundation, 1968.

Savin, Howard.   Personal communication, 1969.

Schaefer, C.E.   The Barron-Welsh Art Scale as a predictor of
    adolescent creativity.   *Perceptual and Motor Skills*, 1968,
    27, 1099-1102.

Scheerer, M., Rothman, E., & Goldstein, K.   A case of "idiot
    savant": An experimental study of personality organization.
    Psychological Monographs, 1945, *58*, (4, Whole No. 269).

Scheinfeld, A.   *Women and men*.   New York: Harcourt, Brace, 1943.

Schultz, K.V., & Knapp, W.E.   Perceptual preferences and self
    descriptions.   *Personnel Guidance Journal*, 1959, *38*, 581-84.

Sechrest, L., & Jackson, D.N.   Social intelligence and accuracy
    of interpersonal predictions.   *Journal of Personality*, 1961,
    29, 167-82.

Smith, J.M., & Schaefer, C.E. Development of a creativity scale for
    the Adjective Check List.   *Psychological Reports*, 1969,
    25, 87-92.

Snedecor, G.W.   *Statistical methods*.   (4th ed.)   Ames: Iowa
    State College Press, 1946.

Stark, S.   Toward a psychology of knowledge: Hypotheses regarding
    Rorschach movement and creativity.   *Perceptual and Motor
    Skills*, 1965, *21*, 839-59.

Stein, M.I.   A transactional approach to creativity.   In C.W.
    Taylor & F. Barron (Eds.) *Scientific creativity: Its
    recognition and development*.   New York: Wiley, 1963.

Stix, D.L. Discrepant achievement in college as a function of anxiety and repression. *Personnel & Guidance Journal,* 1967, *45,* 804-07.

Sticker, L.J., & Ross, J. Some correlates of a Jungian personality inventory. *Psychological Reports,* 1964, *14,* 623-43.

Stock, John D. Personal communication, 1969.

Strong, E.K. Jr., *Manual for the Strong Vocational Interest Blanks for men and women, revised blanks (Forms M and W).* Palo Alto, Calif.: Consulting Psychologists Press, 1959.

Taylor, C.W., & Holland, J. Predictors of creative performance. In C.W. Taylor (Ed.), *Creativity: Progress and potential.* New York: McGraw-Hill, 1964, 27.

Taylor, D.W. Environment and creativity. In D.W. MacKinnon (Ed.), *The creative person.* Berkeley: University of California Extension, 1961, Chap. 8.

Taylor, I.A. The nature of the creative process. In P. Smith (Ed.), *Creativity.* New York: Hastings House, 1959, 51-82.

Terman, L.M. The discovery and encouragement of exceptional talent. *American Psychologist,* 1954, *9,* 221-30.

Terman, L.M. *Manual, the Concept Mastery Test.* New York: The Psychological Corporation, 1956.

Terman, L.M., & Miles, C.C. *Sex and personality.* New York: McGraw-Hill, 1936.

Terman, L.M., & Oden, M.H. *The gifted group at mid-life. Genetic Studies of Genius.* Vol. IV. Stanford, Calif.: Stanford University Press, 1947.

Terman, L.M., & Oden, H. *The gifted group at mid-life. Genetic Studies of Genius.* Vol. V. Stanford, Calif.: Stanford University Press, 1959.

Thorndike, R.L. Some methodological issues in the study of creativity. In: *Proceedings of the 1962 invitational conference on testing problems.* Princeton, N.J.: Educational Testing Service, 1963.

Torrance, E.P. *Guiding creative talent.* Englewood Cliffs, N.J.: Prentice-Hall, 1962.

Torrance, E.P., & Dauw, D.C. Aspirations and dreams of three
    groups of creatively gifted high school seniors and com-
    parable unselected groups. *Gifted Child Quarterly*, 1965,
    9, 177-82.

Tyler, L.E. (Ed.) *Intelligence: Some recurring issues*. New
    York: Van Nostrand Reinhold, 1969.

Van de Castle, R.L. Perceptual immaturity and acquiescence
    among various developmental levels. *Journal of Consulting
    Psychology*, 1962, *26*, 167-71.

Van de Castle, R.L. Development and validation of a perceptual
    maturity scale using figure preferences. *Journal of
    Consulting Psychology*, 1965, *29*, 314-19.

Vernon, P.E. (Ed.) *Creativity: Selected readings*. Baltimore:
    Penguin, 1970.

Vroegh, K. Masculinity and femininity in the preschool years.
    Child Development, 1968, *39*, 1253-57.

Wahba, Michel. Personal communication, 1967.

Wallach, M.A., & Kogan, N. *Modes of thinking in young children*.
    New York: Holt, Rinehart & Winston, 1965.

Wallas, G. *The art of thought*. New York: Harcourt, Brace, 1926.

Watson, W.G. An analysis of responses to the Welsh Figure Pref-
    erence test to evaluate its effectiveness as a measure of
    mental ability. Unpublished doctoral dissertation,
    University of North Carolina, Chapel Hill, 1964.

Weaver, W. The imperfections of science. *American Scientist*,
    1961, *49*, 99-113.

Wechsler. D. *WAIS manual*. New York: The Psychological Corpo-
    ration, 1955.

Welsh, G.S. *A projective figure-preference test for diagnosis
    of psychopathology*. Unpublished doctoral dissertation,
    University of Minnesota, 1949.

Welsh, G.S. Factor dimensions A and R. In G.S. Welsh & W.G.
    Dahlstrom (Eds.), *Basic readings on the MMPI in psychology
    and medicine*. Minneapolis: University of Minnesota Press,
    1956.